MELBOURNE STUDIES IN EDUCATION
1984

MELBOURNE
STUDIES IN EDUCATION
1984

Edited by
IMELDA PALMER

MELBOURNE UNIVERSITY PRESS
1984

First published 1984
Typeset by Dovatype, Melbourne
Printed in Australia by
Brown Prior Anderson Pty Ltd, Burwood, for
Melbourne University Press, Carlton, Victoria 3053
U.S.A. and Canada: International Scholarly Book Services, Inc.,
P.O. Box 1632, Beaverton, OR 97075
United Kingdom, Europe, Middle East, Africa:
HB Sales
Enterprise House, Ashford Road, Ashford, Middlesex,
England TW15 1XB

The editor wishes to acknowledge her indebtedness
to Mrs Gwen McDowall, research assistant in the
Department of Education, University of Melbourne.

CONTENTS

ILLUSTRATIONS

NOTES ON CONTRIBUTORS

BILL CONNELL has had a long and warm association with the University of Melbourne, first as student and lecturer, and more recently as consultant on educational issues. He is currently a fellow of the Faculty of Education at Monash University, having retired from the Chair in Education at the University of Sydney to devote himself to writing. He now holds the title of Emeritus Professor. He is probably best known for his book *The Educational Thought and Influence of Matthew Arnold* (London, Routledge & Kegan Paul, 1950) and *A History of Education in the Twentieth Century World* (Canberra, Curriculum Development Centre, 1980). Works which he has co-authored include *Growing Up in an Australian City* (Hawthorn, Vic., Australian Council for Educational Research, 1957), *12 to 20: Studies of City Youth* (Sydney, Hicks Smith and Sons, 1975) and *The Foundations of Education* (Sydney, Novac, 1962). Professor Connell has an international reputation both in the social sciences and in the history of education.

IAN BIRCH is currently Head of the Department of Education at the University of Western Australia. His teaching and research interests are in the governance of education and, more particularly, in education law. He combined earlier studies in education and jurisprudence with a doctoral study in education law at the Australian National University. Dr Birch made the first Australian contribution to the study of education law with his *Constitutional Responsibility for Education in Australia* (Australian National University Press, 1975) and *The School and the Law* (Melbourne University Press, 1976) and has followed these with articles in *Melbourne Studies in Education*, the *Australian Journal of Education* and the *Journal of Educational Administration*. He has also published a range of books and articles on the governance of education.

MARION AMIES is a research assistant and doctoral student in the Faculty of Education at Monash University; her thesis explores home education

xi

in nineteenth century Australia, a long neglected aspect of Australian education. From a literary background, she has published in the fields of Old English and bibliographical studies. Her monograph, *The Education Pamphlets Collection, State Library of Victoria* (University of New South Wales, for Australia 1788-1988: A Bicentennial History. Historical Bibliography Monograph no. 3, 1981) makes accessible to researchers the extensive and valuable collection of educational pamphlets held by the State Library. She became interested in Matilda Goldstraw when she established that Matilda, writing under the pseudonym Noel Hope, was the author of *Milliara: An Australian Romance* (1893), the story of a colonial governess.

DON SMART is a Senior Lecturer in the Politics of Education at Murdoch University, Western Australia. He completed his Ph.D. on Federal Aid to Schools in the Education Research Unit at the Australian National University in 1975. Subsequently he took up a post-doctoral fellowship in Sociology at the Australian National University and worked on a study of the national power structure with John Higley and Desley Deacon. This culminated in their jointly authored book *Elites in Australia* (London, Routledge & Kegan Paul, 1979). In 1977 Dr Smart moved to Murdoch to take up an appointment in the School of Education. His publications include: *Federal Aid to Australian Schools* (St Lucia, University of Queensland Press, 1978); I. K. F. Birch & D. Smart (eds), *The Commonwealth Government and Education 1964-1976* (Richmond, Vic., Drummond, 1977); Grant Harman and Don Smart (eds), *Federal Intervention in Australian Education* (Middle Park, Vic., Georgian House, 1982).

KEN MCKINNON is Vice-Chancellor of the University of Wollongong, and Chairman (part-time) of the State Board of Education in Victoria. He was appointed foundation Chairman of the Australian Schools Commission from 1974 to 1981. In this role he took the leading part in the preparation of many influential reports, including *Schooling for 15 and 16 year-olds* (Canberra, Australian Schools Commission, 1980). Dr McKinnon is a graduate of Adelaide, Queensland and Harvard universities. He has been a teacher in South Australia and in New Guinea, and from 1966 to 1973 was Director of Education for Papua New Guinea. In the past decade he has participated widely in activities concerned with education and the arts in Australia, and internationally on behalf of Australia.

ANDREW SPAULL is a distinguished graduate of the University of Melbourne, having been awarded the Katherine Woodruff Prize in economic history and the Dwight Prize in education. After a short teaching career in secondary schools, he undertook doctoral studies and then joined the staff of Monash University, where he now holds the position of Reader in Education. His major publications are: *Australian Teachers: From Colonial Schoolmasters to Militant Professionals* (South Melbourne, Vic., Macmillan, 1977) and *Australian Education in the Second World War* (St Lucia, University of Queensland Press, 1982). He is co-author of *Teachers in Conflict* (Melbourne University Press, 1972) and *Politics of Schooling* (Carlton, Vic., Pitman, 1976). Dr Spaull has established an international reputation through his extensive research on teacher unionism.

PETER KARMEL is Vice-Chancellor of the Australian National University. From 1971 he was Chairman of the Australian Universities Commission until, in 1977, it gave way to the broader-based Tertiary Education Commission which he chaired until 1982. The previous decade was spent first in planning for The Flinders University of South Australia and then serving as its Vice-Chancellor. Before that he was Professor of Economics in the University of Adelaide. His work in the economics of education is well known, and includes 'Some Arithmetic of Education', published in *Melbourne Studies in Education 1966* from his Fink lecture given in the Faculty of Education, University of Melbourne. Since 1979 Professor Karmel has been President of the Australian Council for Educational Research.

FRANK NAYLOR obtained his doctorate in the Psychology Department of the University of Melbourne and is currently a Senior Lecturer in the Department of Education. He is co-ordinator of the Master of Educational Psychology programme, in which he teaches differential psychology. His research interests have been mainly in the relations between personality and performance, and research methodology. He is particularly interested in the effects of anxiety and curiosity on classroom learning, and how these relate to the development and maintenance of interests. He has published in education, philosophy, psychology and medicine, including a book on *Personality and Education Achievement* (New York, Wiley, 1972). He is a Fellow of the Australian Psychological Society.

ABBREVIATIONS

ACER	Australian Council for Educational Research
ACSSO	Australian Council of State School Organisations
ACT	Australian Capital Territory
APM	Australian Paper Mills
A/S	Anti-submarine
ASCO	*Australian Standard Classification of Occupations*
AWA	Amalgamated Wireless of Australia
BHP	Broken Hill Proprietary
CAE	College of Advanced Education
CAI	Career Assessment Inventory
CSR	Colonial Sugar Refinery
DDIAE	Darling Downs Institute of Advanced Education
DOGS	Defence of Government Schools
DOT	*Dictionary of Occupational Titles*
EFTS	Equivalent full-time students
EIS	Educational Institute of Scotland
EMTA	East Moreton Teachers' Association
HMC	Headmasters Conference
IFASES (IF)	Industrial Fund for the Advancement of Scientific Education in Schools
MATA	Melbourne Assistant Teachers' Association
MDTA	Melbourne District Teachers' Association
NCIS	National Council of Independent Schools
NCSST	National Committee on Social Science Teaching
NDEA	National Defense Education Act (USA)
NSWTF	New South Wales Teachers' Federation
NUT	National Union of Teachers (of England and Wales)
PLC	Presbyterian Ladies' College
PROV	Public Records Office of Victoria
QPSTA	Queensland Public School Teachers' Association

QTU	Queensland Teachers' Union
RANVR	Royal Australian Naval Volunteer Reserve
RIASEC	Realistic, Investigative, Artistic, Social, Enterprising, Conventional
SAIT	South Australian Institute of Teachers
SAPTA	South Australian Public Teachers' Association
SATA	South Australian Teachers' Association
SCII	Strong-Campbell Interest Inventory
SDS	Self Directed Search
SEMP	Social Education Materials Project
SSTUV	State School Teachers' Union of Victoria
SSTUWA	State School Teachers' Union of Western Australia
SVIB	Strong Vocational Interest Bank
TAFE	Technical and Further Education
TEASA	Tertiary Education Authority of South Australia
TEC	Tertiary Education Commission
TSSTA	Tasmanian State School Teachers' Association
TTF	Tasmanian Teachers' Federation
UK	United Kingdom
USA	United States of America
V2	Long-range German rocket (World War II)
VEF	Victorian Employers' Federation
VIT	Victorian Institute of Teachers
VLTA	Victorian Lady Teachers' Association
VLTR	Victorian Lady Teachers' Resolution
VPI	Vocational Preference Inventory
VPRS	Victoria, Public Record Series
VTI	Victorian Teachers' Institute
VTU	Victorian Teachers' Union
WATU	Western Australian Teachers' Union
WMTA	West Moreton Teachers' Association

1

THE EDUCATION OF A PROFESSOR OF EDUCATION

by W. F. CONNELL

When Burley Griffin's attractive and imaginative plans for Australia's new capital city were translated into practicality by the civil engineers of Canberra's construction authority they lost some of their aesthetic appeal. My father was one of those engineers. In 1916, when I was born, he and my mother lived in a house which still stands near the present Canberra public hospital. My mother, a golf enthusiast, was probably the first person to play that game in Canberra. She had a rough old course below the house on the slope that has now disappeared under the waters of Lake Burley Griffin. When the time came, she went off to her parents' home at Lockhart some 200 kilometres to the west in the Riverina and I was duly produced there—the second of her three sons.

My father's outlook was matter-of-fact and practical. He had a nineteenth century engineer's mind. His job, as he conceived it, was to see that the roads, sewerage and water supply for the new city that was being created out of nothing were efficiently and economically installed. If the plans of some visionary architect decreed otherwise then they would have to be changed. He graduated B.C.E. in 1895, and subsequently M.C.E., from the University of Melbourne and, on one of his first jobs, worked on the west coast of Tasmania at Queenstown and Zeehan. He took part in the construction of the interesting Mt Lyell railway from Queenstown through the rainforest along the course of the King River to Teepookana. I cannot claim that he was the man responsible for one of the first desecrations of one of Australia's finest wilderness areas, nor that he alone engineered the changes that broke Burley Griffin's heart in Canberra. But he was typical of the philistine engineering mind that produced the graceless cities of Victorian England and America, and the country towns and cities of Australia. Yet he was not entirely insensitive. He designed the rather elegant Cotter Dam, presumably where it was possible for beauty and practicality to coincide, and one of his closest friends was my godfather, T. G. C. Weston, who landscaped our capital city, flooding it with native and exotic trees that have helped establish it in a setting of great beauty.

1

After I was born we moved to Melbourne and from 1919 lived in a newly built house on part of my grandparents' land in Hawthorn. My father was soon back in Canberra and spent most of the rest of his working life there until his retirement in the mid-1930s. He became chief civil engineer in the federal Department of Works, moved around Australia a good deal, and visited us on his annual leave in Melbourne or Mornington, where the family had a seaside house. He was a sort of distant influence who kept in touch by a conscientious and affectionate daily correspondence and who would descend occasionally to teach us swimming with his curious old-fashioned trudgeon stroke, bully us over our mathematics homework, and depart once more for some indefinite period to some other part of Australia. His practical streak was constantly communicated to his family. Consequently, although I was not to become an engineer or even to have any interest or competence in mechanical matters, I found a distinct inclination, when I eventually became interested in the educational profession, to set value on educational theories that arose out of an analysis of practical situations and were designed to have an effect on social and educational practice. Dewey's pragmatism, for example, with its concern for building democratic processes through education to control an unfinished and developing world, has consistently attracted me.

The most important educational influence, however, during my adolescence was exercised not by my occasional contact with my father but by constant association with his sisters, my maiden aunts. The Connell family had moved from Prahran to Hawthorn in the 1870s. They had an acre of ground and lived in an attractive slate-roofed, well-lit, single-storeyed house with a wide tiled veranda. It was set in a fine garden; a profusion of fruit-trees and vegetables at the back and walks of shady trees and lawns in the front. It was an exciting garden to explore when we were young. Our place was close to the Yarra River near the present Wallen Road bridge where my aunt told us she remembered as a very young girl hiding her face bashfully in her mother's long skirts when they visited a camp of Aborigines in the 1870s. The camp site fifty years later, when I was a small boy in the 1920s, was part of the Hawthorn tip where we played cricket and football after school and in the weekends. It was an interesting alternative playground to our grandparents' garden, especially as in the early spring it would often be under ten or twelve feet of water. It was part of the bed of the original Hawthorn or Connell's Creek that had been converted into a concrete main drain. When the floods came down the Yarra in September, the water would back up along the line of the old creek, and for a few days the houses below us became uninhabitable and we had a lake instead of a tip to disport ourselves in.

State Schools: Glenferrie and Mont Albert

In 1921, when I was four, I started at Glenferrie State School in the kindergarten class, and remained at the school to the completion of the sixth grade. From this period two teachers stand out. Miss McCrum was the headmistress of the infants' school. She was up-to-date, efficient and, with the children, rather austere. Out of school, however, she was a delight. She and my mother used to get along very well, and as a result she would come to Mornington to spend some of the Christmas holidays with us. We enjoyed her company and for years after my older brother and I had left the school she kept in touch with us.

My other teacher of note was Miss G. Andrews who taught me in the fourth and fifth grades. She was what would probably have been called a good disciplinarian. I can remember being barbarically struck on the hand on cold winter mornings with a heavy strap which she wielded with some vigour, and I cordially detested her for it. But she was thorough in her teaching and interested in her pupils' progress. When, several years after I had left Glenferrie, I won a junior government scholarship, she sent me a postcard of congratulations and encouragement to further effort.

Mont Albert Central School followed in 1927-29. I used to catch the train from Hawthorn to Mont Albert eight stations down the line and walk about a kilometre or so across the streets and paddocks to the school. It was primarily a scholarship shop for the aspiring middle class children of the eastern suburbs. Together with its great rival, the Spring Road School in Malvern, it produced hundreds of scholarship winners and supplied Melbourne's independent secondary schools with many of their brightest students. It was run by Alfred Harley, an eccentric headmaster of uncertain temper. I remember a star performance one day when a wastepaper basket in one of the first floor classrooms irritated him and he kicked it out of the door and pursued it down the stairway yelling 'pig's bucket' as he sent it on its way. On another occasion he surprised the school by suddenly announcing that it was to have a school captain and young 12-year-old Connell was to be it. My duties turned out to be merely that of leaning over the first floor balcony when the headmaster had finished his harangue to the school at assembly each morning, blowing a whistle and bidding each class march off smartly to its appropriate room. School self-government was apparently not something that Mr Harley wished to rush into. It was, nevertheless, an enjoyable and effective period of schooling. It was the beginning of secondary education. We started to learn a foreign language, graduated from primary school arithmetic to the intellectual puzzles of algebra and geometry, started mildly experimenting in a science laboratory, and, every lunch-hour, played cricket or football in the extensive school grounds or on the unpaved tracks that wandered off into the open countryside beyond the school fence. Every Monday morning, too, the boys would start their day at the Box Hill State School in Station St where for half the morning we were taught sloyd, and then made our way back on foot through two kilometres of gorse-covered paddocks to our own school. These lessons gave me a lasting taste for simple cabinet making. The teaching in most of our schoolwork was good, and the teachers were undoubtedly the most thoughtful and professionally competent group that I encountered throughout my schooling.

Melbourne Church of England Grammar School in the 1930s

In 1930 I became a pupil at Melbourne Grammar School and stayed there for the next five years. A half-century has now passed and I understand that the standard of teaching and the level of educational ideas at that school have been raised. They were fairly dismal in the 1930s. I once asked my father, in my Dip.Ed. year at the university, why he had sent me to Melbourne Grammar when the education that it offered seemed to me so appalling. He replied that he judged on results—its pupils consistently gained high honours and exhibitions in the public examinations, and its ex-pupils could be seen in large numbers to be holding important and lucrative positions in business and throughout the professions. Clearly, his observation was right, and clearly, also, it was superficial. The kinds of results he cited were not closely related to the school's contribution to the education of its pupils. The large number of bright adolescents who attended the school succeeded simply because they were bright and aspiring and had the advantage of a middle class background; and those who got good jobs later got them often because they succeeded their parents or they were recognizably of middle class upbringing.

The headmaster, R. P. Franklin, as is usual in independent schools, set the style and tone of the school. He was a good classical scholar, though a poor teacher, and saw that the classics predominated at the school. That suited me well. I liked Greek, Latin, and Greek and Roman History, and was successful in them. The teaching on the language side was systematic and enthusiastic. The same could not be said for the teaching in Greek and Roman History which was the headmaster's responsibility. His method was to prescribe two textbooks, one for Roman and one for Greek History, then, every second Tuesday, to set an examination of two essay-type questions on the next fifty pages of the textbook which he would duly mark and return to us; meanwhile from the beginning to the end of every other class period, he would dictate a set of notes unvarying from year to year and which many of us had inherited from former pupils. Fortunately, the school had a reasonable library and we could get some intellectual stimulus from that source.

My school programme was poorly balanced. I took no science beyond some elementary physical science up to intermediate certificate level, and my mathematics petered out at a similar level, both subjects being taught by singularly uninviting masters. There was no art of any kind taught in the regular school curriculum. For my last three years at the school my programme was confined almost entirely to learning Greek, Latin, Ancient History, French, and a little English. I enjoyed these subjects and did well in them, but it could hardly be argued that they were a very sensible preparation for life in the mid-twentieth century. We were then in the depths of the great depression of the 1930s, but nothing that we did at school had any relevance to it, and I spent my years of secondary education almost unaware of what our society was experiencing.

One of the school's strong points was its emphasis on sport. After school for about two hours on at least three days a week and on Saturday mornings we played cricket or football. It was vigorous and pleasant exercise, and was, no doubt, a good basis for a subsequently healthy life for many of us. It was generally a well-planned activity and involved many of the boys in some responsibility for its organization.

The principal organ through which the older adolescents exercised some authority was the prefect system. Each year a dozen or so boys were appointed by the headmaster as prefects in which post they acted as a sort of executive of the staff to help organize various items of school business and maintain order. There was little that was educational in the system. It was primarily a support and policing function in which the prefects had the power to punish other boys summarily by caning. Corporal punishment in fact was a common feature of the schooling process. It was used for any and all offences—failure to attend a morning chapel service, appearing in the street without having a Grammar cap on one's head, poor or untidy homework, and rowdy behaviour in class all provided an opportunity for a senior adolescent or a teacher to assault an erring pupil.

It is not surprising that a great amount of bullying was associated with the system. This was probably the worst feature of the school in the 1930s. It was not a *Tom Brown's Schooldays* situation but there was enough bullying to make many of the younger and some of the older boys uncomfortable and resentful. Much of it was designed to bolster an expiring and inappropriate public school tradition which in the guise of promoting school spirit promoted many petty and childish activities. It was a symptom of the thoughtless and unstimulating society that the school had lapsed into. Many of the English public schools during the 1930s were starting to pull out of their stagnation, and after World War II became much more educationally alert and interesting places. Melbourne Grammar, when I was there, had not yet felt the stirrings of the new educational breeze. For most of its students it must have been a cultural and intellectual desert. Even for the academically more successful, the work in all our language subjects, for example, was nine parts memorization and one part the development of the kind of style that paid off in examinations in which we were inordinately successful. From this experience I have often wondered why teachers have come to think that learning foreign languages is a difficult process, and one that should be reserved for the brightest pupils. The intellectual effort required in studying the social sciences seems to me to be much more considerable.

Maiden Aunts

During the years when I was at Melbourne Grammar my principal educators were two maiden aunts, my father's sisters, who lived with my grandmother next door. They were part of a talented family of women. Grandfather's sister, great-aunt Isobel Sarah Connell who married Thomas Jackson of Young and Jackson's well-known hotel in Melbourne—her niece, Mary Sophia Connell, married the partner, Henry Young—was a cultivated woman whose Jolimont residence was something of a miniature art gallery. Such are the profits of the hotel trade. I have an exercise book of hers, dated 1856, containing notes on eleven lectures in chemistry which she appears to have attended in that year. There is, unfortunately, no clue as to whether they were part of an early university extension, mechanics institute, or other public course, and it is probable that great-aunt Isobel's interest in chemistry was not pursued very far.

Sustained and systematic higher education among the Connell women began in the next generation with my father's four sisters, Maud, Cora, Rita and Beatrice. Maud and Rita were graduates of the University of Melbourne. Beatrice passed one university subject, Pure Mathematics I, and then decided to become a teacher of physical education. Cora did not attend a university. She travelled extensively, talked interestingly about her travels, developed an interest in music, and spent her spare time working for the newsboys club and later for the Dorcas Society in Brunswick. She had a broad taste for non-conformist religion, and would vary her attendance at the local Presbyterian church with visits to the Independent, Unitarian, and Australian churches in the city to which she would sometimes take me if she thought there might be an interesting sermon. In her youth she had been a leading tennis player at Grace Park, and, when she later turned to croquet, she was reputed to be very hard to beat. Her company was always lively and interesting. As she did not marry, and lived continuously next door to us, I saw a great deal of her.

Rita had the best academic career of the four sisters. She entered the science faculty at the University of Melbourne in 1897 as a non-resident Trinity College student. In her second year she took first class honours and the exhibition in the combined subjects of Biology II and Physiology, and graduated in 1901 with second class honours and a shared exhibition in Biology III. She was an exact contemporary of a later well-known figure in Melbourne's school of history, Jessie Webb, who was also impressively winning exhibitions throughout her course.

Aunts Rita and Beatrice both married and left the Connell household. My main contacts were therefore with the two older, maiden aunts who lived at home during the period of my upbringing. My closest association was with Aunt Maud.

Maud Connell was one of the first women to take a degree at the University of Melbourne. She began in 1887, six years after the first woman was admitted to the university. It was the year in which Professor Masson was reported to have said to his colleagues, 'Gentlemen, the ladies have come to stay'. Maud was also a Trinity College student. She took a Bachelor of Arts degree with second class honours in the School of History, Political Science, and Jurisprudence in 1890 and her M.A. was awarded in 1892. She was 21 when she graduated, and two years later she left to take up a post at the newly established Ipswich Girls Grammar School in Queensland. Ten years later she became its headmistress, and remained there until 1905 when she left to go abroad. On her way back in 1908 she stepped off the ship in Perth and found herself headmistress of MLC Claremont. There she remained till 1913. When, in 1982, the school held a ceremony to name a new building after her, about a dozen of her surviving pupils turned up to celebrate and reminisce about her affectionate firmness. She would share the girls' sport and school walks, tuck the boarders in at night, soothe the apprehensions of the new girls, and at the same time unrelentingly demand the best quality of work from her charges. In 1913 she returned to Melbourne and became the senior language mistress at another new school, University High School. The historian of that school, Alice Hoy, who was a junior mistress at the time, described Aunt Maud as 'formidable', and 'an impressive teacher' of modern languages 'who commanded the respect of all and the affection of those whose good fortune it was to be admitted to her friendship'. At the end of World War I, in 1918, she retired at the age of 49 and lived for the next forty years with her mother and sister Cora in their Hawthorn house. She did some tutoring and examining for the University of Melbourne in French and German and spent much of her time improving the education of her nephews.

Her main interest at all times was in the teaching of languages. While she was at Ipswich, she took two years off from 1894 to live and work in Europe. She stayed for a while in Berlin, and then taught at a girls' Gymnasium in Wolfenbüttel in Lower Saxony, the home of the celebrated Bibliotheca Augusta of which Leibniz and later Lessing had once been librarians. Then this 26-year-old young woman was off to Paris, living in the bohemian Latin Quarter in the exciting *fin de siècle* world of the post-impressionists and the symbolist poets. For the rest of her life she never lost her affection for the literature of that period.

In 1906 she was back in Europe for another two years. She taught at a girls' school in Grenoble in 1907, and acquired there a nicely bound anthology of symbolist poetry which, much read and marked, I later presented to MLC Claremont. In 1908 she completed a diploma in the teaching of French at the University of Geneva, and lived for a while in Italy.

Much later, when she was 66 she decided to learn Spanish and brush up her Italian. She and Aunt Cora went off for another two-year trip. In 1935 they lived in Spain for five months through the beginning of the Spanish civil war and, when they failed to reconcile the conflicting parties, went off touring in northern Europe and finally stayed for a five-month spell in Italy.

Aunt Maud was a woman of great determination. She made great demands on herself and she expected others to act similarly. She lived simply and frugally and devoted herself generously to her students and her family, and to the teaching of language and literature. For the whole time that I was at Melbourne Grammar I used to spend about an hour and a half each evening with her working on Latin, Greek and French, and later we used to read German together. She gave me the run of her study and books, and I would sit for hours through the weekends and holidays reading and working in that little room off the front veranda that looked out on a delicious apricot tree and beautiful Japanese maple. Sometimes the contest between apricots and Greek irregular verbs was resolved in favour of the taste buds, but in Aunt Maud's establishment backsliding was not encouraged.

From her I learnt principally two things. First, that worthwhile achievement usually requires hard work. With her there was, however, no nonsense about work and the Protestant ethic. It was just that there were a lot of interesting things to do and to find out, and if they were really to be mastered you could expect to work hard at the task, and, as Aunt Maud frequently put it, 'not fritter away your time'. Work, and academic work in particular, was a way of enjoying life and getting a lot out of it. The second of Aunt Maud's educational legacies was the revelation that in every language there is a literature of great beauty written in varied form and style. At school we were too busy with the mechanics of language and the niceties of translation to see into and savour the style of the literature we were supposedly studying. Aunt Maud led me through Heine and Goethe, and her favourite, Schiller's *Wilhelm Tell*. We explored with a new perception the pieces of Chateaubriand, Mérimée, and Daudet that we were studying in school, and we caught glimpses of the lyric genius of Horace, Livy's 'milky richness', the emotional appeal of a Euripidean chorus, and a great deal more. This, of course, for me was merely the dawning of sensibility. There were hints at school and later at the classics school at the university that literature was a creative exercise of talented human minds, but, in my experience, little was done in either place to encourage students to appreciate the beauty of expression and the pertinence of stylistic variation in the foreign languages they were studying.

University of Melbourne, Undergraduate Student

In 1933 I won a senior government scholarship, held it over while I stayed at school for another year, and then in 1935 became a student at the University of Melbourne in the faculty of Arts in the combined honours schools of Latin and History, intending subsequently to study law. At the same time I entered Trinity College on a resident scholarship and remained in residence for two enjoyable years. There was good company there in every respect. There were sporting activities that were not taken too seriously. There were social activities for small groups and there were large social occasions. I spent a good deal of time in ballroom dancing and joined classes at a Collins Street studio to improve my performance and to learn steps in the new dances such as the rumba that were beginning to take on. From early in my first year my constant partner was a science student, Margaret Peck, with whom I have been dancing ever since. Trinity also, through its tutorial system, its proximity to university facilities, and its accumulation of bright young men with many common interests and diverse talents, was a place of great intellectual stimulus. In short, the college situation was a good setting in which to grow up intellectually, socially and emotionally. Some of us joined various university clubs— sports, religious, political. I was not conscious of much political activity among the general body of undergraduates. The abdication crisis made a temporary stir, Hitler's activities were keenly watched, but there was little excitement about the local scene. My parents were staunch labor supporters and I joined the Labor Party while I was at the university. I became assistant secretary of the South Carlton branch which met in the Trades Hall. This put us close to the centre of affairs, and we were involved in minor policy making and the usual run of witchhunts.

University work was uneven in its interest and demand. I probably improved my proficiency in Latin very little. We certainly covered new ground by moving into silver age Latin and I began an interest in the Roman imperial period that has been a lasting one, but I gave little attention to my language work to improve it to any great extent. My honours thesis dealt with the spread of Mithraism in the Roman Empire, and this led to my first contact with the University of Sydney. Much of my work had to be done in the Fisher Library, as the main collection of source materials on my topic were housed there. Aunt Maud's influence was at work even there—she was a close friend of the librarian, H. M. Green, and his wife who had been a pupil of hers at Ipswich!

At the beginning of my course, the Melbourne history school consisted essentially of two people, Ernest Scott the professor and Jessie Webb senior lecturer. Scott looked after the European, British and colonial history, and Jessie Webb the ancient history. Both were interesting in their own way. Scott was a polished lecturer, making each hour a set piece on a specified topic with a clear, crisp opening, a complex, full-flavoured development, and a well-rounded finish. It lingered on the palate like a glass of vintage red. Jessie Webb rambled. At one moment she would be clambering up a drain with Sir Arthur Evans in Knossos, and at the next discussing Jane Harrison's views on primitive Greek religion. Her lectures never managed to cover the course; Scott's always did.

The history school put an emphasis on historical method which usually meant principally a reading and appropriate use of original sources. We learnt the techniques by constantly writing essays. In Scott's honours courses we had to present ourselves at an allotted time and read our essay to him, a reading that was punctuated by his comments and occasional discussion. I thought it was an excellent practice and used it with my own honours students some years later. Jessie Webb was my supervisor when I later wrote an M.A. thesis on Roman Historiography from Suetonius to Orosius. Her insistence that I think through again some of the lines of argument and thoroughly rewrite the first draft enabled it to reach a first class honours level.

University of Melbourne, Teacher Trainee

In 1937 I was 21, and supposedly destined for a legal career and eventually the High Court bench! Some of the legal material, however, that I had touched on in my Arts course I found singularly unattractive, and my ambitions in that direction waned. Moreover, Margaret and I wanted to get married. This, according to Aunts Maud and Cora who by then had returned from their stay in Spain and Italy, would be the ruin of my career. Their judgement on this occasion was completely astray and they later graciously conceded as much. In any case we took no notice of it.

What we lacked, however, was an income. By this time Margaret had already taken a course at the Associated Teachers Training Institution with Miss D. J. Ross, and had begun teaching. My attention, too, had been attracted to education by an exciting international conference in 1937. To enable us to marry, therefore, I decided to enter the teaching profession. I was wisely urged by Aunt Maud to take a course of teacher training instead of going off untrained to a job that had been offered to me at that time in a Sydney school. Consequently, in 1938 I entered the faculty of Education at the University of Melbourne.

I enrolled in the first year of the postgraduate Bachelor of Education degree. It was a good decision, and I thought the course was the most stimulating educational experience I had so far had.

The B.Ed. degree had started in 1936. The first year was the existing Dip.Ed. which could be taken at pass or, with an additional subject, at honours standard. Students who took honours could complete the second year while engaged in full-time teaching by taking the subject Experimental Education and writing a minor research thesis.

The inspiration in the course was, without any doubt, G. S. Browne, who at that time was the only full-time member of staff. The part-time staff who numbered about fifteen were mostly concerned with methods of teaching. I studied and did my practical teaching in three methods, Latin, History, and French. For Latin the lecturer was P. Radford who taught classics at Scotch College and did his method work knowledgeably and thoroughly, for history J. R. Peart from the technical schools who, substituting for Alice Hoy then on leave, was pleasant and interesting, and for French W. H. Frederick from University High School, the most exciting and enthusiastic classroom teacher I have ever seen. M. S. Sharman, headmaster of University High School, taught an outmoded and mercifully short course in general method with one extraordinary high spot. Using a class from his school he demonstrated through a lesson on the binomial theory the Herbartian phenomenon of apperception. It was a clever demonstration of the way in which comprehension of a general law or rule gradually dawns on the members of a school class as they move through the Herbartian steps of association and generalization. With K. S. Cunningham, who came to us once a week from the Australian Council for Educational Research, we plodded through educational psychology. He was a sound scholar and a delightful person but an incurably dull lecturer.

Browne, who might have been unscholarly at times, was never dull. We lived, in 1938, to a certain extent still in the euphoria of the New Education Fellowship Conference that had brought a large and extraordinary group of talented and astute educators to tour Australia in August-September of 1937. As an Arts student I had attended many of the sessions which were held at the university during their week in Melbourne. It was my first glimpse of progressive education and its leading exponents and I was greatly stirred by both the educational and social views that they intelligently and attractively put forward. To that company G. S. Browne was a fellow-spirit. One of his main objects in life was to put forward the cause of progressive education. He became a keen critic of existing practices in Australian schools, enthusiastically encouraged innovation, and constantly made known any promising developments from overseas. He did not have a consistent and well-thought out theory of education, and therefore gained a reputation for superficiality. He certainly did not explain and analyse with us the rich underlying layer of theory with which many progressives had struggled in the 1920s and 1930s, for example, on educational and social change, the nature of authority, the significance of community, or the interpretations of individuality, personality and human growth that emerged from diverse psychological schools. But he did introduce us to such problems. His strength was in the improvement of practical teaching. He introduced us, for example, to the details of the Dalton and Winnetka plans, to projects and various activity programmes, and he had us try them out in practice. He was also astute enough to see that these practices raised a number of unsolved problems of both practice and theory for many of us. He made these known. He suggested lines of further study, and he introduced us to a new world of educational literature.

Browne was a questioner and a problem-raiser rather than a systematic thinker. As such he was academically a man for his times, but he was also something more. It was a period in which the university's task was conceived as primarily that of producing critical minds. We learned to dissect, discover arguments, and detect flaws and inadequacies, accomplishments from which it was easy to lapse into cynicism. Sydney's leading philosopher, John Anderson, with his notion that the task of philosophy is criticism, exemplified the academic mind of the 1930s. Literary criticism, book reviewing, legal debate, even biography and academic conversation had this touch about it. It was clever but not productive. It was a useful but, in itself, a barren training that survived for many years in various university departments. Fortunately a more creative counter-stream developed and slowly made its way in post-World War II years. Browne's tendency was to try to raise our thresholds of criticism. He would provoke his classes with unanswered questions and suggested problems. Without himself working in depth to a solution he would demonstrate some of the constructive answers that progressive educators had produced and introduce us to some of their more fundamental work.

From the Dip.Ed. year I gained principally two things. I developed a lasting interest in and love of the history of education and determined that it would be the main area of my research thenceforth. In that matter I made a start in the next year by completing my B.Ed. degree with the subject Experimental Education and a minor thesis on Roman Education in the Antonine Period, and followed it up during my war service by an M.Ed. thesis on Education in the Third Century of the Roman Empire. Soon after, I moved to the nineteenth and twentieth centuries and have recently found a great deal of interest in writing contemporary educational history.

For all the many years of formal education I had had and the multitude of examinations I had passed, I did not learn to think in any but a critical and analytical sense until my Dip.Ed. year. It was Browne's introduction to Dewey that really began my intellectual education. I read Dewey's *How We Think* and began to get an appreciation of what he called reflective thinking. I then moved on to *Democracy and Education*. I found in it the most comprehensive and satisfying construction of the task of education in a potentially democratic society. It is now 67 years since it was published, and it has a number of deficiencies that its critics have enthusiastically pointed out, but it still remains for me the classic exposition of democracy and the manner in which it is underpinned by education. In his 80th birthday speech in 1939, Dewey summarized his view of democracy not as a mere governmental arrangement but as 'a way of life controlled by a working faith in the possibilities of human nature'. The task of education was to reorganize the material of experience, and to create, by conscious and resolute intellectual and educational effort, a sense of community and a habit of amicable co-operation productive of a freer and more humane experience. This gives to education an immense importance and scope. It becomes the central human activity of a civilized community. It is difficult for a budding educator to resist this kind of rhetoric. I did not resist it in 1938-39, and subsequent thought and experience have served to deepen my attachment to it. It has great richness and depth; and it has an appropriateness in the twentieth century that few other educational theories can approach. At all events my struggles to understand Dewey's views and to develop the implications of them, were, for me, the beginnings of serious constructive thinking about education, the nature of society, and social change.

School Teaching in New South Wales

From 1939 to 1942 I taught in two independent schools in New South Wales, first as the history master at Barker College in Sydney, and then as the headmaster of a small and struggling school in Newcastle, the Newcastle Church of England Boys Grammar School. Educationally there was not much to learn from either school. The staffs were pleasant and I made some interesting and lasting friends. I consolidated some teaching skills, and learned some of the technique of administration. I also learnt quite quickly that, for the secondary schools, public and private, of New South Wales, the most important matter was to get the best possible results in the external public examinations. These results were published, school by school, in the daily newspapers, and the worth of a school was judged—and usually announced on annual speech nights—by adding up the number of passes at A and B level obtained by its students. Twenty years later, in exasperation, I publicly described New South Wales as being in danger of becoming the most examined and least educated state in Christendom. Even with the subsequent examination changes in all Australian states I doubt if there has been any substantial change in the emphasis and importance given to examination results.

The World War II Years

At the end of 1939 Margaret and I were married, in 1942 our first daughter was born, and a few months later I joined the Australian navy. My initial rank was Acting Sub-Lieutenant RANVR, a position not regarded with great reverence by other members of the senior service. For the first four months I joined a class of ten other tyros training to be anti-submarine officers at the A/S school on Rushcutters Bay in Sydney. We had courses in gunnery, navigation, electrical theory, radar, and the theory and practice of anti-submarine warfare. At the end of it I was appointed to the instructional staff of the school and for the next year taught the theoretical parts of the course. I was then sent off via America to the UK for posting to the British navy and found myself doing further courses at the main A/S school in Scotland and at Western Approaches headquarters in Liverpool. I finished up as the admiral's A/S officer in Colombo mainly teaching units of the Sri Lankan navy. One of my odd duties there was to be in charge of a small disused lighter tied up in Colombo harbour. As I cannot recall ever handing over my responsibility to anyone when I left to return to Australia, it is possible that the hulk is still there, tied up and pining for its mysteriously absent commanding officer.

During my naval experience I was able to complete my thesis for the M.Ed. degree on Education in the Third Century of the Roman Empire. Like its predecessor for the B.Ed. degree it earned the Cohen Prize at the University of Melbourne and helped to give me entry to doctoral work at the University of London. My naval years were the first opportunity to travel round the world and see something of academic work in education in other English-speaking countries. In my transit of the USA I visited and talked with Harper Swift, then one of the leading historians of education at the University of California, and, on the east coast, spent an afternoon with I. L. Kandel at his home in Connecticut.

In London I was able to talk with the director of the Institute of Education, Sir Fred Clarke. He was interested in having someone make a study of the educational work of Matthew Arnold and suggested that I should do it as a Ph.D. thesis. I was accordingly enrolled, and, whenever I was on leave in London, I attended occasional lectures at the Institute which, after a period of evacuation, had returned to temporary quarters in Portman Square in the West End of London. It was the V2 period in which German-fired rockets would land unheralded on various parts of London demolishing quite substantial buildings on impact. One such landed uncomfortably close to the Institute, and its staff must have wondered whether their return had not been a little premature. Apart from Clarke the star attraction was Karl Mannheim who lectured in the newly developing subject of sociology of education. He was easier to read than to listen to; he had a difficult accent and a lisping speech that made it difficult to understand what he was trying to say to his audience. His writings, however, opened up and explored new worlds in education. From that time, through Mannheim's works and Clarke's enthusiasm for the new area, I began to develop a substantial interest in the sociology of education.

At the end of the war in 1945, on funds supplied by the federal government to help universities cater for an expected post-war influx, I joined the staff of the School of Education at the University of Melbourne as a full-time lecturer in Education. It was the first full-time appointment other than the professor to be made in Education; and even the professor had been part-time principal of the teachers college and part-time university officer until 1939. It seems extraordinary that, from Smyth's first appointment as professor of education in 1919 until 1945, for a period of twenty-six years, a university department could be expected to fulfil its proper functions with an almost entire dependence on part-time staff. Yet it was the same in each of the Australian states. When I became a senior lecturer in 1951 at the University of Sydney, I was again, with a fellow appointee, Morven Brown, the first full-time non-professorial appointment in Education. Obviously, university departments had not been expected to make any sustained study or research in education, but were to concentrate on the practice of training teachers.

My work in Melbourne was mainly that of conducting evening classes in several subjects for first and second year B.Ed. students. During 1946 the John and Eric Smyth Travelling Scholarship was established and I became the first travelling scholar. I held the scholarship for a two-year period. It was supplemented by a Commonwealth Reconstruction Training Post-Graduate Grant awarded for the duration of the Ph.D. course in London.

University of London

By the end of 1946 therefore I was back in London. For a family of four as we were then, the immediate post-war years in England were fairly bleak. There was a near-record cold winter and severe rationing. We remained for two years until I completed my thesis which was subsequently published as *The Educational Thought and Influence of Matthew Arnold*.

I was enrolled both at the Institute of Education and the Institute of Historical Research of the University of London and had two supervisors, Fred Clarke who had recently retired from the directorship of the Institute of Education, and Robert Greaves who was a lecturer at Bedford College with an interest in religious and nineteenth century history. Both were delightful persons who took a great interest in the progress of the thesis. I used to visit Sir Fred at his flat and, in front of a pleasant fire, discuss various broad aspects of educational, moral, and social theory, and Arnold's contribution to them. Each month I would submit a chapter to Robert Greaves for his detailed comment, and we would find a quiet corner in the Institute of Historical Research to discuss that chapter and the next. It was a regular, well-disciplined research and writing programme, and through it I learned to write in a disciplined way, assiduously and carefully assembling the material, searching for its structure and meaning, reflecting on its significant points and relationships, and, from the beginning of the research, constantly writing and developing the narrative.

One of the great advantages of working in a place like London was the richness of the academic environment. There was a great range of general and specialized libraries and archival collections. There were also interesting courses available in the various colleges of the university and I attended many of them. Laski was in full flight in politics at the London School of Economics, Ashton in economic history, and Beales in local government at the same institution; Mace at Birkbeck, and Burt at University College provided attractive courses in psychology; and at the Institute of Historical Research one could occasionally listen to Tawney.

At the Institute of Education, I found Hamley the most interesting person. An Australian, who taught for a while with Aunt Maud at University High School in Melbourne, Hamley was a professor of education in charge of the higher degree students. He lectured in educational psychology and educational statistics with great clarity and precision. He sur-

Maud Mary Connell

Emeritus Professor W. F. Connell

prised me one day by telling me he had put my name in for the vacant chair in the history of education at King's College in the hope that an appointment would be deferred until I had finished my Ph.D. thesis! The King's electors chose to disregard the Australian lobby and appointed, instead, A. V. Judges, a skilful and more experienced historian.

The work on Matthew Arnold introduced me to the great sprawling Victorian Age. To deal competently with Arnold's views on education I had to steep myself in the whole social, economic and intellectual life of that age. Arnold's interest in culture and its intimate relation to education became for me also a lasting interest. His notion of culture, as an active agent of the best elements in human thought being brought to work for the betterment of society, and his commitment to a general humanization of society by the salutary influence of such a culture, is not unlike Dewey's interest in the use of education for the reconstruction of society and for the development of a closer sense of democratic community. It provides the various purposes of education with a strong moral overtone directed to the improvement of human society. By constantly seeking the improvement of thought, skill, and taste, the educator contributes to the improvement of culture; but the person of true culture in Arnold's and Dewey's sense is the one who also relates these activities to the task of raising the sense of mutual respect and obligation throughout human society. My supervisor, Fred Clarke, was of the same persuasion.

Somewhat related to this theme was an important experience that happened in 1947. Unesco had recently been established and had decided to run its first workshop seminar for a group of educators from its member countries. The topic was Education for International Understanding. It was a six-week seminar held at Sèvres on the outskirts of Paris. There were 82 participants from 31 countries, all in residence in a fine old building that Mme de Pompadour had once graced. Four Australians attended of whom I was one. D. J. Ross, headmistress of Melbourne Girls Grammar School was also a participant and the seminar was the beginning of a long and affectionate friendship in which we found much in common between us in our political, social and educational convictions. Howard E. Wilson, a professor of education at Harvard, directed the seminar, and was assisted full-time by an exciting group which included Margaret Mead, Hilda Taba, Robert J. Havighurst and Jean Guiton. In addition, others, such as Léon Blum, Gilbert Murray, Jean Piaget, James Yen, Salvador de Madariaga, and Karl Bigelow, would turn up for a day or so to talk with us. I was much taken with the fact that Gilbert Murray who was then 81 sought out the Australians and in conversation let us know that he still nostalgically thought of himself as one of us though he had left Australia in 1877 at the age of 11. We discussed at length basic ideas about the nature of international understanding, teased out some useful principles for teaching it, and proposed various elements that might be included in a secondary school programme.

The seminar was my introduction to Unesco, to workshop procedures, and to peace education. After our return home I became a member of the Australian Unesco Education Committee and its chairman from 1964 to 1973. Through it we were able to organize a number of workshop-seminars which produced useful materials for Australian schools. One resource document on Education for International Understanding was used for a while in several thousand Australian secondary schools and went through a substantial reprint. Throughout the 1960s there was no federal agency through which educators from all states and overseas consultants could be brought together into a workshop to study ways of improving school curricula. Our Unesco Education Committee took up this task and during that period we held one or two such workshops each year on science, mathematics, languages, music, art and international understanding. Unesco's efforts towards peace have been supplemented by those of many other educational bodies. For one of them, the World Education Fellowship in 1982, I drew on the experience of Unesco's workshops to compose an address and article on the basic considerations involved in designing a curriculum for peace education.

University of Illinois

It was during the Sèvres seminar that our next academic move was planned. I remarked to Howard Wilson that I would soon finish my Ph.D. and I would like to get some experience of American universities before returning to Australia. He suggested writing to the University of Illinois which he regarded as one of the most interesting in the field of education. I followed his advice. In due course an instructorship for the fall semester of 1948 was offered to me and it was subsequently extended to a job for the whole academic year. It was the beginning of a long, affectionate, and scholarly rewarding association.

Illinois in 1948 had a superb School of Education. Spalding, the dean, was an intelligent administrator who kept abreast of the work and ideas of each of the professional fields of education, and was able to attract and keep at Illinois many of the leading figures in each area. At that time there were, for example, in educational philosophy and history, B. O. Smith, Benne, Stanley, and Anderson; in educational psychology, Cronback, Gage, Stendler, and Blair; in educational administration, Trump, Reeder, and Benner; in curriculum, Hand, De Boer, Shores, and Van Til; in special education, Kirk; and in evaluation, Hastings. Each had already made or was to make widely acknowledged contributions to his field. Champaign-Urbana was a university town so we were quickly and constantly in contact with our colleagues. I found the intellectual life had a richness I had not previously experienced in any other environment. This American group were widely read in education and much related literature, they were sharp-witted and probing in discussion, their ideas were innovative, and they were immensely hard-working and productive in research and writing.

I was particularly attracted to the history and philosophy group. They were convinced Deweyans and had the responsibility for editing *Progressive Education*, and later, *Educational Theory*. Smith and Benne had just written, with Raup and Axtelle, *The Discipline of Practical Judgment in a Democratic Society* which grappled with the problem of the kind of education and social processes that are needed in a democratic society to produce action by co-operative agreement instead of through compromise. It was an important and original contribution to educational thinking. Both Smith and Benne were highly stimulating individuals and intellectually the brightest persons I have ever met in any of the social science disciplines. Smith later was the co-author of an outstanding textbook on curriculum development. He retired from Illinois to his native Florida, and, now in his eighties, works at the University of Southern Florida and is still in demand for his superbly incisive judgement as a moderator at conferences. Benne left Illinois in the mid-1950s and spent 25 years at Boston University where he built up an international reputation in the field of group dynamics and the planning of social change. Stanley was a very knowledgeable exponent of Deweyan social theory. I sat in on a semester course which he gave on *Democracy and Education*. It was a detailed, and, for me, illuminating commentary, chapter by chapter, on Dewey's book. Anderson was a specialist in the history of American education, having a special interest in the nineteenth century. I shared a course with him, taught one in comparative education, and also ran an extra-mural course on a Saturday morning in the history of American education, keeping a chapter ahead of the class in the basic textbooks. Before returning to Australia early in 1950 I spent a term at the University of California at Los Angeles, again teaching the history of education and comparative education with Flaud Wooton, a well-known and very helpful scholar in the history of education.

My year and a half in the USA was immensely stimulating. The experience reinforced ideas that I had already been developing, and gave me a much richer perspective of the content of educational studies. American educational literature in the experimentalist tradition seemed to me more extensive and thorough than any to be found elsewhere. In consequence, I have mainly looked since then to American research and writing for suggestion and stimulus in most educational fields. In particular, it was clear in 1948 that the Americans had moved more extensively than academics elsewhere into the serious study of education. The American graduate schools of education had no counterpart elsewhere. They were, and still are, not primarily to improve the training of teachers, but to deepen our knowledge of one of the important social sciences of our time, education.

When I had the opportunity a few years later to develop a school of education at the University of Sydney my main objective was to build a centre which, while providing exemplary teacher education programmes, would be recognized as a leading centre for the study of education comparable with a good American graduate school of education. With its tough honours school in the Arts faculty, and its popular coursework masters' degrees already established, the Sydney education school lent itself admirably to such an ambition.

I rejoined the faculty of education at the University of Melbourne early in 1950. There was a great temptation to stay at the University of Illinois. I was offered an assistant-professorship there during the course of that year and, had a senior lectureship at the University of Sydney not come up at the same time we probably would have moved back to Urbana. Years later, in 1964, there was another strong temptation. A decision was taken at the University of Illinois to establish a full professorship in comparative education and it was suggested to me that I should come and take up the position. It was a flattering proposition, but I was by then too much committed to and interested in working in Sydney to want to migrate permanently to America.

University of Sydney

My job at the University of Sydney began in 1951 and I remained there until my retirement in 1976. I was promoted to a readership in 1953. Two years later, in 1955, with the appointment of the professor of education, C. R. McRae, to the deputy vice-chancellorship of the University of Sydney, and the retirement of Professor G. S. Browne in Melbourne, the chairs of education at the universities of Sydney and Melbourne became vacant. I applied for both. As it happened both selection committees met within a few hours of each other and I was offered both chairs on the same day! They seemed equally attractive. The ensuing days were, consequently, a period of painful decision making. Probably one of the most important influences on my eventual decision to accept the Sydney chair was the Sydney professor of philosophy, John Anderson. We shared an interest in Matthew Arnold and he used to urge me to write another book like my thesis on Arnold. He had been one of the Sydney selection committee, and he suggested to me that there was greater scope for solid academic work in education at Sydney and that, as the Melbourne school had a larger and more settled staff at that time, Sydney was in greater need. Certainly, Melbourne in 1955 had a good nucleus while Sydney where I was already acting professor had, because of recent staff moves, only one other person and he had just been appointed. Sydney was well designed for both teacher training and a range of other educational studies and courses, and therefore seemed to offer the greater possibility for writing and for developing a strong department for the study of education.

To start the process of such a development at Sydney three things were initially necessary, a supply of young staff who understood and had experience of the depth and comprehensiveness of the programme in a first class American school of education, encouragement to the staff to become involved in research and scholarship, and a concerted effort to extend the range of educational studies.

I had already begun to arrange from my earliest years in Sydney to send each year one or more of our best honours students to the University of Illinois for doctoral work. Among those who went in the early years from Sydney to Illinois and subsequently built themselves an academic reputation were Bill Walker, Ray Debus, Joyce Wylie, Malcolm Skilbeck, Jim Bowen, Brian Crittenden, Ken Sinclair and Brian Hill. Over the years students from other Australian universities also went to Illinois, and that university in due course established a Connell Scholarship scheme for Australians to perpetuate the connection that had been steadily built up between Australian and American scholars in education.

To stimulate staff research, I encouraged co-operative research and managed each year to secure the appointment of research assistants and to get some modest financial assistance for research projects from meagre university funds. In 1957 the *Australian Journal of Education* was established, and I became its editor for its first 16 years. The *Journal* was another means of encouraging the development of educational research and good quality writing, not merely by the Sydney University staff but throughout Australia generally. For most of that period Ray Debus and Vija Sierens of the Sydney staff were exacting and perceptive assistants.

To widen the range of subject-matter relevant to the study of education, two of us began to teach educational sociology mainly from American material that the Chicago school had been producing for the past decade on educational opportunity and the impact of social class and environment on education. Mannheim's views on a democratically planned society also came under consideration. From 1951 I lectured also on curriculum development and tried to stimulate an interest in curriculum theory and research.

Gradually the staff of the Sydney department grew and diversified. In the 1950s our student numbers were enormously swelled by returned servicemen. To cater for them we required extra finance and staff, and, although the additional resources went mainly to departments with large undergraduate first-year classes, we managed in Education to add one or two new members of staff year by year and were able to build up a viable department of a respectable size.

From my years at the University of Sydney I have selected in what follows the kinds of experiences which, it seems to me, contributed most to my further education. They were a kind of informal in-service education.

Sydney style

I found very quickly that the University of Sydney was a tough and conservative school. If you had a vacancy on the staff to fill you had to analyse each applicant carefully before a hard-headed committee of senior academics from science and arts departments and carefully justify your personal choice. It was rare for anyone to win an appointment to an initial lectureship without a record of first class honours work and favourable reports from trusted referees whose qualifications were in turn scrutinized. If you wanted additional resources of money, staff or material you quickly learnt the discipline of drafting persuasive memoranda that would meet all the subtle objections that other academics could fabricate to deny your case. On one occasion at the end of 1965 I wrote a different kind of memorandum, trying with poetry to melt the heart of a so-far unresponsive vice-chancellor on the matter of appointing a second professor of education. I sent him and his advisory establishment committee an adaptation of the first two verses of Wordsworth's 'The Solitary Reaper':

> Behold him, single in the field,
> Yon solitary professorial suitor!
> Teaching and searching by himself;
> Stop! grant him a coadjutor!

and so on for another twelve masterly lines supplemented with appropriate explanatory notes. It was all in vain. It was two years later and a new vice-chancellor before a second chair was agreed to and more than three years before the new professor, Don Spearritt, was actually appointed.

The university did not usually warm to anything innovatory, and if you were silly enough to put any interesting change up for approval through the appropriate channels you were almost certainly courting failure or at least inordinate delay. Consequently, except when it was inescapable, I did not refer changes, that the education staff and I wished to make, to faculty or other authorities but simply made them. For many years, for example, our Dip. Ed. course had little resemblance to what was formally stated in the university calendar. I was agreeably surprised, therefore, that we were able to introduce a four-year undergraduate B.Ed. degree in 1960 after about two and a half years of negotiation. Though for several years understaffed, it was a highly successful degree. It was limited to primary, pre-primary, and physical education students. We were unable to win the argument for secondary education students who had to continue from an arts, science or economics degree to a one-year postgraduate diploma in education. The number of B.Ed. students was limited, with the result that only students with high academic qualifications succeeded in gaining admission. This, together with clearly skilled and challenging teaching from the staff running the degree, and highly commendatory reports from the schools on the graduates of the courses, gave the course an excellent reputation both inside and outside the university.

Over the years, one of the more interesting features of university life was the development of various informal groups among the staff. Some were special interest groups such as a mediaeval and Renaissance, or an American or Asian studies group, others centred round sporting or current political issues, and others again were cross-disciplinary luncheon clubs made up of persons who found one another's company congenial. I was an original member of one of the latter type which we called the '54 Club from the year of its foundation. It was limited to about twelve members, each from a different discipline, and met for lunch each Wednesday. I found it always a most attractive occasion. The conversation was interesting and ranged over topics in which there was usually an expert or two present; there was always an interested audience. It was an effective way of getting to know closely and affectionately a selected number of colleagues throughout the university. The club still continues and I revisit the group whenever I am in Sydney on a Wednesday. The general toughness and conservatism of the university tends to take on a more mellow quality over the luncheon wine of the '54 Club.

Fourth year honours classes

A significant and continuing educational experience was my contact with the fourth year final honours students in Education who were studying for a B.A. degree.

Each year I would take a seminar with this group. In the 1950s they were mostly part-time evening students in full-time teaching jobs; by the 1970s most of them were full-time. I do not think that the change in status had any effect on the quality of the students. They were an outstanding group throughout the whole twenty-five years in which I was associated with them. It would be hard to find a comparable group in any other university where Education is studied. By the time they had reached their fourth year they would usually have had a year of psychology or philosophy, and two years of educational studies. In each of their first three years they would have had to maintain an honours standard in the Education subjects. In their fourth and final year they were required to write a research thesis, put together a long, sustained essay on a topic of their choice, and undertake two seminar courses, one in educational evaluation, the other with me. It was an exacting introduction to the study of education. Everyone who completed it was good; those who finished up with first class honours were superb.

In the seminar which I ran with these students I selected about half a dozen books for analysis and discussion. Usually none of them was specifically on education; instead, each dealt with some aspect of modern culture that I thought they should learn to relate to education. R. Jungk, *Brighter than a Thousand Suns*, an account of the Manhattan project and its background, was a good example. On one occasion when it was being considered, S. Kapitza, a Russian atomic physicist and son of one of Rutherford's collaborators, was present to add spice to the discussion. The seminar met every second Wednesday in the evening for two terms at our home in Beauty Point. Margaret provided a dinner about 6 p.m., and from 7 to 9 p.m. we adjourned to my study to consider one of the books under the guidance of one of the students. There was never a set pattern for our activity. For example, one year, with one of the books we did not get past the cover—a reproduction of a Paul Klee abstract—during the whole of our two-hour session. At another session, after duly pondering *Mother Courage*, we decided to go to a theatre where *The Good Woman of Setzuan* was playing. After the play we met the cast and talked with them about Brecht's ideas and techniques, and how, as actors or educators, we could get our respective audiences to comprehend them. On another occasion one of the students started by setting us all an objective test on our knowledge of some of the ideas that he wanted to emphasize in that night's book. Needless to say, some of his views on what were the correct answers were subject to sharp and spirited questioning.

The seminar had several purposes. It was designed to make these potentially leading educators more fluent and penetrating in the discussion of educational issues. We therefore argued without restraint 'to the stumps of our intellects', as one of Matthew Arnold's odd acquaintances put it, and everyone was required to participate fully. It was a serious and sustained exercise in thinking into educational and social problems, and in formulating a sincere and defensible position on them. The seminar was designed also to encourage the students to see education in a wider cultural context. An important part of their task was to detect, clarify and evaluate the relationships between education and a variety of economic, social and cultural activities, and to determine possible lines of educational action arising out of their analysis. The seminar was, in a sense, a way of putting both Arnold and Dewey into action together.

Adolescents, culture, and co-operative writing

When I first went to Sydney in 1951 I started a course with the third year distinction students on the School in the Australian Society. In it we began to look at topics such as Australian cultural and educational traditions, the nature and impact of social class, demographic influences, child-rearing practices, and adolescent experience in Australia. It did not take us long to realize that there was scarcely any material available on the Australian situation. Nothing could bring home more profoundly the derivative nature of our education and culture than the realization that since the beginning of our university courses in education we had initiated no substantial study of the characteristic behaviour, interests and attitudes of Australian children and the way in which they grew up in an Australian culture. In the 1950s we were still teaching our child growth and development courses out of American and English textbooks, and the new subject of educational sociology had almost no local basis. The distinction class and I decided to make a start on the collection of Australian data. We could not cover the whole field, and we therefore chose to concentrate on a study of the way in which an Australian adolescent grows up within an urban Australian environment.

Thus *Growing Up in an Australian City* was conceived. It took several years and several classes of distinction students to complete. We studied nearly 9000 adolescents between 13 and 18 years old in Sydney, in school and out of school; we devised questionnaires that we administered in a large number of schools, factories and businesses; we interviewed various samples of adolescents and read a number of comprehensive and interesting diaries. We discussed our data in seminar sessions, and half a dozen of the group lived with us in our beach home at Collaroy for about three weeks during a Christmas vacation to work the material into presentable form. My family too joined in the work, and ever since, have thoroughly but gently and suggestively, read many of my manuscripts to my great advantage. Finally, two research assistants and I wrote the book, and the ACER published it in 1957.

Growing Up was quite a popular book but, except for one fine study of youth in a rural town by W. J. Campbell who was then on the Sydney staff, it did not lead to the further Australian studies that were needed. It was not until about ten years later that they started to emerge. It did foster my interest, however, in writing on adolescence and secondary education and in further ventures in co-operative writing. My essay on *The Foundations of Secondary Education* in 1961 was an effort to continue the argument on the relationship of education and culture and the schools' role in cultural modification. At the end of the 1960s I persuaded several members of staff to work on a more thorough study of adolescents and in due course we produced in 1975 *12 to 20: Studies of City Youth.*

Meanwhile another highly successful co-operative book had been written. Again we had met the problem of the lack of suitable material for one of our courses. In this case it was the central foundations area of the Dip.Ed. course. Over the years we experimented with various approaches to teacher education from a traditional structure through situational teaching to a school-based programme. About 1960 we had adopted an approach which attempted to tease out the social, psychological and philosophical foundations of education, relate them together in a sensible way, and make them the core of the Dip.Ed. programme. Of course, there was no suitable text for students. The staff therefore set about the task of writing one and speedily produced *The Foundations of Education.*

This book had ten authors and, in sixteen chapters and 300 pages, provided a sound and interesting basic text written primarily for Australian university students but capable of attracting a much wider audience. Since the Sydney Dip.Ed. was available for both primary and secondary teacher education, the book was suitable for intending teachers of both levels. It began by looking at the significant features in the pattern of children's development from birth to late adolescence, moved on to consider the general social and cultural setting of the school and its possible objectives, examined the way school curricula could be designed and the bases for effective teaching and evaluation; and, finally, considered the characteristics of the teacher and the teaching profession. It was just the kind of introduction that we wanted for our own courses. Other institutions apparently had similar thoughts and the book was widely used. During its currency of about fifteen years and three editions about 120 000 copies were sold in Australia, New Zealand, Malaysia, and Great Britain. We subsequently produced a book of readings in the foundations of education which also prospered.

A History of Education in the Twentieth Century World

My major piece of research and writing throughout the 1960s and 1970s was on the development of education in the twentieth century. It arose out of a general interest in the period and a consciousness that when one wanted to teach the recent history of education there was nothing available except a few national histories and specialist studies of isolated problems and periods. I wanted also to try to show the central importance of education and the views of educators in the development of the twentieth century. Education has always seemed to me the basic activity of any civilization, and with the advent of mass education it has become an increasingly important element in the maintenance, modification or reconstruction of existing cultural traditions.

When we began offering classes for M.A. and M.Ed. students in the 1950s with our rather small staff, we selected topics that each lecturer had a particular interest in and wished to pursue further. I therefore began a course on educational thought in the twentieth century which in the 1960s gradually became a history of twentieth century education in general. I began to write comprehensively on each of the topics dealt with in the classes. It was an endeavour, while not neglecting the standard western tradition of courses in the English-speaking world, to step beyond it to consider education in the leading communist countries in a serious non-propaganda way, to look at the recent history of education in some significant Asian countries, and to study the educational growth of a sample of the developing countries of the world.

What I have learnt from two decades of intensive work and unmitigated pleasure with this book is the importance of searching for underlying patterns and movements of explanatory ideas and influences. Many that are found prove to be inadequate, false or short-lived. Sometimes they may fit reasonably well. It is easier to find them in the lives of individuals and institutions than in the cross-currents of national and cultural change. For this reason biography is a more relaxing genre to work in than cultural or social history. My Matthew Arnold, for example, was much easier to write than the twentieth century book. History of education on a broad canvas has to be highly selective and must be seen largely as a thoughtful untangling and clarification of the main themes that are embedded in each period and movement. As the narrative moved from one cultural setting to another, I tried to show the nature of each culture and the way in which the educator, in the light of his current situation, grappled with, made use of, and sometimes succeeded in modifying his cultural heritage. Obviously I have not always been successful and may sometimes, but I hope not too often, have misconceived the task.

During the course of writing the twentieth century book Margaret and I went abroad on study leave several times. The first occasion was in 1959 as a Fulbright scholar to Teachers College, Columbia University, and the University of Illinois. In 1966 I spent a period at the Center for Advanced Study at the University of Illinois, and in 1974 had a semester as a George A. Miller Professor at the same institution. In 1960 and again in 1963 I worked at the Institute of Education, University of London, and in 1974 was a visiting fellow at Wolfson College in the University of Cambridge. Otago invited me as an Evans Visiting Professor for a pleasant stay in the South Island of New Zealand in 1970. These periodical visits helped to build up a knowledge of the recent history of education in the western tradition.

It was also possible to visit the USSR and China and to acquire a reasonable level of familiarity with educational ideas and practices in communist countries. During the last twenty years Margaret and I have made three visits to both the USSR and China and have been interested principally in the way in which, in each country, a long-standing educational tradition has been maintained in some circumstances and reconstructed in others to foster aspects of the newly developing proletarian culture. Educators in both countries have been very co-operative, and over the years we have established a number of warm friendships.

I am now starting to look at the twentieth century again through a series of essays which try to explore these problems and trends in a more comparative way.

Social science education

From the mid-1960s I had an opportunity to take a more practical part in the process of curriculum development in Australia. I have already mentioned the work of the Australian Unesco Education Committee and its part in developing national workshops on various aspects of teaching and curriculum. In 1965 I proposed to it that we hold a workshop on the teaching of social science in secondary schools. This was duly held in Melbourne at Burwood Teachers College in 1967. It was an important occasion. It was the first time on an Australia-wide basis that academics, schoolteachers and administrators had sat together in a week-long workshop to plot the possible future development of an area of the school curriculum. The outcome was the establishment of advisory committees on social science teaching by each of the state departments of education, and, in 1970, a National Committee on Social Science Teaching (NCSST) set up and funded by the federal government. The NCSST lasted until 1978 when its functions were absorbed into the national Curriculum Development Centre. I was its chairman throughout its existence. Its members were co-operative, interested, and prepared to think through and work at the various tasks we attempted.

We ran national and regional workshops, published reports on them, made small grants to teachers to help them with special projects, commissioned several substantial pieces of research, provided consultants for activities initiated by state and regional bodies, and initiated a large-scale programme for the production of social education materials for teachers that became known as SEMP. It was a national exercise in what might be called participant innovation—more or less a translation to the national scene of the techniques of the fourth-year honours class. We worked closely with those whom we regarded as innovative teachers and we encouraged others to join in. As far as possible we worked direct with teachers, involving them in group discussion, classroom experimentation, the practice of new skills and the development of new materials.

Innovation is a complex and subtle matter. If teachers are to change their style and habits, they have to undergo both a cognitive and an attitudinal change. We were involved in both kinds of processes with them, and our experience suggested that success was most likely to be achieved when teachers have the opportunity to participate in all stages of the innovatory process from initial planning to final evaluation, and in a range of mutually reinforcing innovatory activities. The national committee was greatly supported by the Victorian state advisory committee, the only one of the state committees that survived for any length of time. It provided lively staff members for a number of our workshops and produced an excellent quarterly teachers' magazine which we financially supported. Since 1978, when the national committee ceased to exist, the kind of work we tried to develop has been admirably continued through the programmes undertaken by the Victorian committee.

Continuity and Change

Continuity is a difficult matter to assess. I think of myself as a continuator in part of G. S. Browne's work, and also as one who has used the opportunities provided by the structures set up and the foundations laid by C. R. McRae in Sydney. There is, however, more than a subtle difference between the three of us. I am a social scientist who is interested in the study of education as a dynamic and central element in a society's culture. I try to understand it by examining the historical processes through which this relationship has developed. I seek also practical ways of controlling it and of producing educational and cultural change. My predecessors were interested in individual development and the reorganization of teaching and administrative processes in ways best calculated to ensure such an outcome. There is much in their practices with which I agree, but my approach to educational issues is from the opposite direction.

I am not sure that the staff at the University of Sydney would have always shared my educational views. They were a very carefully selected group, and my biases would perhaps have entered in some measure into the selection process. Moreover several of them had followed the Sydney–Illinois track. Over the years, relationships throughout the department were almost uniformly pleasant and mutually supportive. Don Spearritt, Bob Petersen, and Ray Debus, for example, have been some of my most constructive and valued critics; with many others I have had a close and sustained collaboration in research and writing. I am sure they share my sense of the importance of education; they may not share my cultural reconstructionism. Nevertheless, I hope that enough symbiosis has occurred to ensure a reasonable continuity of the educational approach and activity that I have tried to practise and profess.

At the end of 1976 when I was sixty I retired from Sydney to return to Melbourne and concentrate on writing. To my delight, Monash University invited me to become a fellow of its faculty of Education, and provided me with accommodation and a continuing opportunity for academic contact.

One of my long-term projects, on which I have been working at Monash, is an analysis of the factors involved in educational change. What are the general influences, the particular interests, and the mechanisms which promote or inhibit change, encourage or frustrate innovation? This sort of question raises fundamental issues for an understanding of the ways in which education has been changed in the past, and the ways in which it might be induced to change in the future. If we are to have some reasonable control over them they deserve much more attention from educational historians than has so far been the case.

A noted classical scholar, T. R. Glover, once wrote an interesting essay called Springs of Hellas in which he described and commented on the exploration of the numerous fresh-water springs in Greece and their importance in the life and development of that country. A search for the processes of educational change seems to me to be not dissimilar. It is concerned with the sources of energy that underlie educational and cultural development. It is the subterranean task of historians of education—a search for the springs of education. It is to this elusive area that I hope to make some contribution during the next few years.

2

STATE-AID AT THE BAR: THE *DOGS CASE*[1]

by I. K. F. BIRCH

'State-aid is legal', 'State-aid declared valid'—such were the banner headlines announcing the decision of the High Court of Australia in the *DOGS case*, which was brought down on 11 February 1981. The reception given this decision was mild compared with the days of turmoil in the 1960s when state-aid was of such political moment. But just because the issue had become so settled at governmental levels, the High Court's determination of this case was awaited with interest.

Not the least interested was the Victorian Council for the Defence of Government Schools whose initiative and drive brought this action to fruition and which, from the acronym DOGS, gave this case its popular name. The attack which the Council for DOGS led was principally against the funding by successive Commonwealth governments of non-government religious schools. The ground for the legal action was that such aid violated the first clause of section 116 of the Commonwealth Constitution. That clause provided that:

> The Commonwealth shall not make any law for establishing any religion, or for imposing any religious observance, or for prohibiting the free exercise of any religion, and no religious test shall be required as a qualification for any office or public trust under the Commonwealth.[2]

The case was of concern for two reasons in particular. In the first place, the High Court had not previously been required to determine the scope of the clause in question. Its interpretation was of some constitutional moment since the provision in section 116 had clearly been modelled on the provision in the First Amendment of the American Constitution which asserted that 'Congress shall make no law respecting an establishment of religion, or prohibiting the free exercise thereof . . .'[3] The Supreme Court of the United States of America had interpreted that provision as prohibiting aid from the public purse for religious schools. Such rulings had greatly encouraged the Council for DOGS to proceed with its action. The question was whether the High Court of Australia would follow suit.

Secondly, an outcome adverse to the legislature could have serious implications for the government of the day and the schools in question, at least in the immediate future. At risk were programmes of aid to schools in the states spanning almost twenty years and costing millions of dollars. A national commitment by all major political parties in support of non-government religious schools was at stake, not to mention the question of the recovery of moneys already granted were the action successful. On both political and constitutional fronts, therefore, the decision in the *DOGS case* was of seminal interest.

Prelude to the DOGS CASE

In 1956 Prime Minister R. G. Menzies announced that his government was to pay the interest on the capital works loans of independent secondary schools in the Australian Capital Territory. Five years later, this programme of assistance was extended to include independent primary schools. Although this was not the first state-aid assistance by a Commonwealth government to religious schools—assistance had been made available to church schools in some of the non-mainland territories from the first years of federation—these programmes marked the dawn of a political era of considerable turmoil and one of significance for educational policy making in Australia. Documentation of this turmoil and its impact on education need not be rehearsed here.[4] What is important as background to the *DOGS case* is the legislation which came under attack in that action.

The Attorney-General for Victoria granted his fiat to Writ No. 57 of 1973 which launched the formal proceedings leading to the *DOGS case* on 14 December 1973. Five days later the *States Grants (Schools) Act, 1973* and the *Schools Commission Act, 1973* passed into law. Although these Acts were not, therefore, in force when the writ was lodged, they emerged as pivotal pieces of legislation when the DOGS' attack was later broadened to embrace all relevant legislation. The former Act was the most comprehensive piece of legislation providing assistance to schooling passed by a Commonwealth government. As far as state-aid is concerned, this Act both caught up the earlier legislation and provided a model for assistance which subsequent governments followed, regardless of their political persuasion. Further, with the introduction of the Schools Commission (now the Commonwealth Schools Commission), administrative machinery to advise the Minister for Education and to administer programmes approved by Parliament was established. These two important pieces of legislation are discussed in turn.

State-aid legislation

The States Grants (Schools) Act, 1973 made provision for assistance to government and non-government schools. It created new programmes and continued old ones which had provided aid for both government and non-government schools. As for assistance specifically to *government* schools, the minister was authorized to make payments to the states for financial assistance for building projects in primary and secondary schools to a limit of $100 million for the years 1974 and 1975.[5] The main conditions placed on the states were that the money was to be used without delay and that it was not to be used on projects the main purpose of which was to increase the number of student places or provide residential accommodation for staff.

The states had received money for their schools' capital costs, apart from particular programmes such as the science laboratories scheme, before 1973. What was novel in the States Grants (Schools) legislation of that year was that the Commonwealth made assistance available to the states for recurrent expenditure in the government school system. The amount provided for the two years 1974 and 1975 was almost $176 million and the conditions imposed required the use of the grant for recurrent expenditure and the provision of certificates that it had been so used.

As for assistance specifically to *non-government* schools, the 1973 legislation made provision for grants to be made under several heads. Grants were made, for example, to the states for assistance for capital works in schools for the two years of the Act's operation to a total of $16 million.[6] The previous government had, in the *States Grants (Schools) Act*, 1972, made provision for like aid. The 1973 legislation, however, added the significant condition—from the viewpoint of the state-aid debate—that the money was not to be applied to provide facilities for use wholly or principally for, or in relation to, religious worship.[7]

Recurrent grants for non-government schools, first provided for in the *States Grants (Independent Schools) Act*, 1969 (which was under direct challenge in the *DOGS case*) were continued in the 1973 legislation for use in Catholic systemic schools and in non-government non-systemic schools. These latter schools were ranked on a scale 'A' to 'H' on a basis of need and were to receive the amounts prescribed for each category. The Labor government was forced to allow the inclusion of sums payable to 'A' category schools against its wishes in return for Country Party and Democratic Labor Party support for the measure in an otherwise hostile Senate.[8] The conditions imposed on both these types of payments were related to the appropriate payment by the states and assurances from the authority or the schools that the money was, and would be, used as the Act required.

The *States Grants (Schools) Act*, 1973 provided for a number of new programmes for the public and private sectors of schooling. These included the provision of capital and recurrent grants for disadvantaged

c

schools, assistance for handicapped children and programmes for the in-service training of teachers, including the establishment of teacher education centres. A programme to encourage educational innovation was also introduced and an amount of $5 million was set aside for this purpose.

Two programmes of earlier governments were continued by the 1973 legislation and later assimilated into the general grants programmes. These were the science laboratories scheme which was introduced by R. G. Menzies in 1964 and marked the introduction of state-aid for secondary education, and the libraries programme of 1968, under which the Commonwealth made grants to the states for capital expenditure on libraries and the acquisition of library material for all secondary schools.

The passing of the *Schools Commission Act*, 1973 fulfilled a goal which Labor had had on its platform for several years. The Interim Committee for the Australian Schools Commission was appointed on 12 December 1972. The Commission came into being some twelve months later after the Government overcame opposition in the House of Representatives and reverses in the Senate (the Country Party and Democratic Labor Party finally changing their vote and giving the proposal their support). The Schools Commission was provided with a full-time and part-time membership. Its functions were somewhat different and broader than those of the Commonwealth's tertiary education commissions of the day and required it to consult and co-operate with state education authorities. Its main tasks were to inquire into and furnish information and advice to the minister on acceptable standards in schools, the needs of schools, matters related to grants to the states for schools and any matter referred by the minister or investigated on its own volition.

Since 1973 the provision of funds for state-aid has been continued and increased and the Schools Commission has devised indices for determining the needs of schools and has recommended payments accordingly. There is little doubt that, by the time the *DOGS case* was heard, state-aid, as the term is commonly understood, had become a political fact of life as far as national governments were concerned. This is quite evident in the amount allocated for non-government schools in the 1981-82 estimates for the Commonwealth Department of Education.[9] Leaving aside joint programmes, the amount proposed for payment to the states for recurrent expenditure in non-government schools was about $251 million, with an additional $24 million being designated for capital expenditure. The former was a fivefold increase on the 1973-74 figure for recurrent expenditure and the latter three times the like figure for capital expenditure.

Although the *DOGS case* focused attention on the national government's provisions for state-aid, mention should also be made of those of the states. No sooner was the science laboratories scheme in operation than Queensland introduced per capita tuition allowances for students attending independent schools. Western Australia followed suit in 1965 and introduced a scheme to meet the interest on capital works as did New South Wales, Victoria and Queensland in 1966. By the end of 1968 per capita grants to students in non-government schools were common to all the states and the idea of a matching Commonwealth-state contribution which amounted to 40 per cent of the cost of educating a student at a government school was being realized. The Commonwealth did not, therefore, stand alone in governmental support for state-aid. But it alone did have a section 116 in its constitution.

The Council for DOGS

That the case on state-aid is known as the *DOGS case* is a tribute to the tenacity of a Council which achieved what others had failed to accomplish. With the emergence of state-aid programmes described above, there was an accompanying rise of protagonists and antagonists of the schemes promulgated. The Parents and Friends Association in Western Australia was clearly among the first if it were not the first of the former: the progenitor of the latter is more difficult to determine since organizations such as the New South Wales Humanist Society had long opposed state government support of religion and had been instrumental in launching legal action on the issue of religion in government schools, albeit without success.[10] Challenges to Commonwealth support appear to have begun with the Victorian Protestant Federation's unsuccessful attempt in 1957 to mount an action on the basis of section 116 in the High Court. The Labor Party, through its leader, Arthur Calwell, threatened legal action after passing of the science laboratories legislation in 1964, but proceeded no further. That year also marked the founding of the Council for the Defence of Government Schools and, consequently, the planning of a constitutional challenge to state-aid.

1971 to 1973 were the heady years in the preparation for the legal battle. Fighting funds were established, petitions circulated and advertisements were placed in the press enlisting public support. Visitors from the USA (where the decision in *Lemon* v. *Kurtzman*[11] cemented the judicial barriers to state-aid) included the Revd C. Stanley Lowell in 1971 who addressed the meeting launching the DOGS challenge and Dr Leo Pfeffer, an American lawyer who had played a leading role in the processes in that country to withstand the push for state-aid. Institutional support came from groups opposed to state-aid either on sectarian grounds or for political reasons. Included among the former were various alliances of protestants; among the latter, teachers' unions figured prominently. The change of government from Liberal-Country Party to Labor in December 1972 altered little except to make more acute Labor's embarrassment at having members of the Party named as relators. The opponents of state-aid recognized that some issues required particular attention. These included the selection of relators for the action, the obtaining of an attorney-general's fiat, fund-raising and the problem concerning the relator/Schools Commission member, Joan Kirner.

The relators

The relators to this action were intended to 'represent a cross-section of Australian society (symbolically representing the widespread opposition to state-aid)'.[12] The cross-section comprised parents, citizens and teachers opposed to state-aid. As far as representative groupings went there were, apart from members of the Council for DOGS itself, noted members of the Labor Party such as the chairman of its education committee, Bill Hartley, and union leaders including Wally Curran, state secretary of the Meat Employees' Union and John Halfpenny, secretary of the Amalgamated Metal Workers' and Shipwrights' Union. The biggest single group of relators flowed from the DOGS' request to the Australian Council of State School Organisations (ACSSO)[13] that it nominate as relators not only its national president, but also the president or nominee from each state and territory so that in each state an approach could properly be made to the Attorney-General, seeking his fiat. ACSSO's affiliates readily responded to this request, with only the Queensland Council of State School Organisations and the Australian Capital Territory Council of Parents' and Citizens' Associations delaying in their acquiescence.

The involvement of the relators in the action varied considerably. At the centre of the activity were Ray Nilsen and Lance Hutchinson, president and secretary respectively of the Council for DOGS. Nilsen was also co-ordinator of the legal challenge to state-aid. Others, such as Hartley, were treated very nominally in the role of relator, receiving no particular information about the progress of events, nor being sought out for advice as to the conduct of the campaign. The relators from ACSSO and its affiliates occupied a middle position. They were consulted on financial matters in particular, and were kept abreast of developments, though not always as adequately as they would have liked. Relationships between the two bodies were sometimes strained, as when ACSSO learnt from the *Financial Review* rather than from the Council that the writ had been amended to embrace the 1973 legislation on states grants and on the establishment of the Schools Commission.

The reasons for opposition to state-aid varied among the relators. Some, such as Nilsen, reflected the demands of James Madison and Thomas Jefferson for the separation of church and state, both to safeguard the integrity of each and to avoid preferential treatment of any one religion. Others, such as Hartley and Kirner, spurned sectarian motives and opposed state-aid as being in conflict with their political ideology. But all parties, religious or not, political or not, found a common cause under the DOGS' banner.

A problem of some interest to those invited to serve as relators was the question of their personal liability for costs in this case. The president of ACSSO at the time, Peter Jensen, obtained legal advice to the effect that the petitioners would be jointly and severally liable for costs, that is, they would share the liability and if any one petitioner could not meet his obligation, the remaining petitioners would need to meet that liability as well.[14] (It was noted that the Council for DOGS was not an incorporated body and was therefore itself unable to become a petitioner to the writ.) Jensen was advised that if he were a petitioner he should obtain from his Council a guarantee that his costs would be met by the Council. ACSSO and its affiliates did, in fact, undertake to meet the costs of their members who became relators by virtue of their office in the organization, and the Council for DOGS had each relator sign a form of instruction and indemnification such that trust moneys collected for the purpose would be used to pay costs should they be awarded against the plaintiffs.

Fiat

The 1957 legal challenge to state-aid foundered on the failure to obtain a fiat from an attorney-general. Without such a fiat the parties had no standing before the High Court, since that Court declined to acknowledge standing to individual citizens unless particularly affected by Commonwealth legislation. After a nationwide list of petitioners had been established through the good offices of ACSSO, letters were sent to the Commonwealth Attorney-General and all the states' attorneys-general on 16 June 1972, requesting them to grant their fiat to an action declaring invalid Commonwealth legislation which made grants to the states in aid of non-government schools. Prompt refusals were received from the Commonwealth and New South Wales Attorneys-General. The negative reply from Tasmania came a little over a year later and replies from the remaining states came after a further request for a fiat from the DOGS' solicitors on 20 September 1973. The reply in all cases (except that of Victoria) was that no fiat would be granted. The Victorian Attorney-General indicated his willingness to grant his fiat provided that a bond against costs was lodged; the relators bore the responsibility for advancing the case; and he retained his right to intervene in the proceedings at any time. The conditions were accepted and the Attorney-General, Vernon Wilcox, signed the High Court writ (number 57 of 1973) on 14 December 1973.

Reasons for the denial and granting of the writ have been discussed by Dr M. J. Ely and will not be rehearsed here.[15] It is worth noting, however, that though Ely seems to share Nilsen's churchman-conspiracy theory in general, she does at least hint (against Whitlam's view that Wilcox was using the courts to challenge Labor's policies) that the Victorian Attorney-General was acting as an attorney-general should, in making it possible for the citizens of his state to approach the High Court.[16]

Finance

The Council for DOGS decided early in 1972 to launch a public appeal for the $20 000 deemed to be required to meet the costs of the action. By that time it had already expended $3000 from its own sources. After discussions with ACSSO, it was decided to establish what became known as the High Court Appeal Costs Trust Fund into which would be paid moneys from the appeal for the $20 000 which was to be set against any costs to the relators, but not against the general running of the campaign. Two forms of agreement were made available: one in which people agreed to make a cash donation which was paid into the Trust Fund and one in the form of a promissory note against a call for support, should the relators have to bear costs. The public response was heartening and by the end of 1972, DOGS was able to report that $14 450 had been promised by eighty-eight guarantors.[17] The financial situation continued to improve and in October 1973 DOGS advised ACSSO that the amount received for the fighting fund and the trust fund amounted to $37 000.[18] But costs were also mounting, with some $11 000 having been paid out, principally in legal fees.

In 1973 a reasonably speedy hearing was assumed. Delays in the case and, finally, its outcome resulted in costs and burdens little expected. Although—and much to the surprise of the Chief Justice—the Commonwealth did not ask for costs against the relators, the other defendants did. At the time of writing the issue of costs had not been resolved.

Relator/Schools Commissioner

Amongst the relators on the writ lodged in the High Court on 14 December 1973 was the name Joan Kirner: amongst the names of those appointed to the Schools Commission on 19 December 1973 was that of Joan Kirner. The ACSSO executive which met on 24 March 1974 resolved that she should remain as a relator but DOGS put the view that the writ should be amended to delete her name. Legal advice given to ACSSO was of the opinion that (1) the amendment sought by DOGS was appropriate, (2) that it should be a mere formality to delete Mrs Kirner's name, (3) that there would be a problem in respect of costs since the other relators would have to bear more of the cost, and (4) that there was no necessity for Mrs Kirner to withdraw, as the matter at issue was one of law and not of fact.[19] ACSSO was persuaded in time that it was in the best interests of all parties for an alternate to be nominated in her place. DOGS' solicitors were asked to give effect to this decision and to the request to delete a Mr Wajsbrem from the list of relators. The Victorian Attorney-General would have none of this. Asked for an explanation, Wilcox intimated that he saw no reason why the group of relators to whom his fiat had been granted should be altered, and that the case was to proceed on the basis of the relators named or not at all.[20] On obtaining further legal opinion, ACSSO was advised that a name could normally be withdrawn from a writ on an application to a judge in chambers and that it was difficult to see how the Attorney-General could oppose such an application. It was pointed out, however, that an applicant could expect to meet the costs of such an application and be required to guarantee his or her part of the total costs of the trial of the action.

The Council for DOGS and its solicitors both asked ACSSO to retain Joan Kirner in a nominal way among the relators. The former, in words which drew a sharp retort from the president of ACSSO, suggested that 'it would be an ironical tragedy if ACSSO's representative was used as the instrument to prevent the case coming to court'.[21] Both DOGS and ACSSO were unsuccessful in having Wilcox change his ground and ACSSO continued to remain under pressure from DOGS to have Joan Kirner continue. 1976 saw a change of attorney-general in Victoria. Wilcox's successor, Haddon Storey, proved less obstructive to DOGS in altering the writ as far as incorporating amendments to accommodate new legislation was concerned. But he, too, baulked at permitting changes to the list of relators. The matter was finally and simply resolved when ACSSO followed the legal advice it had received and Mrs Kirner obtained an order from Mr Justice Murphy removing her name from the list of relators. That occurred immediately prior to the beginning of the hearing on the facts on 6 March 1979.

The Kirner matter was significant for several reasons, not the least being the strain on the person herself. First, it may be seen to be responsible in part for the delay in having the *DOGS case* heard. Certainly, practically all else came to a standstill in 1975 while the matter was under discussion. Secondly, it reflected the change in approach by ACSSO to the state-aid issue. From total opposition to state-aid in 1972, ACSSO had, at its Darwin conference in 1976, decided that state-aid was a political reality and, therefore, its approach should be one of safeguarding the interests of the governments sector by having stringent conditions apply to the receipt of state-aid. Thirdly, it marked a considerable rift in the relationship between DOGS and ACSSO, which appears to have been ambivalent at the best of times. Finally, the affair cost ACSSO about $2000, which was a salutary reminder of the fact that the 1972 commitment had a cost price-tag.

Statement of claim

The years 1973 to 1978 witnessed activity on many fronts as the foregoing suggests. The effect of the time lapse and the influence of the factors discussed led to changes in the approach of the plaintiffs; these changes are reflected in the alterations to the statement of claim between the years in question. The major alterations were to the named defendants and the legislation under attack. There was also considerable refinement given to the final statement on which the action was based.[22]

Changes on the political scene led to alterations in the naming of the defendants, with the then Treasurer and Minister for Education (F. D. Crean and K. E. Beazley respectively) being replaced in 1978 by the then Treasurer, Minister for Education and Minister for Finance (J. W. Howard, Senator J. L. Carrick and E. L. Robinson respectively). The plaintiffs' list was also varied so as to comprise the Attorney-General for Victoria, suing on the relation of 28 named residents of Victoria, six taxpayer residents of Victoria, two of the Australian Capital Territory, four of New South Wales and two of Tasmania.

The 1978 statement of claim provided particulars of legislation which the plaintiffs claimed was for the benefit of religious schools. The list included the Science Laboratories and Libraries Assistance Acts, dating from 1964 and 1968 respectively, all the Acts passed to 1978 providing assistance to schools, the Schools Commission Acts and the loans assistance legislation passed by the Commonwealth. A table of expenditure on capital and recurrent programmes accompanied these particulars.

The plaintiffs asserted in the claim that the religious schools receiving aid could be characterized by one or more traits, including the imposition of religious observance, required attendance at religious activities, the teaching or receiving of religious doctrine, the subjection of secular activities to the demands of religion, and control by churches or church appointees.

The crux of the claim was that the laws mentioned

> constitute laws for establishing any religion and as such are beyond the power of the Commonwealth and are void and of no effect and ... are not authorised by section 96 of the Constitution or alternatively are invalid by reason of the provisions of Section 116 of the Constitution.[23]

In the language of American decisions on church-state relations, the laws were said to have the purpose and effect of Commonwealth support

for religion, and to impose on the Commonwealth an excessive entanglement in the affairs of religion. The plaintiffs sought both a declaration
that the nominated legislation was invalid and injunctions restraining the
defendants from implementing provisions of extant legislation.

Preliminary hearings

Three formal preliminary High Court proceedings were heard before the
DOGS case came before the Full Court. In the first of these, determined
on 17 May 1978, Mr Justice Aickin dealt with two summonses, one from
the plaintiffs and one from the defendants, which were concerned with
the discovery of documents. Aickin J decided for the defendants. The
Chief Justice, Sir Garfield Barwick, presided over the second hearing
which began on 5 October 1978. The matter at issue was a summons for
directions issued by the plaintiffs. The Chief Justice ruled on 20 November that in the absence of agreement by the parties on the facts, a trial
before a single judge would be necessary to determine these facts. This
third hearing was held before Mr Justice Murphy and continued from
6 March 1979 until 9 January 1980, when the judge directed that the
case should go to the Full Court of the High Court.

The drawn-out preliminaries to the final action have been described
as being delaying tactics employed by the defendants.[24] In particular,
criticism has been made of the fact that the defendants declined to enter
a demurrer, which would have had the effect of allowing the case to go
to trial on the points of law involved, regardless of the fact situation. The
Commonwealth did hint at adopting the demurrer approach at the hearing before the Chief Justice, which is discussed below. It would seem,
however, that the independent school defendants, when admitted to the
case, were far from satisfied with the facts as evidenced by the plaintiffs
and were determined not to be compromised were the case to go against
them. The defendants jointly, therefore, declined to demur, closing off
any short-cut to an answer to the constitutional questions involved.

In their search after the facts, the plaintiffs sought delivery of what
would have amounted to hundreds of documents from the Commonwealth Department of Education and the Schools Commission. Those
bodies declined to co-operate and the plaintiffs sought orders for the discovery of documents. The Commonwealth replied with a summons of
its own seeking that the question raised by the plaintiffs be reserved until
a determination had been reached on 'whether it is permissible in
determining the issues in this action to look beyond the terms of the Acts
which are challenged to evidentiary matters relating to the administration of those Acts'.[25]

In argument before Aickin J, the plaintiffs outlined their case as to the
interpretation to be given to sections 116 and 96,[26] and the consequent

violation to those sections perpetrated with the passing of the States
Grants (Schools) legislation and other challenged legislation. They
claimed that it was necessary to establish the administrative detail
attached to the implementation of the legislation, since this was material
in determining the validity of the impugned acts. The Commonwealth,
for its part, argued that the administration of the acts challenged by the
plaintiffs was an irrelevant consideration in deciding that constitutional
validity.

Aickin J was of the opinion that details of administration could not
'throw any light upon the question of whether any of the Acts were
invalid by reason of contravention of s.116 or by reason of falling outside
the ambit of s.96'.[27] He did not deny, however, that evidence of background facts might be useful for an understanding of how legislation was
applied and noted that this was particularly the case in the interpretation
of state-aid in the American Supreme Court, given the doctrines and tests
applied by it.

The plaintiffs' summons was dismissed with costs, and defendants'
question was answered as follows: 'Evidence of the manner in which the
Acts referred to are administered is not relevant to any issue arising on
the further amended statement of claim dated 24th August 1977 and the
defence dated 20th September 1977'.[28]

The question of facts continued as a dominant issue in the development
of the *DOGS case* throughout 1978. On the one hand, the plaintiffs had
compiled a considerable dossier with little hindrance from the Aickin ruling. On the other hand, the National Council of Independent Schools
(NCIS) which was emerging as the second defendant wanted to contest
the facts as submitted, but appeared to be in no hurry to do so. For the
plaintiffs, the facts were of considerable importance in that these were
the evidence for establishing, on the basis of the American test of excessive entanglement, that the state-aid legislation was in violation of the
establishment provision. For the defendants, the principal constitutional
issues could be decided with little reference to the tome of facts assem-
bled by the plaintiffs. More difficult than assigning a role to the facts
was the matter of agreement as to their veracity. Some matters such as
published government statistics could readily be agreed upon. Others,
such as the profile of a church school, found little agreement. In an effort
to speed up proceedings without a lengthy and costly part of the process
being devoted to establishing the facts, the parties appeared before the
Chief Justice, Sir Garfield Barwick, with a proposal to resolve the issue.

Given that there were matters which the parties could agree upon and
some they could not, the suggestion made to the Chief Justice at the hearing on 5 October 1978 was that the legal issues be decided before the
facts were established. The method proposed was that the Chief Justice

should admit the facts as submitted by each of the parties and answer the question as to whether, in the light of those facts, the acts in question fell within the Commonwealth's power. In order to pave the way for an opinion of this sort, the Solicitor-General, Mr M. H. Byers Q.C., suggested that the plaintiffs and defendants could demur to each other's pleading of facts. This would provide, in theory at least, a basis of admitted fact upon which the case could proceed.

Counsel for the plaintiff, Mr N. R. McPhee Q.C., concurred in this approach to the Court on the grounds of the cost that would be involved, were the facts to go to trial. He did, however, express two reservations— one was that the statement prepared by the plaintiffs was not the whole case to be presented from his side: the other was the concern that a reply from the defendants was so long in coming; this was delaying the plaintiffs in the preparation of their reply.

The Chief Justice put the approach in the context of being asked to give an advisory opinion, a procedure eschewed by the High Court but familiar to the American judicial system. He was immediately cautious about this. 'This is in the nature of casting a fly over me, is it, to see how far I would go?'[29] was his first response. Further questioning of counsel confirmed the situation that neither side had a statement of fact in a final form. Barwick CJ was concerned about this in that if he responded to the request and referred the questions of law to the Full Court, an amendment to a statement of claim might be made. He was assured, however, that statements of fact from all the parties would be available in a matter of days.

Before adjourning the proceedings, the Chief Justice raised the question of Sydney as a likely venue for proceedings and was advised by Mr McPhee, for the plaintiffs, that about 100 Victorian witnesses had been subpoenaed for the action. Barwick CJ undertook to try and arrange an early trial and adjourned the hearing to consider his response to the matters before him.

On 20 November 1978 the Chief Justice advised counsel that, given their failure to agree on the facts, the questions of law were not to be discussed until the facts had been established. He therefore ordered a trial on the facts to be heard before a single justice of the High Court. The Chief Justice also agreed to additional persons being added to the plaintiffs (residents of the states with and without children at school) and allowed the National Council of Independent Schools and Father F. M. Martin, as representative of the independent schools, to be joined as defendants.

Mr Justice Murphy began hearing the case on the facts on 6 March 1979 and had before him plaintiffs who had subpoenaed a formidable array of witnesses and amassed considerable documentation for presentation to the court, and defendants not prepared to allow the plaintiffs' submissions to go unchallenged. A drawn-out hearing appeared inevitable and, indeed, ten months were to pass before the case was concluded. During that time the court sat on twenty-eight days, heard fifty-four witnesses and canvassed well over one hundred exhibits.[30] One significant change in the parties to the action occurred after the first adjournment in the case when the states (except New South Wales) and the Northern Territory sought and were permitted to intervene in the case with the defendants.

The plaintiffs' aim was to demonstrate that the Commonwealth's funds went to religious schools whose purpose was to evangelize through education and with whom the government was intricately involved as far as the management of the funds was concerned. As far as Catholic education was concerned, it was intended to show how central Catholic schools were to the life of the Church in terms of the physical placement of buildings and use of teachers from amongst the priesthood and religious orders. From a spiritual perspective, it was intended to show that religious teachings and practices permeated the school organization and curriculum. The religious school defendants, ready to concede on some points of fact in terms of numbers of, and in, church schools and amounts paid to them, attempted to show that the schools they represented distinguished the sacred and the secular, and that their institutions were primarily educational institutions like those operated by governments. Murphy J let in much evidence, subject to a later determination on its validity and, as the sitting days passed, the evidence assumed considerable proportions.

The plaintiffs appeared to have had difficulties from the beginning in evincing from the witnesses the damning evidence which was sought. This may have been a consequence of the process used in selecting witnesses and the reticence of witnesses to co-operate any more than the occasion required. Whatever the reason, the first witnesses, the Bishop of Sandhurst, together with his director of education and his co-ordinator of education provided minimal assistance to the plaintiffs' case. As Mr McPhee Q.C., for the plaintiffs, tried to establish that a bishop of a diocese effectively exercised authority over Catholic education, Bishop Stewart informed counsel that he had not been in a school class in the previous twelve months. The director of education, Monsignor Decampo, who occupied several other positions as well, also claimed not to have visited schools in his parish and to have paid only spasmodic visits to schools in the diocese. Father Duffus, the co-ordinator for religious education, admitted to his appointment only 'in a vague kind of way'. In response to further questioning, he claimed that very little of his time was devoted to educational duties. In all, McPhee's task over the first few days proved to be a difficult one and it continued in this vein as witness after witness replied with ordered responses to the litany of questions put by counsel.[31]

With the completion of the hearing of witnesses, Mr Justice Murphy intimated on 10 October 1979 that the case was one which probably should go to the Full Court. Although he had begun his own summary of the evidence, Murphy J asked counsel to prepare summaries of evidence and adjourned the sitting. On its resumption on 9 January 1980, Murphy J indicated that the parties agreed that the case should be referred to the Full Court, but differed on how this should be done.

> I have considered whether such reference should be by way of stating a case or reserving certain questions for the consideration of the Full Court or whether to direct that the case be argued before a Full Court. I have been very concerned with enabling the matter to come before a Full Court in a state in which the consideration of the case would not be unduly burdensome because of the large amount of oral and documentary evidence.
> The parties have, at my request, engaged in a detailed and thorough examination of the factual and legal issues and this has, in my opinion, overcome the problem of referring the matter to the Full Court. I have decided that of the methods of reference available under Section 18 [of the Judiciary Act] the most appropriate for an expeditious disposition of the case is to direct that it be argued before a Full Court.[32]

Murphy J directed the parties to file submissions on the facts and law with the High Court by 14 February 1980. So the stage was set for the final legal determination.

The DOGS CASE

The plaintiffs to this action were the Attorney-General for Victoria acting on the relation of residents of that state, and a number of other citizens who were residents of Victoria, New South Wales, Tasmania and the Australian Capital Territory, some of whom had children attending government schools. The defendants were the Commonwealth government and three of its ministers, the National Council of Independent Schools and Father Martin as representing the non-government schools.

Under challenge was Commonwealth legislation including several States Grants (Schools) Acts and States Grants (Schools Assistance) Acts, the *Independent Schools (Loan Guarantee) Act*, 1969, Appropriation Acts in so far as they made provisions for payments to and for non-government schools in the mainland territories of the Commonwealth, and the *Schools Commission Act*, 1973. The plaintiffs to the action alleged that the Commonwealth Acts were in violation of section 116 of the constitution and, in particular, its provision that 'The Commonwealth shall not make any law for establishing any religion ...' They claimed that that prohibition limited the power of the Commonwealth in respect of sections 81, 83, 96 and 122 under which the impugned legislation fell.[33] They further claimed that the States Grants legislation was in violation of section 96 of the constitution in that the laws were not laws granting 'financial assistance to any State'. The defendants, for their part, resisted these several claims and challenged the standing of the plaintiffs to this action.

The Court decided, with only Murphy J dissenting, that the laws challenged did not violate section 116 of the Commonwealth constitution. All the judges were of the opinion that the Commonwealth had acted within the ambit of section 96. The remaining sections of the constitution, upon which the plaintiffs' challenge was based, received comparatively little attention and will not be discussed further. Some observations were made, however, about the question of the standing of the plaintiffs and these are mentioned below.

Section 116

In this first decision in which the establishment clause of section 116 was squarely before the Court, it comes as no surprise to find that matters of established principle were considered. Two attracting specific mention, given their importance to the plaintiffs' case, were:

(i) the role of the constitution of the USA and its interpretation by the Supreme Court in that country *vis-a-vis* the Australian constitution, and
(ii) the importance to be attached to the debates of the Federal conventions which were held from 1890 to 1898 and the historical context in which the constitution emerged.

As to the former, the Court was divided in its opinion. Barwick CJ was prepared to see usefulness in American law and decisions only if there were ambiguity in an Australian provision: for him there was no ambiguity in section 116. Gibbs J regarded American precedent as being of little assistance, given the difference in wording in the constitutional provisions and the inconsistency in the US courts' decisions on the establishment provision. Wilson J exhibited a like cautious approach. Murphy J, however, adverted to the comment of the first Chief Justice, Sir Samuel Griffith, in *D'Emden* v. *Pedder* that American decisions were to be regarded 'not as an infallible guide, but as a most welcome aid and assistance' when the constitutional provisions were similar.[34]

Despite the holding of the majority of the Court on this issue in this case, it is interesting to note the readiness of some judges, Gibbs J, for example, to use very American phraseology such as 'primary purpose' and 'fundamental human right' and that Wilson J framed part of his rebuttal of the plaintiffs' case in the language of the threefold test enunciated in *Lemon* v. *Kurtzman*,[35] which required examination of the challenged legislation in terms of its secular legislative purposes, its primary effect and the excessive entanglement of church and state which might result. Clearly, the American connection was not as unimportant as a first reading of the judges' opinion might suggest.

The second issue of principle was the role of the convention debates and their historical interpretation in assisting the Court to arrive at a decision. The Chief Justice reiterated the established position of the Court, that the convention debates could not be used in determining the construction of the constitution. Barwick CJ further asserted that historical analysis might be of assistance where there was ambiguity in the Australian instrument, but that such analysis might 'distract the mind' from the proper meaning of unambiguous words.[36]

No judge was at variance with the Chief Justice on this matter yet all either commented on the convention debates or reflected on some of the historical issues at stake. Wilson J, for example, found interesting the developments at the conventions which led to the inclusion of section 116 and rehearsed aspects of them. Mr Justice Stephen commented on the history of the withdrawal of state-aid in the colonies and found, from his analysis, support for his interpretation of the establishment provision. Attention was paid to historical developments in the USA in the opinions of Gibbs and Murphy JJ with the former claiming that, at federation, American state-aid decisions had not built the wall between church and state, which the latter (and the plaintiffs) claimed they had.

Broad and narrow interpretations

In approaching their exegesis of section 116, the judges were divided in deciding the weight to be given to the establishment clause as against the remaining parts, although all adopted a very literalist approach. In his minority opinion, Murphy J argued for a broad interpretation of the establishment provision such as to allow it to dominate the section. He perceived the clause as one to be read widely as 'a great constitutional guarantee of freedom of and from religion'.[37] He argued that the whole section should not be read as a tenancy agreement such that the establishment provision was pared down on account of any overlap with the remaining clauses in the section.

The majority opinion adopted the view that each of the four parts of the section was to be given its full weight and that the establishment provision was not to be given special treatment. Gibbs J was not prepared to see the establishment clause as being in protection of 'a fundamental human right', a description which he hinted should properly be applied to the clause on the free exercise of religion. The central comment from the majority on this issue was that, if the establishment clause were treated broadly, the remaining three clauses were otiose—an interpretation they were not prepared to accept.

Exegesis

All the judges, except Murphy J, were agreed that the term 'respecting' in the American provision was conducive of a much broader meaning than 'for' in section 116. The latter term was deemed narrow in operation and purposive in character. The most narrow reading was that of Barwick CJ who asserted that for a law to fall within the establishment provision it must have the establishment of religion as its express and single purpose. Murphy J argued that 'for' embraced 'with respect to' and quoted the Oxford Dictionary, a former chief justice and a marginal note in the constitution in support of his position. The first two sources were distinguished by judges in the majority and Murphy J found no support from his brethren for his conclusion that marginal notes (on which little value is traditionally placed in the interpretation of Acts) were 'part of the Constitution'.[38]

Holding in common a determination to interpret the establishment provision narrowly, it is not surprising to find a like definition of 'establishing any religion' among the majority judges. Their position was encapsulated in the opinion of the Chief Justice:

> establishing a religion involves the entrenchment of a religion as a feature of and identified with the body politic, in this instance, the Commonwealth. It involves the identification of a religion with the civil authority so as to involve the citizen in a duty to maintain it and the obligation of, in this case, the Commonwealth to patronise, protect and promote the established religion.[39]

For his part, Murphy J asserted that:

> The purpose of our establishment clause is the same as that in the United States' Constitution ... Section 116 of the Constitution does not assert or deny the value of religion (including religious teaching). It secures its free exercise, but denies that the Commonwealth can support religion in any way whatsoever ... Section 116 recognises that an essential condition of religious liberty is that religion be unaided by the Commonwealth.[40]

He arrived at this conclusion on the grounds that:

> (1) the American provision has been interpreted as one of total separation of church and state;

(2) that conclusion had been reached prior to 1900;

(3) total separation embraced those meanings of establishment advanced in this case, namely, the establishment of a church or religion and the preferring of any one church or religion by, or by more, sponsorship or support over against any other;

(4) total separation implied that any support is in establishment of a religion or church; and

(5) the Australian provision was clearly intended to include a separation clause in the constitution.

The points raised by Murphy J, which reflected the position advanced by the plaintiffs, were commented upon by several of the majority judges. There was argument from some of the majority that the separation pleaded for by him was not in fact in vogue prior to 1900. Stephen J, for example, claimed that American interpretation prior to the sealing of the Australian constitution was slight, and limited to denying preferential treatment to a church or religion. He added that, if section 116 were reflective of the American provision, it would mean only that no national church or religion could be established, and that preference could not be given to any one church or religion. Mason J, who treated section 116 as a law directed to the preservation of religious equality, held that preferential treatment was not of itself an establishing of religion unless the preference shown was of an order such as to meet the definition of 'for establishing any religion' determined by the majority of the Court. The claim for the total separation in the USA was challenged as a matter of fact by Gibbs J who mentioned several cases, albeit mainly ones related to higher education, in which the Supreme Court had validated the provision of state-aid.[41]

Given the majority's interpretation of 'establishing any religion', its corollary was that Commonwealth assistance or support for any religion did not offend section 116. Barwick CJ and Gibbs, Mason and Wilson JJ all affirmed that the purpose of the challenged legislation was to aid education in Australia. The Chief Justice, for example, noted that the legislation was directed to educational ends and was limited to educational activities. He went further in asserting that, if laws for educational purposes were passed, which did not prohibit the use of funds or buildings in advance of religion, they would not offend section 116. Indeed, for Barwick CJ, section 116 'does not involve a prohibition of any law which may assist the practice of a religion and, in particular, of the Christian religion'.[42]

The Chief Justice and Murphy J represented the extremes in the determination of 'establishing any religion'. Other members of the court were prepared to hold that the act of establishing was a complex matter but declined to allow that any one law which might lead to an establishing was in violation of section 116. Stephen J asserted that:

> Because the status of establishment is, in England, the outcome of a complex of relationships does not make a law which creates one element of that complex a law 'for establishing' a religion [*sic*]. Still less does it mean, as the plaintiffs also contend, that any law which may represent a step in the direction of, or may be thought to have a tendency towards, producing the end result of the establishment of a religion is a law which offends against s. 116.[43]

Mason J offered a similar opinion noting in addition that the claim that the Roman Catholic church was being particularly advantaged failed to recognize that its greater amount of funds received corresponded with its greater involvement in the provision of schools.

Section 96

The Court was unanimous in holding that the plaintiffs failed in their attempt to challenge the legislation on the grounds that it was *ultra vires* section 96 of the constitution. Whilst Murphy J dismissed the contention in a sentence, other judges were a little more expansive. Mason J, for example, echoed earlier judgments of the Court to the effect that laws passed under section 96 could treat the states as mere 'conduit'. Others to reflect this position were Barwick CJ, and Stephen and Wilson JJ. But these three also affirmed that the grants in the challenged legislation fell decidedly within the wording of section 96, in that the laws were in assistance of the states. They held that non-government religious schools were part of the school system approved by the states and that support of such schools was assistance to the states which were relieved of a financial burden to the extent of the assistance.

The argument of the plaintiffs—that *Moran's case* (in which section 96 was used to implement a wheat stabilization programme initiated by the states) could be distinguished on the grounds that section 96 was being used in this instance at the will of the Commonwealth—failed. The capacity of the states to reject grants under the section was adverted to. In short, the broad interpretation of section 96 enunciated by Dixon CJ in the *Second Uniform Tax case* prevailed.[44]

One restriction which was applied to section 96 was that it could not be used to accomplish what was forbidden by section 116. A law making a grant to a state on condition that funding be made available to a religion such as to establish that religion or a law with a condition that religion be suppressed would have been held to be in violation of the constitution. Laws in aid of education conditional on the observance of religious practices would be within power, provided there was not any establishing of religion, while laws prohibiting such practices could well transgress the free exercise provision.

Standing

The Attorney-General for Victoria (a minister in a Liberal Party government) provided the fiat which enabled this case to come into court. A number of other attorneys-general (Labor and Liberal), including the then Commonwealth Attorney-General, Senator I. J. Greenwood, declined to support the action in this way. The very process which had to be pursued by a number of plaintiffs and the issue of the role of the remainder highlight the question of standing particularly as it affects citizens.

All the judges who considered this question were agreed that the standing of the states' attorneys-general was well established. Gibbs J discussed the only contentious issue on this point—whether those officers had standing in actions related to the Commonwealth's laws passed in respect of its territories—and asserted that that standing did extend to all Commonwealth laws.[45] Murphy J was alone in holding that all the plaintiffs had standing. This broad view which has some currency in North America asserted the right of the taxpayer *qua* taxpayer to standing in respect of laws passed by a federal government. Stephen and Wilson JJ decided that the question of standing need not be answered, although the latter spelled out the issues in full and highlighted the question of taxpayers' rights, in general, and those rights when an attorney-general denied his fiat, in particular.

Conclusion

The *DOGS case* was decisive if one looks to the unanimity of the decision in respect of section 96, the 6:1 majority opinion on the scope of the 'for establishing any religion' provision in section 116 and the attitudes of the members of the court to matters of principle concerning the relevance of American decisions or the federal conventions. Other matters raised, such as the other constitutional provisions under which the state-aid legislation was challenged, were only lightly touched on and the question left most open was that of standing.

The overwhelming decision in favour of the defendants in this case stands in stark contrast with the expectation of that equally conclusive victory which the members of the Council for DOGS held and proclaimed would be theirs. The fatal flaws in the plaintiffs' legal approach to the state-aid issue were both their heavy reliance on American cases on state-aid wherein like groups had been so obviously successful, and their expectation that one or two straws proffered in earlier High Court cases on the grants power could lead to a major change in its interpret-

ation of a quite settled line of decisions. In terms of constitutional outcomes, a not unexpected determination of the scope of the establishment
provision was arrived at. In political terms, the High Court returned the
question to the Parliament. In the words of Gibbs J:

> No doubt some members of the public hold strong and sincere views
> on the question whether any government should provide financial aid
> to church schools, but the resolution of the differences that exist must
> be left to the democratic processes which exist under the Constitution;
> s. 116 does not resolve them.[46]

NOTES

[1] *Attorney-General for Victoria (ex rel. Black and Others) and Others* v. *Commonwealth of Australia and Others* (1981) 33 ALR 321 (hereafter cited as the *DOGS case*).

[2] *Commonwealth of Australia Constitution Act*, Canberra, 1970, p. 27 (hereafter cited as *Constitution*).

[3] *The Constitution of the United States of America*, United States Information Service, n.d., p. 30.

[4] See G. S. Harman, *The Politics of Education: a bibliographical guide* (University of Queensland Press, St Lucia, 1974), ch. 3 and G. S. Harman, *Research in the Politics of Education 1973-1978: an international review and bibliography* (Education Research Unit, Australian National University, Canberra, 1979), ch. 5, for basic biblio-graphical information. To this should be added Michael Charles Hogan, *The Catholic Campaign for State-Aid: a study of a pressure group in New South Wales and the Australian Capital Territory* (Catholic Theological Faculty, Sydney, 1978).

[5] Section 4 and Schedule 1 of Act no. 214 of 1973.

[6] Section 7 of Act no. 214 of 1973.

[7] Sections 65 and 6(2)(b) of Act no. 214 of 1973.

[8] The House of Representatives agreed to the Senate's amendment to this effect on 12 December 1973 (*CPD*, HR87, p. 4660).

[9] Commonwealth Government, *Estimates* 1981-82, p. 227.

[10] *Benjamin* v. *Downs* [1976] 2 NSWLR 199.

[11] 403 US 602 (1971), 29 L Ed 2d 745.

[12] Letter from DOGS to ACSSO, 16 March 1972.

[13] The support of ACSSO in making their files available for perusal is gratefully acknowl-edged.

[14] Letter from Marian and Co. to Jensen, 31 May 1972.

[15] See M. J. Ely, *Erosion of the Judicial Process: an aspect of church-state entanglement in Australia* (Council for the Defence of Government Schools, Melbourne, 1981), p. 9.

[16] Ibid., p. 12.

[17] Letter from DOGS to ACSSO, 22 December 1972.

[18] Letter from DOGS to ACSSO, 8 October 1973.

[19] Advice from Abbot, Tout, Creer and Robinson, solicitors in Canberra, reported in let-ter from ACSSO president, Geoff Helyar, to the vice-presidents, 20 June 1974.

[20] Letter from J. N. Zigouras to ACSSO, 19 February 1975.

[21] Letter from DOGS to ACSSO, 27 February 1975.

[22] *DOGS case, Submission of the Plaintiffs*, 3 volumes, n.d.

[23] Ibid., vol. 1, p. 57.

[24] Ely, op. cit., pp. 14-16.

[25] *DOGS case*, transcription of judgment of Aickin J, 17 May 1978, p. 1.

[26] The text of section 116 appears in the text at note 2 above. Section 96 of the Common-wealth Constitution reads:

> During a period of ten years after the establishment of the Commonwealth and

thereafter until the Parliament otherwise provides, the Parliament may grant financial assistance to any State on such terms and conditions as the Parliament thinks fit.

[27] *DOGS case*, transcription of judgment of Aickin J, 17 May 1978, p. 12.

[28] Ibid., p. 15.

[29] *DOGS case*, transcript of proceedings before Barwick CJ, 5 October 1978, p. 7.

[30] *DOGS case*, transcript of proceedings, 6 March 1979–9 January 1980, passim.

[31] The transcript of this hearing provided some lighter moments for the reader. These included:

1. An exchange between Mr N. R. McPhee Q.C. and Mr B. J. Shaw Q.C. (at p. 112);
Mr Shaw: I object to that question.
Mr McPhee: I have not quite finished it yet.
Mr Shaw: Well, I object to it already.
His Honour: Well, let it be completed first.
Mr McPhee: Now I have forgotten what I was going to say, Your Honour.
2. Mr McPhee examining Bishop Stewart on the employment of teachers (at p. 127):
Mr McPhee: Well, would you not employ an atheist?
Bishop Stewart: No.
Mr McPhee: Would you employ a Presbyterian?
Bishop Stewart: What is wrong with a Presbyterian?
Mr McPhee: Would you permit a Presbyterian to teach religious instruction?
Bishop Stewart: No because he would not agree with the Catholic position: he would put the Presbyterian position—not that I have anything against the Presbyterian or his position . . . of course, I come from Presbyterian stock.
3. Mr Shaw cross-examining Bishop Stewart (at p. 186):
Mr Shaw: How old are you, my Lord?
Bishop Stewart: Well, I will tell you a little story. I was putting in my immigration ticket in Bombay last year and when the man in charge of immigration, an Indian, looked and saw 4/8/1900 'a last century job', he said, 'You are an old man' and I said, 'Well, do you know a cure for that?' He let me through without any trouble.
4. Mr McPhee interrupted Bishop Stewart who was answering a question (at p. 112):
His Honour: I do not think that he is finished.
Mr McPhee: I am sorry. I interrupted you. Would you like to finish what you were going to say?
Bishop Stewart: Forgotten now.
Mr McPhee: He has forgotten.
His Honour: Well, let us say he was interrupted rather than forgotten.

[32] Ibid., p. 2502.

[33] The wording of the sections referred to here for the first time is:

81. All revenues of moneys raised or received by the Executive Government of the Commonwealth shall form one Consolidated Revenue Fund, to be appropriated for the purposes of the Commonwealth in the manner and subject to the charges and liabilities imposed by this Constitution.
83. No money shall be drawn from the Treasury of the Commonwealth except under appropriation made by law. But until the expiration of one month after the first meeting of the Parliament the Governor-General in Council may draw from the Treasury and expend such moneys as may be necessary for the maintenance of any department transferred to the Commonwealth and for the holding of the first elections for the Parliament.
122. The Parliament may make laws for the government of any territory surrendered by any State to and accepted by the Commonwealth, or of any territory placed by the Queen under the authority of and accepted by the Commonwealth, or otherwise acquired by the Commonwealth, and may allow the representation of such territory in either House of the Parliament to the extent and on the terms which it thinks fit.

For sections 96 and 116, refer to the text at note 2, and note 26 respectively.

[34] *The DOGS case*, per Murphy J at p. 367.

[35] Ibid., per Gibbs J at pp. 345-6 and per Wilson J at pp. 388-9.

[36] Ibid., per Barwick CJ at p. 325.

[37] Ibid., per Murphy J at p. 361.

[38] Ibid., per Murphy J at p. 360.

[39] Ibid., per Barwick CJ at pp. 328-9.

[40] Ibid., per Murphy J at p. 368.

[41] Ibid., per Gibbs J at p. 344. It is important to note that the Supreme Court in the USA did allow state-aid in the case of higher education under certain conditions.

[42] Ibid., per Barwick CJ at p. 330.

[43] Ibid., per Stephen J at p. 348.

[44] *Victoria* v. *Commonwealth* (1957) 99 C.L.R. 575, 605-11.

[45] *DOGS case*, per Gibbs J at p. 334.

[46] Ibid., at p. 346.

3

THE CAREER OF A COLONIAL SCHOOLMISTRESS

by MARION AMIES

On 3 December 1855 Miss Matilda Broadbent commenced her duties as a Work Mistress in the Warrenheip Gully National School. The school, a rotten canvas tent pitched near the mines and mullock heaps of the Ballarat diggings, measured twenty-eight feet by fifteen feet, reached to fifteen feet at the ridgepole and, as a school inspector ironically reported, there was 'abundant ventilation'. The earth floor, ankle deep in mud in winter, dried under the summer sun to gritty dust that swirled into the faces of the pupils when stirred by the hot north wind. There were no privies—a hole in the ground was used but it was fully exposed to the view of passers by. The master had to walk one and a half miles to collect wood, but water was available from the nearby creek although this proved a mixed blessing as flooding in winter prevented many children from attending. On the other hand, the school was sufficiently removed from the diggings not to be disturbed by drunken miners or the noise of mining operations.[1]

Matilda's teaching career spanned the years 1855 to 1878; it included twelve years in various National and Common Schools and seven years in private schools during which she was the foundation principal first of Alexandra College, Hamilton, and then of Queen's College, Ballarat. Her story is of importance for several reasons: it throws light on an area which has not been illumined by previous research—the role of the colonial schoolmistress within the government schools; it acknowledges the existence in Victoria in the 1870s of an academically-oriented college for girls established by a proprietary company of local shareholders; it provides additional evidence for current research which explodes many of the myths relating to girls' schools (those 'foolish and expensive establishments', conducted by 'needy ladies of undoubted refinement but slender educational qualifications');[2] it demonstrates that it was possible for a schoolmistress from the government system to be accepted as the lady principal of a private school; and it indicates that there were colonial women educators whose roles not only as everyday toilers in the classroom but as leaders in educational thought and practice, deserve the recognition already awarded to their male counterparts.

Apart from a few formal documents and letters written by Matilda, her story must be told from public sources—shipping records, inspectors' reports, schools' correspondence, newspaper reports and birth, marriage and death certificates. No personal letters or diaries have survived to give depth and colouring to the public image but her novel, *Milliara: An Australian Romance* (London, 1893), provides insight into her attitudes to children, education, marriage and her years spent in the Western District. On the other hand, the richness of the public sources for the twenty-odd years that she lived as a public figure is surprising—especially for a woman—and it contrasts sharply with the spasmodic references to her later life as the wife of a leading teacher.

Is Matilda's experience representative of colonial schoolmistresses? How unique is her achievement as the foundation principal of two prestigious colleges for young ladies? Neither of these questions can be answered, for as yet we know so little of her sister schoolmistresses and lady principals. There was scant acknowledgement of schoolmistresses in the daily press and, while literature from the 1860s and 1870s presents the vicissitudes and romances of private and daily governesses and apportions blame or praise to the ladies responsible for private finishing schools and young ladies' colleges, the schoolmistress is missing from its pages until the 1880s. However, in keeping with the Victorian view of femininity, there is an impression that the women who became schoolmistresses did so through necessity, not choice, that they lacked intelligence, were ineffectual in their teaching duties and could not cope with the harsh conditions in the bush or on the goldfields but remained in the larger town schools under the protection and guidance of men. James Bonwick, recalling his tours of inspection of denominational schools, does refer to mistresses but in terms that support this view. The mistress of one tent school was described as being disorganized and incapable of maintaining discipline or inspiring 'maidenly modesty'; another bush mistress was devoid of even the most basic skills in spelling and arithmetic, that 'foe to female peace of mind'. Bonwick did mention one notable exception but she had had the good sense to remain in a town school where she had a cleric as protector and mentor and her domain was limited to the infant department. Bonwick also made reference to the difficulty of the task facing tent schoolmasters:

> His tuition is one continual struggle with destiny. He has to teach reading without books, and writing without slates. He has to keep spirits in order brought up amidst the lawlessness of the diggings. He has to train in morals a race of Bedouins whose youthful ears and eyes are open to almost unchecked vice and disorder. He has, in the midst of his own peculiar trials, and his constant exposure to what is degrad-

ing and deteriorating, to set an example of rigid self control, high moral integrity, gentle suasion, and of simple love.

How much more of a challenge and an ordeal was it for the mistresses (many of whom were scarcely teenagers), women nurtured within the protection of Victorian morals and imbued with Victorian sensibility?[3]

A Goldfields Schoolmistress

The report of the Royal Commission on Public Education, 1867, while statistically acknowledging the presence of mistresses, generally refers only to schoolmasters; there are a number of discussions concerning the character of 'teachers' (i.e. schoolmasters) and schoolmistresses are mentioned only when the question of mixed classes is raised with regard to the dubious moral character of the masters.[4] Such concern for the propriety of masters teaching girls was instrumental in Matilda's appointment to the Warrenheip Gully National School. The local patrons of the school were concerned that because they had no female teacher they were losing girl pupils to the denominational schools. They requested that when next at Ballarat the National School Inspector would examine thirteen-year-old Miss Matilda Broadbent with a view to her being appointed Work Mistress or Assistant Teacher. On 15 November 1855 Inspector Thomas Walker examined Matilda and he was pleased to recommend her appointment as Work Mistress.[5]

Matilda had been educated at a National Society School near Halifax, Yorkshire. She arrived in Melbourne on 19 December 1854 on the *Lincluden Castle* with her parents, James and Hannah Broadbent, Mrs Broadbent's four brothers, and Matilda's sisters, Julia and Louisa. Although James Broadbent was a dyer by trade, he had decided to try his fortune on the goldfields. At first he tried Bendigo where Matilda taught for six weeks at a Presbyterian Denominational School until the family moved to Ballarat where they set up in a tent and Matilda began teaching at the Warrenheip Gully National School.[6]

For the first few weeks Matilda worked with A. K. Sparke whom Walker described—with some ambivalence—as 'painstaking & persevering' but in manner 'inelastic and uninteresting'. Matilda was pleased when he was replaced by Alexander Millie, an excellent teacher, with a quiet manner, a positive attitude and the ability to interest children and keep them working happily: his influence was soon reflected in her teaching and in the general improvement in the school. There was, however, little improvement in the conditions under which they worked. In September 1856 a gale blew the rotten tent away. The local patrons acted promptly and within two weeks a weatherboard building was erected close by on Red Hill. New desks and forms and other little requisites, such as hangers for caps and bonnets (luxuries not provided in the tent school), a large blackboard, arithmetical tablets and a ball frame, were quickly installed. There were still no privies and no playground, however, and the new site proved disastrous. In September 1857 Inspector Glen reported that 'stagnant water may be discerned through the chinks of the floor'; he urged the speedy removal of the school to a better site but in May 1858, when Inspector Venables visited the school, they were literally teaching ankle deep in mud: 'The rain collects behind the building and runs through the schoolroom; the floor was during my inspection covered with mud and water, the classroom (a tent) deep with mud could not be used'. In this less than ideal environment Alexander Millie and Matilda taught from 54 to 122 children—depending on the whim of their parents, the vagaries of the weather and the influences of the latest gold rushes.[7]

Matilda regarded teaching as a career and was perturbed when, after teaching for sixteen months, she had not been 'summoned for examination in order that she might be classified according to rule'. With more earnestness than tact she wrote to the National Board urging an explanation for the oversight—the letter ended 'An early answer would greatly oblige'. Benjamin Kane, the Board's secretary, instructed—somewhat tersely—that she be informed that 'none but literary Teachers have been summoned to the Examination, and that, as she is only a Work Mistress her attendance has not been required'. An alternative tactic was then put forward by Inspector Glen who suggested to the local patrons that Miss Broadbent should go to the Training Establishment in Melbourne. The patrons agreed as they were not only impressed by Matilda's ability and assiduity but appreciated Glen's argument that such training, while of advantage to Matilda, would secure to the school the benefit of her improved services. In August 1857 Glen proposed to Kane that she be accepted as a trainee; on 22 October the patrons also made representation on her behalf stressing that although she had originally been appointed as a Work Mistress, she had since been promoted to the 'position of a full teacher'. Kane's response was prompt; on 26 October he instructed that Matilda report to the Training Establishment on 2 November to join the third intake of trainees.[8]

Of the thirty-one teachers in that intake, Matilda, despite being one of the youngest, was one of the most experienced, for only she and three others had prior teaching experience. The training had a strong practical foundation. Seven hours each week were spent in the schoolroom learning the practice of teaching under the supervision of Jane Pullar, the superintendent of the girls' section. Two other sessions each week were devoted to lesson books and the art of teaching. The trainees were also expected to improve their academic qualifications so that the afternoons were taken up with grammar, dictation, arithmetic, geography, drawing, vocal music and natural philosophy but, although the male teachers were encouraged to attend Saturday morning lectures at the University, Matilda and the other female teachers received instead additional lectures related to teaching. There was, however, no time given to needlework: these women were to be qualified literary teachers, not sewing mistresses.[9]

Of Matilda's reaction to those five crowded months we have no indication, but her enthusiasm, determination, willingness to learn and talent for teaching impressed the training staff. Upon inspection after the course she was classified in the 3rd Division of 1st Class: none of the fifty-six trainees in the previous intakes had achieved such a classification. This meant that of the certificated and classified women on the roll she was now placed fourth, Jane Pullar being first.[10] Equally important to her future career, she had realized that if she was to succeed in a society controlled by a male hierarchy she must learn their rituals and conventions, in particular how to capitalize on the system of patronage. The intervention of the patrons and the inspector had succeeded where her eager efforts had failed. Her family was well established in the town and through its reputation and connections, her skill as a teacher and her influence on the patrons and parents, the foundations for patronage were being established. Each of the following men was to be influential in furthering her career: James Oddie, the first mayor of Ballarat and an active patron of the Red Hill School; the Revd John Potter (later Archdeacon Potter), of Christ Church, where Matilda's sisters Louisa and Julia taught at the Denominational School;[11] the Revd James Bickford, a Wesleyan minister vitally concerned with education in Ballarat;[12] and Inspector A. B. Orlebar. On 29 April 1858 Chief Inspector Orlebar visited the school and the impression he gained of Matilda remained with him through the years. His comments show that the school had indeed gained the benefits of her having been allowed to train:

> Miss Broadbent is also an admirable teacher. So great is the discipline into which she has brought her pupils, by flexibility & firmness, that after setting a lesson on the tables to an infant class to chant, she dared to leave it for another class and they continued the chant without a monitor over them for some minutes in perfect order. I never saw such a thing before.[13]

A Brief Marriage

The school's benefit was short-lived. In June 1859 she forwarded a letter of resignation and on 5 July married Joseph Dixie. Joseph, aged 34 (twice Matilda's age), and his brother had come to Ballarat from Cape Town in 1856. They had decided to try their luck on the goldfields not as diggers but as goldbrokers and mining agents. During Matilda and Joseph's brief marriage, they lived in Errard Street, Ballarat, in a cottage furnished with all the chiffoniers, whatnots, engravings, books and ornaments so dear to Victorian respectability; and, presumably, from Joseph's business profits they lived comfortably. On 10 July 1860 a son, Arthur Willoughby, was born. A few months later advertisements appeared in the *Ballarat Star* stating that Mr Joseph Dixie was selling his household furniture (down to the last kitchen utensil and chamber service) as he was leaving the colony for the benefit of his health. Three weeks later, at Walkerville, South Australia, Joseph died, leaving Matilda homeless and with only her clothes and personal possessions. It would have been acceptable, if not the 'proper thing', for the young widow to have lived with and been supported by her parents. Instead, Matilda chose to return to teaching. Through the intervention of Inspectors Venables and Orlebar and the support of the Revd Potter and James Oddie, an appointment was arranged.[14]

Return to Teaching: The Ballarat Benevolent Asylum School

Scores of orphaned and deserted children left destitute in the wake of the shifting and shiftless population on the goldfields and the crushed dreams of many fortune seekers, were taken into the Ballarat Benevolent Asylum where they were housed, fed and given a basic education. The National Board, though loath to grant aid to the Asylum School, preferred to keep the Asylum children out of the National Schools for fear of infection and moral contamination. In 1861 the number of children in the school did not warrant the salary of a fully trained teacher but the Asylum Committee agreed to subsidize the Board's contribution. On 26 October 1861 Inspector Venables put this proposition to the Board and noted that there was 'a person on Ballarat in every way suitable', a young widow named Mrs Dixie. There was also, he added, 'the additional motive of securing to the service of the Board a really efficient teacher'. On 2 November Venables wrote again, stressing that the patrons (including James Oddie and the Revd John Potter) were anxious to appoint Mrs Dixie and that she was 'known to the Chief Inspector', Mr Orlebar: Orlebar initialled this comment, adding 'She is an excellent teacher'. Matilda began teaching in the Benevolent Asylum School on 2 December 1861.[15]

As there was no male teacher in the school, Matilda was classed as a headmistress. She was responsible for the organization of the school, teaching her classes, supervising the assistant mistress and for the complex and time-consuming monthly statistical returns required by the Board. Her stay in the Asylum School was dogged by periodic withdrawals, or threats of withdrawal, of aid. Not only was her salary at first below what it should have been for a teacher of her qualifications, but there were months when the Board's contribution towards it was not forthcoming. The patrons argued that the school should be treated as a special case because of its reformatory nature, the desirability of keeping the children isolated within the institution and the impossibility of the children attending outside schools because of their inability to pay fees. Eventually they recommended that the committee pay Mrs Dixie a fixed salary of £150 per year and that if and when she received payments from the Board she would reimburse the committee.[16]

From thirty-three to seventy children, aged from under seven years up to twelve years, were at the school: their attendance was most regular due to their confinement in the Asylum. The contrast between the external architecture of the Asylum and the conditions of the children's dormitory and schoolroom mirrored the ambivalent nature of Victorian charity, as did the austerity of the children's daily routine compared with the intermittent treats provided for the children by the committee. The Asylum was 'a palace in the Elizabethan style, with well-kept grounds, a magnificent home such as the English poor . . . have never dreamt of in their wildest flights of fancy'. Inside, however, things were not quite so magnificent. The thirty-four children resident in June 1862 slept in one dormitory where there were only seventeen beds. A partition partially separated the girls from the boys. The schoolroom was equally crowded and poorly ventilated. When Matilda's pupils were not in the schoolroom, their companions were the blind, the chronically afflicted in body or mind, the aged 'looking tranquilly at nothing but . . . shadowy memories of the past', and the young girls and babies in the lying-in ward. The faces of many of the inmates wore 'the look of witless deference which is so common to men in their dependent position'. Until 1863 the children's diet was probably inadequate. At the end of that year the committee reported that, with the establishment of vegetable beds and a dairy, there was a sufficient supply of vegetables for the inmates, and the children could drink milk instead of coffee. In sharp contrast, in June 1862 a splendid soirée was held to mark the opening of a new wing. Matilda's pupils, 'that sadly interesting collection of waifs and strays from the way-ward current of social life', were permitted to peep at the visitors and to sing the two opening numbers of the 'oratorial and musical programme [held] for the delectation of the guests'. The irony of the titles of their songs—'Oh, come, come away' and 'Marching along'—was probably lost on the thousand visitors who joined in the 'general outburst of roystering merriment', partook of the 'heaps of plum cake . . . and other extremely seductive edibles', then passed out through the gates and beyond the enclosing walls of the Asylum.[17]

With the loss of her husband, the demands of caring for a young child, a depressing institutional environment and the financial problems of the school, it is not surprising that Matilda's teaching lacked a little of its former confidence and inspiration. The Inspector noted that she 'has not succeeded so well in this School as in others of a different class' but, he added, 'this is to be attributed in part to other causes besides the teacher'. However, the Asylum committee and the people of the town were pleased with her endeavours and with the progress of the children.[18]

In 1868 the children from the Benevolent Asylum were transferred to other institutions. Their destinations are indicative of how they were regarded by the Asylum authorities. The majority went to the newly-opened local industrial school, some of the boys were sent to Melbourne to join the Training Ship, several boys and girls were 'let out' either as apprentices or domestic servants, and the remainder were removed to the District Orphan Asylum.[19] This would seem to indicate that with her pupils, especially the older boys, Matilda had to cope with troublesome or unruly behaviour demanding a firm hand and an uncompromising Victorian attitude to the sin of disobedience. It is, perhaps, surprising that her attitude to discipline remained humane and that she retained a firm belief in the value of reward for good behaviour in preference to punishment for misbehaviour. In regard to discipline she wrote :

> I keep a conduct roll, which I call over daily—the child who breaks discipline loses his marks. I give a prize every half-year for the greatest number of good conduct marks; finding the hope of reward more efficacious than the fear of punishment. When this negative kind of punishment is too mild for the case, I resort to positive—extra work after school-hours, or corporal chastisement.[20]

These comments form part of her reply to the questionnaire which, at the behest of the Royal Commission on Education, was circulated in 1866. They are in marked contrast to the summary of other responses regarding discipline: 'Detention in play hours, extra lessons as tasks, and corporal punishment, used sparingly. In a few schools rewards for exemplary conduct are said to be distributed once a year'. The Commission received 440 responses to the questionnaire sent to the teachers in charge of the 720 Board schools in the colony. Of the 720 schools only twenty-four were in the charge of headmistresses, five of whom replied; in another thirty-one schools there was a mistress as well as a master and in all but two of these schools the answers were supplied by the master. Thus the Commission received the opinions of only seven female teachers. Apart from Matilda, all were in schools connected with the Church of England; they competently supplied the information required but, except in the matters of compulsory attendance and religious instruction, ventured few opinions.[21]

Matilda had obviously given much thought not only to the problems of teaching within her own school but to wider educational issues. She wrote confidently and at length, castigating the majority of private schools at the elementary level as being expensive, inefficient and ill-adapted to the needs of young colonists. On the other hand, while acknowledging that the system administered by the Board had weaknesses, she noted that it was 'an incalculable benefit to the major part of the population of the colony'. Because of the good and practical education available in Board schools they were being used by children whose parents could afford fees and who were thus drawing on government aid intended for poorer families. She proposed an extension of government influence and a dual school system:

Let there be [elementary and high schools for both boys and girls] called 'Unaided Government Schools' in contradistinction to the present Common Schools, which might be called 'Aided Government Schools'. Let these 'Unaided Government Schools' be subject to the Board of Education, only in the matter of inspection. They would be private ventures, but under the cognisance of the government . . . the teachers need not be troubled with government returns, or to be tied up as to the number of pupils in attendance. The inspection might be once a year . . . The present shams would soon be swept out of the field and replaced by realities. The few worthy private-school teachers, who may exist, need have no fear of such an innovation . . .[22]

In August 1868 the children were treated to another gala evening to mark the occasion of their departure from the Asylum. The entertainment consisted of an elegant repast, musical and comedy items, games, presents (work boxes and dolls for the girls; books and knives for the boys) and a grand pyrotechnic display. The children closed the evening by leading the singing of the national anthem: a performance calculated to wring the heartstrings and twitch the hip-pocket nerves of the worthy citizens of Ballarat. Matilda's pupils were then dispersed and the Benevolent Asylum School closed on 21 September 1868.[23]

A 'Christian Lady of unblemished moral character'

For nearly two years Matilda was without a teaching post. She continued to live in Ballarat and on several occasions wrote to the Board regarding employment. On 20 June 1870 she was appointed to School No. 383, Lonsdale Street, Melbourne, in the grounds of Wesley Church. Erected in 1859, the school had originally comprised the upper storey with a book depot below, hence particular attention had been paid to the provision of adequate lighting and the installation of insulation to minimize noise.

While Matilda was there both floors were used, the 160-odd children being divided between two separate schools, one in the upper room with Mr Ingamells, the other downstairs with Mrs Dixie.[24]

Little evidence exists regarding her time at this school. The Revd James Bickford, formerly of Ballarat, was correspondent for the local committee. He noted that the committee unanimously agreed to Mrs Dixie's appointment and 'earnestly desired' the Board to grant her a salary equivalent to a head teacher in keeping with her high qualifications and despite the presence of a male teacher. Bickford appended a personal recommendation: 'I have known Mrs Dixie for about twelve years as a Christian Lady of unblemished moral character and of excellent deportment'. She was granted the full salary.[25]

Lady Principal of the Alexandra College, Hamilton

In January 1872 the *Argus* advertised the positions of lady superintendent and governess at the soon-to-be-opened Alexandra College, Hamilton. The decision to open the college followed the successful establishment of the Hamilton and Western District College for boys. Three years earlier a group of settlers and businessmen had observed the absence of the means of affording a good education for the local boys and had formed the Hamilton and District College Company to rectify the need. They then considered their daughters' education. A second company was set up, registered as the Alexandra College Company (Limited) and, at the first public meeting of shareholders on 11 June 1872, the provisional committee members were confirmed as directors of the company. They were advised by Henry Beresford de la Poer Wall, principal of the boys' college, who acted as visitor and examiner.[26] They aimed to provide not a finishing school but an academic college, and influenced by the recent admission of girls to the matriculation examinations they looked to those examinations as a guarantee of equal educational opportunities for their daughters:

> The Matriculation examination ... is valued by our best teachers as affording a safe guarantee to parents that they are doing justice to our boys, and I think we may also rest satisfied with it as a fair test of the education of our girls.[27]

In their endeavours they were supported by the proprietors of the *Hamilton Spectator* who gave generous coverage to all the activities of the committee and the college, and featured supportive editorials and items that looked forward to the day when the University of Melbourne would admit females.[28]

Applications for the positions of lady superintendent and governess closed on 18 January 1872 on which day Wall was at the Menzies Hotel,

Alexandra College

Matilda Goldstraw

Melbourne, to interview applicants. The fact that Matilda was 'a lady holding a distinction enjoyed by only two others in the colony, viz., a first class certificate from the Board of Education', impressed him but not sufficiently to recommend her as lady superintendent. Instead, he proposed Mrs Pauline Bracken who had been the principal of a ladies' college—a finishing school—for, she claimed, the past twelve years. Despite the emphasis on establishing an academic college, Mrs Bracken's experience in a finishing school was probably the main factor in her favour. The school aimed to be select: Mrs Bracken was used to teaching young ladies; Mrs Dixie, although she was an excellent teacher, had taught only in elementary schools including a charity school. Despite her apparent gentility, was she a suitable person to undertake the nurture of ladylike manners and demeanour? Matilda was offered the post of resident governess but paid the amount budgeted for two governesses.[29]

The College opened on 12 February 1872. The twenty girls took their classes in the Masonic Hall; Matilda and three boarders lived in a cottage in nearby Chaucer Street. Between 14 February and 15 May there were no reports of college activities in the *Hamilton Spectator* but one suspects that there was considerable activity and growing tension as two strong-minded women strove to assert their ascendancy: one clinging to 'what-we-have-always-done-for-our-young-ladies'; the other, with a vision of what education for girls could be, challenging the directors to put their rhetoric into practice. Matilda was determined that the young ladies of Hamilton would have the opportunity to learn more than to 'write a three-cornered note, ... play a set of quadrilles, embroider a rose in wool, and answer a question or two in the heathen mythology (vide Mangnall)'. On 15 May a small paragraph in the *Hamilton Spectator* noted that Mrs Bracken's desire to leave had been agreed to and that Mrs Dixie was now principal.[30]

By 15 June, resident governesses, music and drawing teachers had been engaged. A few days later, a prospectus-like advertisement gave the first definite statement of the college's aims, subjects and fees:

> The object is to afford a thoroughly sound education of the highest kind, and to give young ladies the necessary polish in manners, litera-ture, and accomplishments ... The young ladies will be prepared for the Matriculation and Civil Service Examinations and *it will be the aim to bring all the pupils to this standard.* [My emphasis]

The subjects offered were English, Latin, French, German, arithmetic, euclid, algebra, history, geography, drawing and painting, vocal and instrumental music, use of globes, geology, botany and astronomy. Lessons in dancing, deportment and callisthenics would ensure the girls' health and reassure those afraid that the programme was not feminine.

D

The fees, two to four guineas per quarter for day girls, sixteen to eighteen guineas for full boarders, guaranteed a select enrolment. Two final paragraphs, in businesslike tone, stressed that students must attend regularly and be prepared for hard work and self-discipline. Classes would occupy five hours daily and homework, which parents were urged to supervise, would be given each night.[31]

Enrolments rose throughout the year to forty-three pupils. On arrival, their standards varied greatly as did the subjects they had previously studied at private schools, with governesses or parents, or, possibly, at Common Schools. Matilda used the first year to group the girls into classes, establish how much they did know, repair deficiencies in subjects in which they had some knowledge, and introduce them to new subjects. By mid-year she had chosen the matriculation class but although, at the 1872 speech night, Wall (who stressed that he examined the girls according to the same standards as his boys) reported that a few girls might well have passed, Matilda did not allow them to sit for the matriculation examination. She believed that cramming was bad for the health and unacceptable as an educational method.[32]

In view of the successful first year, the directors turned their energies to providing a permanent home for the college. In August 1873 tenders were accepted for the erection of the first part of the building. Appropriately, the foundation stone was laid on 10 November, 'the birthday of the royal husband of that illustrious lady' after whom the college was named. Being a proprietary venture the college was not attached to a church but present at the foundation ceremony were three ministers, including Revd J. K. Macmillan of the Presbyterian Church. Macmillan, a man of religious tolerance and an active worker for government schools, rebuked those who clung to the belief that domesticity was a woman's only option and that a little knowledge and a smattering of accomplishments would fit her splendidly for that sphere. In 1875-76 Macmillan was active in planning and setting up the Presbyterian Ladies' College, Melbourne, and to those deliberations he carried the knowledge of the achievement at Alexandra College and Mrs Dixie's capabilities.[33]

While the directors turned their energies towards bricks and mortar, Matilda concentrated on building upon the academic foundations laid in the first year. Preparation for the matriculation examination began in earnest and, while it was pleasing that the *Hamilton Spectator* gave their endeavours so much coverage and support, it was unnerving to know that the whole district and overseas relatives (their activities were regularly reported in 'Our Letter Home') were awaiting the outcome of this experiment in female education. On 27 January 1874 the *Hamilton Spectator* published the examination results: of the three candidates, two passed the Civil Service examination. Despite disappointment that the coveted matriculation pass had eluded them, the girls' achievement was considerable and the directors expressed their pleasure at their success and gave due credit to Mrs Dixie and her staff.[34]

By the end of June 1874 the commodious Italian Style building was ready, a monument to the directors' belief in a sound education for girls. On the ground floor, on either side of the elegant staircase, were visitors' parlours. One wing comprised two classrooms with a cloakroom and toilet for day girls while in the other were the dining room, pantry and kitchen. Upstairs, the two dormitories were divided into single bedrooms. Adjoining them were a toilet, two bathrooms (complete with jets for shower baths) and a capacious wardrobe room. Nearby were the principal's and mistresses' bedrooms and a sickroom. While the architect may have won premiums for his designs for state schools, this building was obviously in a different class. The attention paid to privacy and ample accommodation for the girls' voluminous dresses and petticoats, bustles, bonnets and boots bears the stamp of Matilda's advice.[35] In May 1874 a new staff member was appointed: in addition to teaching she took over the domestic management, freeing Matilda for academic matters. The extra time Matilda spent with the matriculation class and the fact that they had now had three years to prepare, brought pleasing results. Of the five candidates all except one passed matriculation and she succeeded at the February examination. Between them they accumulated five credits in French, English and geometry and trigonometry, though all failed in Latin. By comparison, of the eight candidates from the boys' college, three passed matriculation and five the Civil Service examination.[36]

Speech night 1874 was a gala occasion. The town hall, tastefully decorated with garlands and evergreens, was crowded with parents and local dignitaries who applauded the chairman of directors' acknowledgement of Matilda's burden of responsibility and day-to-day teaching, her achievements, and the high regard in which she was held by the directors:

> I have much pleasure in testifying tonight, that whatever success has been achieved by the institution, reflects the greatest credit on . . . Mrs. Dixie, whose rare abilities and devotion to her work, deserve a rich reward, she having, besides supervising the whole work of the school, and teaching other classes, taught the Matriculation class five of the eight subjects they had studied.

He also presented her report: Matilda briefly summarized the year's achievements, paid tribute to her staff and the girls (particularly their 'industry, docility and eagerness to learn') but unfortunately merely alluded to her educational aims and beliefs, promising to dilate on them at a future date.[37]

Matilda was obviously a success as a principal and respected by the directors and the parents. Did this respect and acceptance extend beyond that sphere? Reports of church, charity and social functions show that she was accepted by the leading families of the town and that, with her ability as an organizer, she was a leader at such functions. She was an active member of the Ladies Benevolent Society, represented the Church of England ladies on the Visiting Committee set up to supervise the boarding-out of Industrial School girls as domestic servants and was the correspondent for the committee, responsible for reporting on the suitability of the girls' placements and their progress in their new lives. At church, charity and social functions she tackled such varied tasks as providing afternoon tea for the Bishop of Ballarat, Dr Thornton; making hearthrugs and mats for bazaars; singing at concerts; and acting as the energetic, painstaking honorary secretary who organized the grand bazaar in September 1876. The staff and the girls from the college were also encouraged to take part in such activities. M. B. Macdonald, who in 1875-76 was the full-time classics and mathematics master, organized a concert for the Church of England in which Matilda sang and the girls formed a tableau on the stage. Matilda arranged excursions such as a wagon ride to the fern-bedecked Byaduk caves where, together with the other teachers, she sang operatic selections in the natural amphitheatre. The girls took advantage of the opportunity for practical geology observations and the study and collection of ferns. In later years this excursion was recalled by Matilda and formed the setting for a crucial scene in her novel. Such a busy, efficient, vibrant and talented woman scarcely matches the *Argus*'s representation of lady principals as 'starched and prim ladies of uncertain age'.[38]

Counterpointing these reports of success and enjoyment were others indicating that there were growing tensions in Matilda's life which resulted in the directors accepting her letter of resignation in July 1876. Throughout the early months of the year her father became increasingly feeble. When he died, on 8 March 1876, Matilda went to Ballarat to be with her mother but attended not one funeral but two: five days after he father died her sister, Louisa, succumbed to the epidemic of scarlet fever which was sweeping the colony. Her other sister, Julia, was also dangerously ill.[39]

On 13 May a small paragraph appeared in the *Argus* which caused the directors of Alexandra College to fly into a fury and the editor of the *Hamilton Spectator* to burst into indignant prose. It noted that Mrs Dixie was to join the staff of the Presbyterian Ladies' College, Melbourne, after the winter holidays. The management of PLC must have held her reputation in high regard and considered that her name would help attract students, as the advertisement appeared two months before she could take up the position. Its appearance at such an early date probably suprised Matilda, for it is obvious that she had not yet communicated her intentions to the directors of Alexandra College. Whether Matilda sought this appointment or whether an offer was put to her—perhaps at the behest of, or through, the Revd J. K. Macmillan—is unknown: she later indicated that she had already decided to leave the college and that the position had been offered to her. Faced with the proprietorial anger of the directors, Matilda agreed to withdraw from the PLC offer and remain at Alexandra College until the end of the year but only after the directors agreed to pay her a bonus of £20 a year for both 1875 and 1876. In terms that must have riled Matilda, the *Hamilton Spectator* righteously informed its readers that 'we are glad to be able to state, for the benefit of the pious conductors of the Melbourne establishment with the religious title, that Mrs. Dixie has elected not to desert her matriculation class . . .'[40]

Although not leaving until the end of the year, Matilda began planning and negotiating for her next teaching venture. With the death of her father, thoughts of moving to the city were put aside: she must return to Ballarat to be with her mother. She leased a large, two-storey, brick building (known as the Red House) at the corner of Dana and Raglan Streets then, in consultation with H. R. Caselli, the well-known architect and family friend, set in motion the extensive remodelling necessary to convert the building to a boarding school, to be named Queen's College. She also began negotiations for staff and to activate her networks of influential friends in Ballarat to gain publicity for her new venture. Items appeared in the *Ballarat Star* on 30 November and 1 December 1876 announcing the college, the December item being reprinted, without comment, in the *Hamilton Spectator*. At Hamilton she had the teaching year to complete, including preparing students for the matriculation examination. She had to ensure the smooth handover of the college to the directors and the new incumbents, to organize the Church of England grand bazaar and prepare for speech night. In the background all the time were the ill-feelings that remained from the earlier contretemps with the directors over the PLC affair.[41] At the speech night Laidlaw paid the necessary, but rather restrained, tribute to Matilda's five years at the college. A few days later, Matilda was waited upon by a deputation of eleven gentlemen, from which the directors were notably absent. They presented her with a timepiece and an address signed by the mayor and seventy-seven gentlemen of the district. Matilda's response is curiously worded:

> Everyone tells me that I have made the Alexandra College. This may or may not be true. I will content myself, therefore by saying that . . . through much toil and weariness of mind and body, I have fairly started a good work . . . I came to Hamilton five years ago a young

and sensitive woman, beside being a perfect stranger. Consequently I had much fainting of heart, and many hours when a little sympathy would have been like water to a traveller dying of thirst in a sandy desert . . . This present will be a silent reminder that I had sympathy in past days when I thought I had none and will nerve me in many a moment when my poor courage shall fail me . . .

Few passages in her novel are as melodramatic as this speech although perhaps the sophistic ingenuousness of the poor, orphaned governess, Miss Bentinck comes close. Given Matilda's capabilities and acceptance in the district, and the obvious success of the college, why did she write in this fashion? Did her sense of the dramatic overcome her normal propriety? or was she playing the role expected of a woman who had moved into the public sphere in Victorian society: there a woman supposedly was a 'perfect stranger' who could not be expected to succeed because of those stereotypical feminine attributes, a poor fainting heart and a failing courage.[42]

A School of Her Own: Queen's College, Ballarat

Settled in Eureka Street just a short distance from Queen's College, Matilda supervised the arrival and arrangement of the furniture and linen, the kitchen pots and pans, the slates, books and the piano and was 'at home' to interview parents. The layout of the college was similar to that of Alexandra College in that the principal's office, the spacious, well-ventilated and well-heated schoolroom, the music room, drawing room, dining room and kitchen were on the ground floor while the dormitories, mistresses' rooms, bathrooms and wardrobe room were on the upper floor. Mostly the dormitories were divided into single bedrooms but there were also larger ones for the convenience of sisters. Both hot and cold water were available in the bathrooms and the college was lit by gas throughout. No expense had been spared in providing an efficient, comfortable and homely environment.[43]

The college, it was claimed, was to be conducted along the lines of its namesake, Queen's College, Harley Street, London. How familiar Matilda was with the ideals and performance of Queen's College is unknown. By 1878 it was no longer the leader in the field of academic education for girls but its reputation was sufficiently well known in the colony for Matilda's claim that her college would emulate it to imply innovativeness and status but yet be classed as safe and respectable. Certainly Queen's had been in the news in relation to the setting up of PLC and probably Matilda had discussed Queen's and the aims and ideals of PLC with the Revd J. K. Macmillan, if not with Charles Henry Pearson, headmaster of PLC, at the time she was offered the position there. Little in the operation of Matilda's college stamped it as being like its name-sake: it was strictly a girls' school and there were no afternoon lectures for ladies and those who desired to fit themselves as governesses.[44]

Throughout December and January advertisements appeared in the Ballarat papers announcing the opening of the college, and from 6 January 1877 a conspicuous and carefully planned advertisement appeared in the *Hamilton Spectator*. Matilda well knew what appealed to the families of the Western District. The advertisement for Queen's appeared under a newly·designed Queen's crest, listed the teaching staff, described the college and gave the measurements of the various apartments; it was, Hamiltonians were assured, a college as substantial as Alexandra College. Besides Mrs Dixie, there was a classics master, a resident and junior governess, and visiting masters and mistresses for accomplishments. In mid-1878 another governess was appointed, a former pupil at Alexandra College and daughter of the editor of the *Hamilton Spectator*.[45]

On opening day, 22 January 1877,[46] Matilda was faced with a mixed group of girls, ranging in age from five to twenty-one years, with varying educational backgrounds. They were quickly sorted into five classes and started work on a carefully planned programme of studies (see Table). As Matilda believed that French should be introduced as soon as the child could read words of one syllable, French was taken at all levels. There were daily walks in the gardens by the lake, games and country excursions and, at the suggestion of the Anglican Bishop, Samuel Thornton, chemistry was added to the curriculum in 1878. The lectures, by Dr Flude, were given at the School of Mines so that the girls could use the facilities for experiments. Thornton, who, with Archdeacon Potter acted as a referee for the college, stressed the importance of scriptural studies. During 1877 Matilda had devoted one hour per week to scripture but in 1878 it was

TABLE
Course of Study

Class	Subjects	
Fifth or University Class	English grammar, spelling and composition, Latin, French, geography, history, arithmetic, euclid, algebra, needlework	
Fourth Class	As for Fifth Class but in an easier form, with the addition of reading and writing	Scripture, singing, drawing, music & daily exercise
Third Class	Reading, writing, spelling, grammar, composition, arithmetic, history, French, geography, needlework	
Second Class	As for the Third Class with the exception of composition	
First Class	Reading, writing, arithmetic, spelling, geography and French	

arranged that Dr Craig, Potter's successor, should visit the school to give these lessons. Thus began the association of Queen's with the Anglican Church although it was not until 1918 that the college was formally purchased by the Church.[47]

At the end of the first term Matilda selected her potential matriculation candidates, aiming for them to sit not in 1877 but in 1878. She knew that eighteen months' preparation for the matriculation exam was 'all too short when taking into consideration the fact that a girl's education, unlike a boy's, has had no tendency whatever in this direction in the majority of cases'. Maggie M'Intyre and Mary M'Intyre each attempted seven subjects in December 1878, while Alice Du Rose sat for six. Only Mary passed.[48]

The announcement of Mrs Dixie's retirement from teaching was made at the 1878 speech night: the long, trying winter, and the burden of a large school had proved to be more than her health could bear. After twenty-one years her teaching career had officially ended. In some ways her achievement at Queen's seems less than at Alexandra College but two years at Queen's was too short a time to bring to fruition the good work she had fairly started. It must also be remembered that Queen's was entirely Matilda's responsibility: there was no finance from a proprietary company; no board of directors to oversee the finances and to look after the bricks and mortar; no Henry Wall to offer academic advice; no newspaper editor (with shares in the company and a daughter in the school) to promote the ideal of better education for girls and to keep the activities of the college constantly before the town. The success or failure of Queen's rested solely on Matilda and, through her vision of what education for girls could be, her reputation as a lady of 'unblemished moral character', her skill as a teacher, her careful planning, and managerial skill, Queen's was successfully established.[49]

Mrs Frank Goldstraw: Helpmeet and Novelist

While the announcement marked the official end of Matilda's teaching career it did not end her close association with teachers and teaching. A few days later, in St John's Church, Ballarat, she married Frank Goldstraw. Frank, aged 28 (eight years her junior) was a master at Wesley College and, as Matilda was no longer a public figure, it is largely through his career that her activities must now be traced. Frank Goldstraw was born in 1851 at Heaton Mersey, Lancashire, the youngest son of Charles and Mary Ann Goldstraw (née Motley). The family had migrated to Melbourne in 1857, and from 1861 they lived in Elgin Street, Carlton. Frank attended the Model and Training School where, in 1865, he became a pupil teacher. He taught until 1869 when he was awarded the first Central Schools Scholarship of £50 which enabled him to continue his degree at the University of Melbourne. He graduated with a B.A. in 1871 and completed an M.A. (with first class honours) in 1873. In 1872 he began teaching at Wesley College and in 1882 was promoted to Second Master. Frank was a dedicated, enthusiastic and talented teacher, the '*beau ideal* of a public school master'. A member of the Victorian Academy of Art, his paintings were regularly hung at its exhibitions and received enthusiastic reviews in the press but few sold and fewer have survived.[50]

How Matilda, who had spent the last seven years in Hamilton and Ballarat, met the handsome, witty and unfailingly courteous Frank, is unknown. For several months in mid-1878 he was seriously ill with typhoid. Perhaps at that time he convalesced at Ballarat. In 1880 Frank purchased an elegant, eight-roomed brick house at 652 High Street, Armadale, where, apart from their years at Wesley College, they lived until Frank died in 1909. On 19 November 1880 Matilda gave premature birth to a daughter, Winifred, who died eighteen days later. A second daughter, Amy Rose, was born on 15 May 1882, at which time her son, Arthur, was mid-way through an Engineering degree at the University of Melbourne.[51] Little is known of Matilda's life from 1879 to 1892 and, as there are no private papers, there is no indication as to whether she was happy to move from the public sphere into the domestic roles of wife and mother. It is hard to imagine that she became a stereotypical 'middle-class lady' but perhaps, like Bell Newton in *Milliara*, she enjoyed the relative lack of responsibility: 'It was inexpressibly sweet to be cared for, after having been the caring one for so long'. Amy's upbringing and education would have taken up much of her time and she nursed Julia's daughter for five months until she died in 1884. Another of Julia's daughters, Lucy Dickinson, lived with Matilda and Frank from 1893 (possibly earlier) to 1898, partly to be a companion for Amy and partly to escape the annual discomforts of sandy blight that plagued her family at Forbes. Matilda would have been a loyal supporter and intelligent critic of Frank's educational and artistic activities and a regular visitor to Wesley on formal and social occasions.[52]

The writing of her novel, *Milliara: An Australian Romance*, occupied many hours in 1891-92. Published under the pseudonym 'Noel Hope', it was released in September 1893 and was widely and favourably reviewed in European and Australian newspapers and journals, the only dissident voice being the reviewer for the Melbourne *Argus*. Despite this, *Milliara* proved popular in Melbourne but few readers, except those associated with Wesley College, knew that it was written by Matilda. Although it was common for nineteenth century female writers to adopt pseudonyms, it seems uncharacteristic of Matilda to do so. If it was because it was 'not proper' for the headmaster's wife to write novels, why was its publication so proudly announced in the *Wesley Chronicle*? Her choice of the name 'Noel Hope' may have alluded to the Goldstraw's plans for Wesley or, more likely, to Matilda's hopes for a future career as a novelist. The novel is well written and although it draws freely upon Matilda's experience of life in the Western District it is not a family saga describing 'the-way-we-live-in-the-colonies' for the edification of friends at home in England. The heroine, Bell Newton of 'Milliara' station, bears a distinct resemblance to Matilda in that she is an attractive, well-educated, young woman with heavy family responsibilities. Due to her father's death and her mother's long illness, Bell brings up her youngest sister as her baby (shades of the young widow and her son) as well as overseeing the household and the running of the property. Incidents from Matilda's own life are used; for example, at a concert in Hamilton Matilda sang accompanied by a soaring flute obbligato; Bell performs similarly at one of her social triumphs. Bell is modelled on the type of young woman that Matilda strove to send forth from her schools. At the picnic at the caves, Bell easily engaged Mr Bolton, a young academic from Melbourne, in conversation, explaining the volcanic formations and identifying the native ferns and flowers. Mr Bolton, 'looking at Bell's upturned face, . . . thought her a very charming companion, . . . not in the least blue, but having a mind to think and observe, and using it whenever occasion arose'. Though the action of the novel begins in the late 1860s, it mainly takes place during the time that Matilda was in Hamilton, the 1870s, and the geography of the setting, from Bell's first journey to Grazington (Hamilton), to descriptions of the volcanic landscape and its formation, is realistic. The development of the district is sketched into the background of the plot: references to events such as the completion of the rail link and the establishment of the Hamilton and Western District College help to locate the action in time and place. Apart from Bell, the other main character of the novel is Miss Adela Bentinck, the governess at 'Milliara', whose presence and similarity to her literary predecessor, Becky Sharp, cause havoc with Bell's suitors. Of more interest, however, is what the novel reveals of Matilda's understanding of children and her feelings regarding teaching methods and the value of education. The six young Newtons are real children, country children, self-reliant, grubby and unruly but intelligent and with the clear-sightedness of childhood that sees through pretence. In the classroom they are quick to 'try-out' their new governess. Willie gives an excellent imitation of an idiot and pretends not to be able to speak while the older girls, sensing that Miss Bentinck's antecedents are not quite as genteel as she claims, pretend colonial gaucherie. Miss Bentinck's disciplinary tactics are swift but not approved of by Matilda: Willie receives a smart box on the ear and Conny is spoken to most sharply and threatened with being sent to stand in the corner.[53]

At the beginning of 1893 Goldstraw became headmaster of Wesley. His acceptance of the position at the depths of the depression and under the terms proposed by the Executive Committee was quixotic. He quickly realized that it was impossible for the school to show a profit but it was not until mid-1895 that the committee released him from the agreement. The cryptic wording of the Executive Committee minutes and the spectre of the balance sheets obscure the positive contribution made by the Goldstraws during those dark years to the rise in the level of academic attainment and to the quality of school experience within the college. Frank's appointment was welcomed in Methodist circles: the *Spectator* commented that he was 'the man of all men to attract Australian boys, and gain a lasting influence over them'. He was regarded as having a considerable asset in his admirable helpmeet, Matilda, whose academic successes at Alexandra College were noted, though greater emphasis was laid upon her experience in the domestic supervision of a boarding school. In an endeavour to attract students, Frank published a glossy promotional pamphlet, *In and about Wesley College* (Ballarat, 1893), which lauded the academic virtues of the college and stressed its healthy family atmosphere. The Goldstraws had obtained permission to farm the grounds, and the orchard, vegetable plots and dairy supplied all the produce used in the college. The homely atmosphere and the feeling that the Goldstraws personally cared for the boys was heightened by the fact that Matilda and Frank took their meals with the boarders, while on weekends there were tennis and croquet parties in which old boys and young ladies were included and all were treated to afternoon tea. Matilda kept watch on the boarders' behaviour as well as their appetites and provided an annual prize for punctuality in the house.[54]

Valuable as Matilda's role as helpmeet was, she also contributed to the life of the school in ways that were distinctively her own and gave rein to her dramatic flair and sense of humour. In 1893 she wrote, produced and made the costumes for three short plays which satirized the foibles and follies of Victorian society. With their topicality and obviously Australian characters, such as Lord Fitzboomerang and Mr John Woolcrop, the plays appealed to the boys and to visitors alike. One was presented at a Moonlight Entertainment and Strawberry Fete held to raise funds for the Games Committee. Considerable thought was given to its staging, the platform being illuminated by a large star of gas jets, while overhead were scores of Japanese lanterns whose light mingled with the silver streams of moonlight that poured down from the cloudless sky.[55]

At the Goldstraws' farewell, tribute was paid to the manner in which Mrs Goldstraw had looked after the comfort and well-being of the boys and the fact that 'she never seemed to consider or spare herself in the least'. The masters, in appreciation of her kindness to them, presented her with an elegantly bound copy of *Milliara*. In his response, Frank invoked the prayer, 'Lord, keep my memory green': victims of the depression, and overshadowed later by the reputation of Adamson, the Goldstraws' devotion to Wesley and their brave efforts to turn the tide of decline during the depression years have been largely forgotten.[56]

Toorak Grammar School and the Registration of Teachers and Schools Act

Throughout the remainder of 1895 the Goldstraws reassessed their situation and then planned for their future. The natural thing to do was to open another school, despite the depression. Their home at 652 High Street was altered to provide a school wing with a separate entrance, and in February 1896 Toorak Grammar School opened with twelve pupils. By 1898 it was necessary to add an upper storey as well as a large weatherboard schoolroom at the back. Precisely what role Matilda played at this school is unknown. There was accommodation for fifteen boarders who came from Western Australia, Thursday Island and the Philippines to enjoy 'the comforts and sociability of home life'. Their comfort was in Matilda's hands but, as money for staff wages must have been short, she probably taught during the early years of the school. Certainly Amy, who by 1898 was sixteen and had passed matriculation, was pressed into service as a music teacher.[57]

Both Matilda and Frank inspired loyalty and affection in the boys at the school. Lawrence Ralph, who attended in the last year of the school, recalls that:

> I went for one year only to Toorak Grammar School and I learned to love its Headmaster and his family . . . at times I was invited to lunch with them . . . Mrs Goldstraw . . . was a charming stately lady with grey hair dressed in the fashion of the time, who smiled at you and notwithstanding the great differences in age and station made you feel completely at ease and welcome . . .

Apart from the school, the family picked up the threads of their life in the community. They re-established their connection with the Anglican Church (severed when Frank became headmaster of Wesley) and became active members of St Alban's Church, Armadale. Matilda, accompanied by Lucy, attended social functions such as the annual reception given by the Mayoress of Prahran together with the mothers and sisters of the boys who attended their school.[58]

Toorak Grammar seems to have been at least a modest success until the intervention of the Registration of Teachers and Schools Act. It was well accepted in the district and some old boys moved on successfully to university although mostly they took their places in the commercial world. But from 1906 numbers began to decline, partly because it was no longer possible to receive boarders due to Matilda's long illness. Then, throughout 1907-8, Frank's health began to fail as the increasingly debilitating effects of Bright's disease limited his ability to work effectively. The falling enrolments and his failing health, together with the difficulty and expense of fulfilling the requirements for registration, forced Frank to decide to retire at the end of 1908. The school was to be leased in the new year by Stanley Coad and Hyman Miller but Frank did not live to hand over the premises to them: he died on 2 January 1909. Matilda and Amy moved to a small cottage in Malvern Grove, Caulfield. Apart from the little that Amy made from teaching the piano, they had an income of £170 p.a. from the five-year lease on Toorak Grammar. For Messrs Coad and Miller to be able to continue with the school, extensive alterations were necessary to conform with the new health regulations. In this Matilda refused to co-operate (or could not for financial reasons) unless they would agree to take up a further five-year lease, so they decided to abandon the school which was closed shortly after Matilda's death on 21 June 1911. It is sadly ironic that this strong-minded woman who had 'fairly started' two schools that have survived as memorials to her devotion to education, should have inadvertently destroyed the school that might have kept green the memory of her husband.[59]

Matilda's teaching experiences may not be typical. The mud and discomfort of the turbulent years on the goldfields were shared with scores of other women, though few had the opportunity to train at the National Model and Training Schools and no other teacher on the goldfields—male or female—held her high classification. For nearly seven years Matilda coped with the education of waifs, strays and 'problem' children in a charity/reformatory school within the depressing confines of the Ballarat Benevolent Asylum, an experience shared by few women. In providing a sound academic education for girls, Alexandra College was not unique but it was in the vanguard and it seems that the establishment of a college by a proprietary company was unusual in the Australian colonies. Thus, Matilda's situation as lady principal but answerable to the college directors was also unusual. On the other hand, Queen's College was established and operated in a manner similar to the many ladies' colleges owned and operated by enterprising and intelligent women who devoted their skills to the education of girls although, as with Alexandra College, it began at the time when the implementation of the ideal of an academic education for girls was becoming more acceptable. But whether her experiences were typical or not (and later research may show that there were other colonial women educators whose achievements match Matilda's), it is possible through her story to illuminate the life of one of the thousands of invisible women who have borne the brunt of educating generations of Australian children.

NOTES

[1] Victoria, Public Record Series (VPRS) 880, National School Board, Inwards Correspondence Files, Box 4, 55/1798; VPRS 1406, Inspectors' Reports, National Schools, vol. 1, 55/1626.

[2] Kathleen Fitzpatrick, *PLC Melbourne: the first century 1875-1975* (Presbyterian Ladies' College, Burwood, 1975), pp. 32, 33; Marjorie Theobald, 'Tradition and Change in the Education of Girls: Victoria 1839-1885', research in progress.

[3] See, for example, 'Hope Morton', serialized in *The Australian Woman's Magazine and Domestic Journal*, 1883-1884; James Bonwick, 'Rambles of a School Inspector', first published in *Rides Out and About: a book of travels and adventures* (The Religious Tract Society, London, [1862]), rpt. in *Leisure Hour*, 1863, see ch. XIII, 'The Kneeling Scholars and the Learned Mistress', ch. XIV, 'The Portland Infant School', ch. VI, 'The Wandering Teacher'.

[4] *Royal Commission on Public Education, 1867*. Facsimile published as *Sources in the History of Victorian Education*, No. 2 (Burwood State College, 1978), p. 36.

[5] VPRS 880, Box 4, 55/928. See also VPRS 1406, vol. 1, 55/1626; VPRS 880, Box 4, 55/1624.

[6] VPRS 880, Box 4, 55/1624; VPRS 947, Inwards Shipping, 1854; VPRS 880, Box 4, 55/1624.

[7] VPRS 1406, vol. 1, 53/1626; VPRS 880, Box 4, 55/1846; VPRS 1406, vol. 3, 58/1093, 58/1245; VPRS 880, Box 4, 56/1785, 57/512, Box 58, 57/1963; VPRS 1406, vol. 3, 58/1093; VPRS 880, Box 58, 57/1963.

[8] VPRS 880, Box 4, 57/629. Kane's response is recorded on the cover of 57/629; VPRS 1406, vol. 2, 57/2349; VPRS 880, Box 4, 57/2505; VPRS 878, National School Board, Letter Books, vol. 10A, 57/3156.

[9] VPRS 878, vol. 10A, 57/3725; VPRS 880, Box 4, 55/1624. VPRS 880, Box 42, National Training Establishment, Timetables for the Male and Female Departments, November 1857.

[10] Victoria, Education Department, Transcript of Service Record. From 1 March 1864 she was classified as equivalent to 1st Honours. In 1866 only six men and three women out of the 779 classified teachers held such a high classification: see *Royal Commission on Education, 1867*, p. 36.

[11] Victoria, Education Department. Transcripts of Service Records. Julia Broadbent taught at Common School 57, Ballarat (formerly Christ Church Denominational School) from 1 August 1864 to 31 December 1869. Louisa Broadbent commenced teaching on 1 August 1864 at Common School 587, Soldier's Hill. On 1 January 1870 she was appointed to Common School 57, consequent to Julia's resignation, and remained until the school closed on 31 December 1873.

[12] Bickford was the correspondent for all the Wesleyan Schools in the Ballarat area: *James Bickford: an autobiography of Christian labour* (Charles H. Kelly, London, 1890), p. 161. See also Douglas Pike (ed.), *Australian Dictionary of Biography*, vol. 3, 1851-1890 (Melbourne University Press, 1969), p. 162.

[13] VPRS 1406, vol. 3, 58/1245.

[14] VPRS 880, Box 4, 59/1791; Marriage Certificate, 59/3461; *Ballarat Star* (BS), 16, 17 December 1860; Birth Certificate, 60/13506; BS 16, 17 December 1860; Death Certificate, South Australia, 61/1859.

[15] VPRS 880, Box 5, 62/1914; VPRS 903, Board of Education, Inwards Correspondence Files, Box 6, 63/1704. This did not prevent epidemics, however: see VPRS 903, Box 47, 65/2272; VPRS 880, Box 5, unregistered item attached to 61/2029, 61/2048, 61/2104, 61/2365.

[16] VPRS 1226, Chief Secretary's Correspondence, Box 23. A Return Shewing the Names of Teachers and Correspondents of Common Schools, September 1866, p. 5; Annual Report of the Benevolent Asylum of Ballarat, 1865; BS, 4 November 1864; VPRS 880,

Box 5, 62/33; VPRS 903, 64/8186, 64/10035, 65/578, 65/5857; VPRS 880, Box 5, 62/1914; VPRS 903, Box 6, 63/1704; *BS*, 4 November 1864.
[17] *BS*, 7 June 1862, 23 January 1868; VPRS 880, Box 5, 62/33; W. B. Withers, *The History of Ballarat from the First Pastoral Settlement to the Present Time* (2nd edn, Ballarat, 1887), pp. 259-60; *BS*, 7 June 1862, 23 January 1868, 7 June 1862, 27 August 1862.
[18] VPRS 1406, vol. 7, 62/1888; Annual Report of the Benevolent Asylum of Ballarat, 1864, 1865.
[19] Annual Report of the Benevolent Asylum of Ballarat, 1868; *BS*, 21, 26 August 1868.
[20] VPRS 1226, Box 21, Response to Questionnaire, Royal Commission on Education, Q.10.
[21] *Royal Commission on Education, 1867*, Appendix C, Q.10; VPRS 1226, Box 23, A Return Shewing the Names of Teachers and Correspondents of Common Schools, September 1866; VPRS 1226, Boxes 21, 22, Responses to Questionnaire.
[22] VPRS 1226, Box 21, Response to Questionnaire.
[23] *BS*, 21, 26 August 1868; VPRS 903, Box 113, 68/13520.
[24] Victoria, Education Department, Transcript of Service Record; VPRS 898, Registers of Inward Correspondence, 70/6940, 8013, 9979; VPRS 903, Box 158, 70/10447; Minute Book, Lonsdale St Wesleyan Church, 15 July, 1859; VPRS 903, Box 185, 71/9259; VPRS 903, Box 179, 71/3727.
[25] VPRS 903, Box 158, 70/10447; Box 159, 70/11651.
[26] *Argus*, 9 January 1872; *Hamilton Spectator (HS)*, 12 November 1873: speech by D. Laidlaw, chairman of directors, at the laying of the foundation stone, recalling the setting up of the company; *HS*, 25 May, 15 June 1872; Elise Robertson, *A Brief History of Hamilton District and Alexandra College* (Hamilton, 1972), n. pag.; *HS*, 7, 14 February, 26 June 1872. Proprietary schools were relatively common in England from 1830: see Donald Leinster-Mackay, 'English Proprietary Schools: A Victorian Marriage between Commerce and Education', *Education Research and Perspectives*, vol. 8, no. 1, June 1981, pp. 44-56. Apart from the two Hamilton companies, the only other known Australian company was that formed in 1839 in an attempt to establish a school at Honeysuckle Point, NSW: See Bruce Mitchell, 'Honeysuckle Point, Blandford and Armidale: The Story of a School', *Proceedings of the Twelfth Annual ANZHES Conference, Hobart, 1982.*
[27] T. H. W. Leavitt, *Australian Representative Men* (Wells and Leavitt, Melbourne, 1887), n. pag.; *HS*, 19 December 1874.
[28] See, e.g., *HS*, 6 July 1872, 16 August 1873, 14, 25 February, 19 September 1874; 14 February 1872.
[29] *Argus*, 9 January 1872; *HS*, 27 January 1872; *HS*, 27 January, 7, 14 February 1872. The *Ballarat Directory* (James Curtis, Ballarat, 1869) lists 'Pauline Bracken, Teacher, 24 Ligar Street'; *HS*, 27 January 1872.
[30] *HS*, 14 February 1872; VPRS 1226, Box 21, Response to Questionnaire.
[31] *HS*, 1 June 1872; 26 June 1872.
[32] *HS*, 18 December 1872; VPRS 1226, Box 21, Response to Questionnaire, Q.11; *HS*, 21 December 1877.
[33] *HS*, 9, 13, 30 August, 1873; *HS*, 12 November 1873, Leavitt, op. cit., Fitzpatrick, op. cit., pp. 36-7.
[34] *HS*, 5, 12 November, 3 December 1873; University of Melbourne Archives, Matriculation Records; *HS*, 4 February 1874.
[35] *HS*, 27 June, 8 July 1874; *Australasian Sketcher*, July 1874.
[36] *HS*, 13 May 1874; University of Melbourne Archives, Matriculation Records; *HS*, 20 January 1875. To the financial gain of one local gentleman who had laid 6 to 4 on the girls gaining better results than the boys: *HS*, 19 December 1874.
[37] *HS*, 19 December 1874.
[38] *HS*, 22 April 1874, 15 March, 19 July 1876; *HS*, 15 September 1875, 27 March, 2, 16, 30 September, 7 October 1876; *HS*, 8, 27 March 1876; *Milliara*, vol. 2, pp. 155ff; *Argus*, 13 July 1871.
[39] *HS*, 29 July 1876; *Ballarat Courier (BC)*, 16 March 1876; *HS*, 18 March 1876.
[40] *BS*, 21 December 1877; *HS*, 29 July, 17 May 1876.
[41] Ballarat, List of Owners and Occupiers, 1877; *HS*, 2 December 1876; *BS*, 22 January 1877; *HS*, 16 November 1876, 9 January 1877; *HS*, 30 November 1876.
[42] *HS*, 14, 19 December 1876; *BS*, 20 December 1876; Robertson, op. cit.

43 *BS*, 20 December 1876; *BS*, 22 January 1877; *HS*, 6 January 1877.
44 *BS*, 1 December 1876; Elaine Kaye, *A History of Queen's College, London 1848-1972* (Chatto & Windus, London, 1972), passim; Fitzpatrick, op. cit., pp. 64-5.
45 *BS*, 27 December 1875; *BS*, 16 January 1877, 3 July 1878.
46 A myth has grown up concerning the date of establishment and the name of the founding mother of Queen's. It asserts that Queen's was founded by Mrs Abbott in 1868 although there were antecedents as far back as 1856. See, e.g. Robert Gay, *Some Ballarat Pioneers* (Mentone, Victoria, 1935), p.41; Weston Bate, *Lucky City: the first generation at Ballarat 1851-1901* (Melbourne University Press, Carlton, Victoria, 1978), p. 237; *Queen's Centenary Magazine*, 1968, p. 5. The myth is to be discussed in full in the forthcoming history of Ballarat and Queen's Anglican Grammar School to be written by Sue White. Nina Valentine, of B.Q.A.G.S., has contributed substantially to research in relation to the myth.
47 *BS*, 21 December 1877; *BS*, 18 December 1878, 29 March 1877, 18 December 1878; Elaine Pascoe, 'Co-education in Independent Schools of Victoria', unpublished paper, 1975.
48 *BS*, 21 December 1877, 18 December 1878; University of Melbourne Archives, Matriculation Records.
49 *BS*, 18 December 1878.
50 Marriage Certificate, 78/3933; VPRS 947, Inwards Shipping, 1857; J. A. Allan, *The Old Model School* (Melbourne University Press, 1934), p. 198; Victoria, Education Department, Transcript of Service Record; *Age*, 10 April 1869, 26 April 1870; University of Melbourne Archives, Student Record Card; *Wesley Chronicle* (*WC*), April 1882; *WC*, December 1895; for his contribution to Wesley College see, e.g. *WC*, December 1877, October 1882, July, October 1889, May 1891, October 1890; Index to Exhibition catalogues, Victorian Artists Society, at State Library of Victoria; e.g. *Daily Telegraph*, 14 March 1881.
51 Letter, Goldstraw to Victorian Academy of Art, October 1878. Papers of V.A.A., State Library of Victoria, Box 578; Prahran Council, Rate Books; Birth Certificate; Death Certificate, 80/11033; University of Melbourne Archives, Matriculation Records and Student Record Card.
52 *Milliara*, vol. 2, p. 207; Death Certificate, 9 June 1884; *WC*, July, October 1893, *Prahran Telegraph*, 22 May, 19 December 1897, Marriage Certificate, 29 December 1898, personal communication from Mrs M. Browne, Lucy's daughter.
53 See M. Amies, 'The Author of Noel Hope's *Milliara: An Australian Romance*', *Bibliographical Society of Australia and New Zealand Bulletin*, vol. 6, no. 2, 1982, pp. 65-7; *WC*, December 1893; *Milliara*, passim; *HS*, 7 October 1876; *HS*, 8 March 1876 cf. *Milliara*, vol. 2, pp. 155ff; *Milliara*, vol. 2, p. 168; *Milliara*, vol. 2, pp. 77ff, 74, 234, vol. 1, pp. 205, 211, 221.
54 Wesley College, Minutes of the Executive Committee, October 1892-November 1895; Geoffrey Blainey et al., *Wesley College: the first hundred years* (Robertson and Mullens, Melbourne, 1967), pp. 89-91; *Spectator*, 3 February 1893, *Prahran Telegraph*, 21 January 1893; *Spectator*, 14 July 1893; *WC*, April, September, December 1894.
55 *WC*, July, October, December 1893, September 1894; Wesley College, Sports Committee Minutes, 6 October, 27 November 1893; *Spectator*, 8 December 1893.
56 *WC*, December 1895.
57 *Prahran Telegraph*, 19 December 1897; Prahran Council, Rate Books; VPRS 10300, Closed Schools Files, School 300, Item 5; James Smith (ed.), *The Cyclopedia of Victoria*, vol. 2 (Melbourne, 1904); VPRS 10061, Teacher Registration Files, Application No. 2654.
58 Personal communication; *Prahran Telegraph*, 17 July 1897, 5 February, 26 November 1898; *Prahran Telegraph*, 22 May 1897.
59 *Prahran Telegraph*, 19 December 1897, 17 December 1898, 19 December 1908; VPRS 10300, School 300; *Prahran Telegraph*, 19 December 1908, 9 January 1909; VPRS 10300, School 300; Death Certificate; Sands and McDougall's *Directory of Victoria*, 1910, 1911; VPRS 10300, School 300; Death Certificate.

4

THE INDUSTRIAL FUND:
A HIGHLY SUCCESSFUL MODEL OF BIG BUSINESS
COLLABORATION WITH THE HEADMASTERS
CONFERENCE IN THE
INTERESTS OF SCHOOL SCIENCE

by DON SMART

The Industrial Fund for the Advancement of Scientific Education in Schools (henceforth IF) was a non-profit-making organization registered in the ACT in September 1959. Inspired by a United Kingdom model, the Fund was formed by a small exclusive group of Australian business leaders to enable industrial and commercial companies to make financial grants to secondary schools to increase both the quality and quantity of science education. These grants were restricted to Headmasters Conference (HMC) schools[1]—in effect, largely élite schools—and were to be used for laboratory construction only.

This article is an historical account of the Fund derived from its records, which are lodged with the Academy of Science in Canberra.[2] It addresses three issues. How and why was the IF established? How did it grow and operate? And, finally, what was the relationship between the Fund and the Menzies Government's commonwealth science scheme which was enacted in 1964? The latter scheme is extremely significant, as it represents the very small beginnings of federal aid for schools which in less than two decades has blossomed into a mammoth one billion dollar enterprise.

The Establishment of the Fund

The formation of the IF in Australia in 1958 must be seen against a background of prior international developments. Few events have had as striking an impact on modern western education systems as the successful Russian launching of Sputnik 1 in October 1957. Not surprisingly, perhaps, the United States of America reacted most dramatically. In that country, Sputnik sparked off many educational reforms including the National Defense Education Act (NDEA) of 1958, and a widespread questioning of the prevailing 'democratic' secondary educational practice of catering for the 'average child' at the expense, amongst other things, of consistently under-taxing the abilities of the gifted segment of the school population. Out of the NDEA and similar initiatives grew a host of innovatory and supplementary science programmes, many of which were to have some impact on science in schools in Australia over the next decade.

Perhaps more immediately relevant to Australia were events which had taken place since 1953 in Britain.[3] In that year a number of UK companies engaged in the chemical, electrical, and mechanical engineering industries,[4] conscious of the impending shortage of qualified secondary students in relation to the number of available university places in science, considered what additional corporate action industry could take to expand the number of scientists both for industry and for the country as a whole.[5] The solution was considered to lie in increasing the output of science-trained secondary students and, with this end in view, the Industrial Fund for the Advancement of Scientific Education in Schools (IFASES) was established on 1 November 1955. It was decided that these objectives could best be achieved by giving financial assistance for building, expanding, modernizing and equipping science buildings, whilst taking into account the volume and quality of existing science teaching.[6] A conscious decision was taken to aid only non-state schools, for these schools were ineligible for government aid for buildings, and as a result, were having great difficulties in providing science accommodation for all those students wanting to switch to science.[7]

Of special interest (due to its absence in Australia) is the understanding which the executive of the UK Fund reached at the outset with the Ministry of Education. It got from the Minister an undertaking that he would announce publicly that he welcomed the scheme, and that if the Fund looked after the non-government schools, he would make special provision for the government schools. Thus, there was to be an element of reciprocity on the part of government in the UK, due to a skilful manoeuvre of the Fund to ensure maximum return for its effort. Despite the fact that it was doubtful whether the British Government 'fully honored' this undertaking, considerable gains for government schools had undoubtedly resulted from the Fund's astute bargaining.[8]

The UK Fund executive was aware that as well as a shortage of accommodation, there was the complementary problem of shortage of science teachers, but it considered this problem less acute in the non-state schools and less open to solution by the Fund.[9] By May 1957 the UK Fund had succeeded in raising just over three million pounds and had made building grant offers to 187 schools and apparatus grant offers to 328 schools.[10]

Returning now to the Australian context, the link with international events will become clear. The beginnings of the Australian IF can be traced to a dinner, purpose unspecified, at the University Club in Sydney during November 1957. Before dinner F. E. Trigg, senior partner of Price Waterhouse and Company, and L. C. Robson, ex-headmaster of the Sydney Church of England Grammar School, were amongst a group who decided to listen to Prime Minister Menzies' address to Parliament on his Government's proposals in relation to the recent recommendations by the Murray Committee on universities. They heard him tell Parliament of the Government's intention to provide substantial new funds over a period of three years to stimulate university development, particularly in the basic sciences.[11]

Robson observed that given Menzies' proposals, unless enough secondary students were science-trained, the universities might well find themselves with more places than could properly be filled. If this occurred, the fundamental problem of producing and improving the number of scientists, for industry and Australia generally, would not be solved. Trigg and Robson agreed that a solution should be found or the Government's proposals might result in a 'white elephant'. Both men were aware that industry in the UK had established the IF to tackle the same problem there in recent years. Robson had been most impressed with the work of the IF during his visit to the UK in 1956 and now he and Trigg agreed that something similar could and should be tried here.[12]

Subsequently they sought information from the IF and after sounding out some leading industrialists in Sydney, Trigg arranged a meeting of about a dozen of them under the chairmanship of Sir Edward Knox, chairman of the Colonial Sugar Refinery (CSR).[13] At this meeting on 20 March 1959 it was resolved to establish the Australian IF.[14] The IF's objectives were stated to be:

a. to increase scientific awareness in the community;
b. to increase the number of well qualified scientists and technologists for the future;
c. to make the most of suitable talent;
d. to contribute to increased productivity; and
e. generally to encourage and promote scientific progress throughout the country.[15]

At the meeting, a small but extremely influential executive committee was appointed, consisting of R. G. C. Parry-Okeden,[16] D. B. Lewington,[17] G. H. Rushworth,[18] G. C. Remington,[19] F. E. Trigg as chairman, and L. C. Robson.[20] This set the pattern for the tight, closed and exclusive leadership which was to characterize the IF's operations and decision making in Australia. The UK IF's policy of restricting assistance to non-state schools was explained, and the meeting agreed that the Australian Fund should follow suit by focusing attention 'first upon those schools of standing which cannot look to Government sources for capital funds'. It was agreed that HMC schools met this definition.[21] This vital decision taken by the small group present was never altered and effectively ensured the permanent exclusion of both government schools and non-government girls' schools from a share in the Fund's financial assistance. It is probably significant that none of the six members of the executive committee had been educated at a government school.

At the first meeting of the executive committee in May 1958 Robson reported that he had devised and sent out a questionnaire to HMC schools in New South Wales and, on the basis of the replies, he estimated that £300 000 to £350 000 was required to provide adequate laboratory construction in that state alone. The meeting was told that Dr W. C. Radford of the Australian Council for Educational Research (ACER) had written to the Fund recently, stating that he had been approached by several 'interested individuals and organizations' about the possibility of creating something like the UK Fund in Australia. Radford had sent out a questionnaire to all non-government schools to assess their science needs, but was unsure whether the matter would be pursued further by the 'interested' parties. Robson reported that he had replied to Radford, suggesting that the initiative for establishing such a Fund 'should come from Industry itself' and expressing the hope that 'ACER might move forward in this matter in co-operation with what was being developed in NSW'.[22] One of the 'interested organizations' was the Victorian Employers Federation (VEF), although Radford may not have specified this in his letter to Robson.[23] If he did, then it seems Robson was probably anxious to promote his own organization before any Victorian body and had possibly discouraged Radford for this reason. Certainly, the VEF scheme was still being mooted in 1960 but was dismissed as 'hopeless' and 'insubstantial' by influential members of the Victorian committee of the Fund established in that year.[24] Part of the Fund's objection, no doubt, centered on the VEF's desire to make the scheme include more than just HMC schools.

Radford persisted with his survey and came up with two major conclusions about science and the non-government schools. The first conclusion must have been disturbing for the newly founded Fund, in light of its recently avowed policy: 'If a quick increase in the numbers of students studying science subjects is required, the obvious place to concentrate on is the girls' schools'. The second conclusion was reassuring in that it stressed the great need for funds for laboratory construction and science equipment.[25] Surprisingly, there is no record of the executive committee's ever having discussed the ACER's survey. Yet, its existence was certainly known, for Robson used its financial data in calculating the cost of upgrading laboratory accommodation in HMC schools in 1959.[26]

In keeping with its tight rein over information, the Fund committee advised the standing committee of the HMC about its plans and progress in August, 1958, but individual school governing bodies had still not been informed some twelve months later.[27]

The Growth and Operation of the Fund

In 1958 Trigg visited the UK on business and also spent a good deal of time meeting members of the Fund there and gaining valuable experience about its general mode of operation and fund-raising methods. Peter Ashton, secretary of the UK Fund, wrote for Trigg a lengthy memorandum, encapsulating the essence of the Fund's operations and the keys to its success. The document in many ways became a blueprint for the Australian Fund. Ashton attributed the success of the UK Fund to three factors:

> First, it was a good scheme; secondly, the Chairman and the Committee were really good and really prepared to work, with an inner nucleus which kept all the strings in hand; thirdly, the assessors were professionals, knew exactly what they were doing and were, therefore, very acceptable to the schools.[28]

As will be seen, the 'inner nucleus' concept was very successfully employed in the Australian organization. Undoubtedly, Robson was a very professional assessor and, as an ex-headmaster, was highly acceptable to the schools.[29] Composition of the UK Fund's executive committee was largely determined by the inclusion of a top board member from each company which agreed to contribute the maximum 'stake'. On the question of fund raising Ashton emphasized that it had mostly been done at top level, by discussion, and the ten largest companies (out of 150) had contributed half the total sum raised. He emphasized that usually only one man in a company decided what the company would give and that he must be tackled 'on at least his own level', so it was vital for the executive committee to include 'top men with the widest contacts'.[30]

The Australian committee later adopted the UK committee's fund-campaigning methods by tackling five major companies on an informal basis and then using their influence to broaden the circle of contacts; preparing lists of potential donor companies from which the members could choose the ones they would approach; and organizing selected committee members to tackle whole industries. Ashton also alerted Trigg to the corporate phenomenon of 'keeping up with the Joneses' and its implication that early contributors must be persuaded to come in at a high level of contribution.[31]

In February 1959, having returned with a useful blueprint for action, Trigg called the executive committee of the Fund together in Sydney, told them of his UK visit, and suggested that the companies represented at the first meeting be asked to contribute £100 each to meet the cost of incorporating the Fund. These companies would then become foundation members of the Fund.

The committee, probably at Trigg's suggestion, agreed that it was time to test the feeling of some of the big companies which had so far tentatively agreed to support the Fund. Probably influenced by Ashton's advice, the committee hoped that some of the companies would be prepared to support the Fund to the extent of £50 000 over a period of five years, and thus set a high initial standard of contribution. It was decided to make immediate approaches to the Bank of New South Wales, British Tobacco, Unilever, CSR, and Amalgamated Wireless of Australia (AWA). Three committee members volunteered to approach the respective company or companies with which they had influence and contacts.[32] The committee's future course of action was to be decided on the basis of these initial approaches. The results were presumably fairly acceptable to the committee: CSR promised £50 000; AWA £25 000; British Tobacco £20 000; Bank of New South Wales £15 000; and Unilever £10 000. Three committee members making personal approaches at top levels in big companies as Ashton had suggested thus netted the Fund £120 000 very quickly. This was remarkably successful, given the traditional Australian conservatism about private investment in education, and says much for the persuasive power of personal contact in big business. By July 1959, when the committee met at Unilever House, firm promises from industry were approaching £200 000, and further approaches were discussed and planned.[33] No doubt the fact that the committee was able to assure prospective donor companies that all donations were likely to be accepted as tax deductions[34] and could be spread over five years[35] were additional incentives to contribute.

About August 1959 the committee was informed by Robson that on the basis of his earlier NSW questionnaire, and consultations with an architect and numerous HMC Headmasters, he considered that the amount required to bring science accommodation in all HMC schools to a good standard was £1.2 million. This estimate was on the basis of UK laboratory standards, providing building only, and contributing only 80 per cent of the cost.[36]

A document, probably drafted by Trigg and/or Robson about August 1959, provided a programme for action by the Fund prior to its public announcement on 2 February 1960. It proposed a preliminary administration to operate until the permanent organization was established, and a permanent organization consisting of an executive officer, and a committee of advice. It was further suggested that a questionnaire be prepared and printed, ready for sending to schools; that a letter to contributors, a letter of announcement to schools and press announcements be prepared; and that a statement of support by the Prime Minister be arranged.[37]

The Fund was incorporated in the ACT on 28 September 1959. Companies subscribing to the incorporation were AWA, CSR, Australian Electrical Industries, British Tobacco, John Lysaght, Bank of New South Wales, Commercial Banking Company of Sydney, Unilever, J. C. Ludowici and Son, Ltd., James N. Kirby Pty. Ltd., and the Commonwealth Bank of Australia.[38] With success of the Fund more or less assured in NSW, Trigg and Robson next sought to extend the Fund by establishing committees in other states. By November 1959 approaches were being made by the Sydney committee to find suitable chairmen in Melbourne, Adelaide, Brisbane and Perth to establish committees in those states. With the aid of Essington Lewis, retired managing director of Broken Hill Proprietary (BHP), they persuaded Charles Booth, chairman of the Australian Paper Mills (APM), to be chairman of the committee to be established in Victoria. Following discussions between Robson and Booth, and in accordance with the August blueprint, a committee of advice was established in October 1959 with Robson as chairman.[39] In early 1960 A. G. C. T. Carver, a retired CSR employee, was appointed executive officer of the Fund. CSR provided him with an office in Chatsworth House, Bent Street, Sydney.[40] On 2 February 1960, by prearrangement with press and radio, the existence of the Fund was simultaneously announced across the nation.[41] It received a good deal of news coverage in the ensuing months. Favourable editorials, some of them probably solicited, appeared in the *Daily Telegraph*, the *Sydney Morning Herald*, the *Age* and the Adelaide *News*,[42] while supporting statements were made by prominent Australian scientists such as Sir Mark Oliphant, Sir John Eccles and Professor Harry Messel. Despite the mostly favourable comment, there were some letters to editors and other comments critical of the exclusion of state schools and non-government girls' schools from the Fund.

At the executive committee meeting in February 1960 the members agreed to systematize the fund raising by drawing up a list of companies not yet approached, and then forwarding to them a covering letter and brochure, to be personally followed-up by committee members where possible. Robson reported progress in the preparation of a questionnaire for distribution to all HMC schools to assist in assessing the relative needs and priorities amongst the schools. Presumably Robson regarded Radford's ACER data as unsuited to his purpose or already outdated, otherwise he could have saved much time and effort. At this meeting it was decided that Robson should visit the UK and possibly the United States and Canada to learn as much as possible about the latest laboratory construction and fittings, and to study the English Fund's method of assessing the needs and priority of schools.

In April 1960 Robson gave an executive committee meeting a preliminary report on his allocation of priorities and needs amongst the forty-one schools which had so far returned their questionnaires. He calculated that £822 000 would be needed to provide adequately for the science laboratory needs of these schools. The meeting was told that after approaches to another 115 companies, the total amount promised had reached £294 037, and that state committees had been successfully established in Perth and Adelaide under the chairmanships of D. W. Brisbane[43] and Roland Jacobs[44] respectively. It was hoped that efforts to find a suitable Brisbane chairman would soon be rewarded.

Formation of the Victorian Fund

It was also reported that, hopefully, the Fund would now get under way in Victoria. To that end Charles Booth and Ian McLennan, chief general manager of BHP, had arranged a dinner for about forty industrialists at the Australian Club in Melbourne, to launch the Fund in Victoria, to explain its purpose, and secure promises of contributions. This dinner was an interesting example of big business fund-raising methods and the employment of Ashton's 'keeping up with the Joneses' principle. Trigg and Robson, as founders of the Australian Fund, were invited to attend the dinner and tell of their activities to date. Four days earlier, with Booth, McLennan and R. Selby-Smith, they were also invited to a preliminary dinner at the Melbourne Club to plan the strategy for the Fund dinner. At the planning dinner McLennan, who was pre-eminent in the Melbourne business community, compiled a list of what the major companies would probably give and said he was usually 'pretty right'. His total came to £285 000.[45]

All agreed that the list of contributors being proposed by the Sydney Committee should not be published until after the Melbourne promises were made at the dinner. This was because many companies would wish to be in the first list. It was also agreed that rather than separate lists for each state and potential rivalry, there should simply be one list compiled on an Australia-wide basis. Trigg said that some Sydney companies would not be contributing until after 30 June, or after approval from the UK, or after certain Melbourne companies had 'come in'. The latter point indicated that many companies adopted a 'wait and see' approach, so that if a Fund member could persuade a rival company in that industry to contribute at a high level, then others might well follow suit. This was also borne out by Trigg's description, on another occasion, of how £250 000 had already been raised in NSW by April 1960 through a series of personal approaches to some of the big industrialists: 'we did not cast the net too wide at first, as we felt that if we could get the initial support at a sufficiently high level this would encourage others to come in on a basis which was appropriate to their "place" in the industrial pattern'.[46]

At the prior strategy dinner it was agreed that a Victorian IF committee of six would be set up during the industrialists' dinner and three members of the committee would be nominated as councillors of the Fund. They felt that the other states should be given more than one representative on the council, as they were 'inclined to be touchy' about the size and power of NSW and Victoria. Trigg explained that the executive committee in NSW was a committee appointed by the first NSW council to carry on the day-to-day activities of the Fund. The first council, the local NSW committee and the executive committee all had the same people on them.

At the preliminary dinner, too, the question was raised as to whether the Fund should be doing anything about alleviating the teacher shortage. This was a not uncommon criticism of the Fund. Moreover, Trigg, Sir James Vernon, and Robson had feared it might become a major issue at the Melbourne dinner, as it was known that Syme, the chairman of BHP, was critical of the Fund on this issue and planned to raise it at the dinner.[47] However, Syme apparently overcame his misgivings, and assured McLennan of his support for the Fund. McLennan and Selby-Smith told Trigg and Robson they were of the opinion 'that adequate facilities were necessary to attract teachers. As far as they were concerned, the schools had to be put on a proper basis first'.[48] They were probably reassured by the fact that the UK Fund had adopted a similar attitude.

Robson was very hesitant about attending the Melbourne industrialists' dinner, no doubt because he was aware of the importance of the impact of the dinner on the success of the Fund, and was very conscious of the Sydney–Melbourne rivalry and the danger of his being seen as an interfering outsider. He expressed to Trigg his reluctance to attend without the presence of Trigg as well:

> My experience of Melbourne suggests that I would not carry enough weight on my own: the school association is too strong. Our combined weight is considerable. If x and y° could soften up a few men in advance (and it is up to them to do so), our weight would make a deeper impression. However, I'm ready, with reluctance, to be a candidate for a martyr's crown.
> [° x and y were two senior Sydney CSR executives.][49]

Thus, Robson was keenly conscious of the possibility that he and Trigg might be resented as interfering New South Welshmen. Such inter-state sensitivities were a factor which the organizers constantly had to allow for.

The guest list for the Fund's dinner at the Australian Club was a veritable *Who's Who in Industry in Melbourne*. Virtually all the biggest industries were represented and mostly at the top level by chairmen or managing directors (see Appendix I, pp. 101-2). Over thirty people attended. The main proceedings of the evening were Charles Booth's explanatory speech, the election of a Victorian committee to launch the Fund in Victoria, and the announcement of some donations.

In his address Booth revealed that, in 1958, Sir Edward Knox had approached Essington Lewis, then head of BHP, suggesting that Lewis might launch a nation-wide public appeal to raise money for the Fund. However, their discussion led them to agree that 'funds for a purpose such as this would not be raised by way of public appeal, but rather, by individual approaches'.[50] They agreed that Knox should try such an approach to the main companies in NSW and, if successful, they would then extend to Victoria. Now, as a result of NSW having successfully raised £300 000, it was decided to commence in Victoria.

Was Knox and Lewis's preference for individual approaches to companies rather than a public appeal inspired by the feeling that the latter might not be at all popular with the public at large, or did they simply believe the former to be the more effective fund-raising device? They may have believed, perhaps realistically, that the general public viewed the HMC as élitist and would not, therefore, have supported a public appeal. Certainly part of Booth's speech is open to the interpretation that he was expressing an élitist viewpoint to an exclusive audience whom he knew to be sympathetic:

> Let me say just this in conclusion. Those of us who have studied this subject accept the fact that many of the future industrial leaders and those who provide the most promising material for such leadership commence their lives in the schools which we plan to aid—in what would be called the Public Schools in England.[51]

The above statement seems to have been regarded as sufficient justification in this gathering for aiding HMC schools to the exclusion of others. During the course of his speech Booth explained the reason for Tasmania's absence from an otherwise Australia-wide Fund. Tasmania, influenced largely by Harry Hey of Electrolytic Zinc, had decided to establish an independent IF, raising finance purely for its own schools. Electrolytic Zinc had promised £25 000 provided other Tasmanian companies in aggregate matched this contribution. Booth said that all members of the council of the Fund would have preferred Tasmania to participate in a nation-wide Fund. This claim does not appear to have been completely accurate, for at the Sydney executive committee meeting on 5 February 1960 Robson informed the committee of Tasmania's determination to have a separate Fund, and commented that 'it would not be a disadvantage to us if Tasmania wishes to look after its own affairs as we would be relieved of embarrassment in dealing with a leading independent school which is co-educational'.[52] It would seem from Robson's comment that concern over setting a precedent of providing aid for girls' schools was one factor which discouraged the mainland Fund from actively pursuing union with the Tasmanian Fund. It is interesting to note that the Hobart *Mercury*, on the date of the Australian Fund's announcement, ran a news item under the heading 'State's Lead on Technology Followed' in which it emphasized that the 'mainland' was simply copying the Tasmanian idea.[53]

Presumably, the Fund regarded the Melbourne dinner as only moderately successful, for firm promises reached only £106 500 despite McLennan's prediction of £285 000. However, many companies which later contributed funds could not do so until after consultation with their boards, and so the £106 500 represented only those companies which had previously determined their donation and declared it at the dinner. Victoria's total grew quickly in succeeding months.

Implementation of the Laboratory Building Programme

It is not simplifying things too much to say that while Trigg exercised national supervision of the fund-raising and business side of the Fund, Robson did the same for the educational side. From the beginning of 1960, with the Fund already assured of considerable finance, Robson's time became increasingly absorbed with putting into action a nation-wide school laboratory building programme. Robson's first job had been to assess the science accommodation needs of all the HMC schools by questionnaire.[54] In early April, just before leaving for the UK and North America on a six-week study tour for the Fund, Robson wrote a report for the executive committee on his preliminary processing and analysis of questionnaires from the first forty-one schools to reply. Robson's procedure was to give each school two ratings. The first was a priority rating on a four-point numerical scale based essentially on the criterion of 'productivity' or current size and quality of senior form science output to university and industry. For example, Priority I ratings were only given to big secondary schools of 600 or more pupils with big sixth forms, good standards, and a fairly high rate of supply of boys to university and industry. Potential for improved productivity was also considered. The second rating was a needs rating (on a four-point alphabetical scale) based on their present laboratory accommodation and their ability to find their own finance. Robson suggested that the Fund should commence by aiding those schools which rated Priority 1 and Need A. According to his analysis, there were eleven such schools. However, he emphasized that there were many good Priority 2 and 3 schools to be considered also.[55]

In a shorter typed version of this report, dated 4 April 1960, Robson concluded by emphasizing that if the full £1.2 million target was not achieved, the council of the Fund would have to decide whether to choose a limited number of schools and provide 80 per cent of costs, or provide less than 80 per cent of costs for a larger number of schools.[56]

On his return from the UK and North America at the end of May 1960 Robson wrote an interesting report for the Fund. He described the general UK standards with regard to number, size, and type of laboratory and ancillary rooms. These he recommended as a suitable Australian guide. Robson emphasized the importance of emulating the UK example by providing some laboratories purely for advanced work. He then offered a series of recommendations for discussion by the Council:

(a) that applications be invited only from 'some twenty or more [schools] which we consider to be of first priority . . . until we have one million pounds at our disposal;

(b) that the Committee of Advice consist of only three members;

(c) that Council consider the possibility of appointing an Advisory Architect;

(d) that the working procedure should be for school applications to be considered by the Committee of Advice and sent with a recommendation to the Executive Committee, which would then appoint a small committee (one executive member and one member of the Committee of Advice) to negotiate with the school; and

(e) that Council consider the desirability of either encouraging or insisting upon schools employing laboratory assistants.[57]

It will be seen below that most of these recommendations were adopted within a few months. At the executive committee meeting held in the CSR board room in Sydney on 14 July 1960 it was clear that the Fund was rapidly gathering momentum. It was decided to reconstitute the executive committee due to the growth of the Fund in other states. The committee was reduced from six to four members with Trigg, Parry-Okeden and Remington being re-elected from NSW and Booth elected from Victoria. Total funds promised had now reached £496 000 and spokesmen from New South Wales, Victoria, South Australia and Western Australia all expressed confidence in raising much more. All states except Western Australia considered that publicity of contributions to date would disadvantage their present campaign of personal approaches to companies. A suitable Queensland chairman had not yet been found. The question of utilizing some funds for science equipment was raised, but the meeting concurred with the chairman's view that this would contravene the tax concession agreed to by the Commissioner, which specified that funds were to be used only for building. Robson reported on his trip and decisions were taken on his recommendations. There was some disagreement with Robson's motion that the Fund would have to be selective in its aid—Booth said every HMC school should receive some assistance from the Fund. It was decided that letters should be sent to all HMC schools acknowledging receipt of the questionnaires and informing them that the Fund would soon begin to help a limited number of schools. Robson's advice recommending a smaller technical committee was accepted and it was reduced from five to three members. On 24 August 1960 Robson, who had spent much of the year visiting and assessing the needs and priorities of HMC schools in all mainland states except Western Australia, submitted a detailed report on these schools. Robson nominated fourteen schools (seven in New South Wales, five in Victoria, and two in South Australia)[58] which he said should be invited to apply for assistance by submitting sketch plans and first estimates. He recommended no schools from Queensland, as he had not completed his survey of its schools.

In his report Robson indicated the general line of thinking behind his allocation:

> In recommending schools for early invitation, I have in mind the balance between States, and between denominations. In fact, there are more direct and appropriate cases in NSW than in Victoria: and there are really no Catholic schools in these two big States which, for various reasons, seem to be urgent cases at this early stage of our work.
> I feel that it is also most desirable that a good number of jobs done at the early stage of the Fund's operations should be such as to exhibit the Fund's ideas and standards and to set an example in laboratory buildings. Hence, I have leant strongly towards jobs which will be new buildings rather than re-arrangements within existing walls. I have in mind that those recommended contain several in which the Fund's representatives have had, or will have, a good say in the drawing of the plans. It would be wise also to bear in mind the special cases of Wesley (Victoria) and Geelong: these provide the possibility of interesting new contributions to the field of science teaching.[59]

By the 6 September meeting of the council, he had also visited Western Australia and chosen two schools there which should be invited to apply for assistance.[60] The council agreed that Robson's recommendations should be acted upon. On 15 September the sixteen schools were invited to submit applications to the Fund, complete with sketch plans and a first estimate of cost.

Once schools had been invited, the Fund followed procedures laid down by Robson:

1. The school will be invited to submit a project for consideration, with at least sketch plans and estimates.
2. The Committee of Advice will examine the project with a view to determining:
(a) The number of rooms needed according to the Fund's standards.
(b) Whether the rooms proposed are suitable, according to the Fund's standards, in regard to size and design. (It is hoped that in most cases, the Fund's representative will have been consulted during the planning stage.)

3. The Committee of Advice will consult with the Fund's architect in accordance with my report.

4. The Chairman of the Committee of Advice will submit to Council:
(a) His report, embodying a recommendation as to the amount of assistance, and other details, required for negotiation of the agreement with the schools, and
(b) The architect's report.

5. The Council will consider the reports as in (4.) and will appoint one of their number to act with the Chairman of the Committee of Advice in negotiating agreement with the school to such extent as they may approve.[61]

It seems that by December 1960 unsuccessful schools were expressing to councillors their criticism of selection procedures, for Robson wrote to Carver, providing him with information constituting a defence of the Fund's policy to date and suggesting that it should be forwarded to Victorian councillor, Seddon, and NSW councillors, Trigg and Knox.[62]

King's School was clearly dissatisfied with its relatively low priority. In his August report on schools Robson had stressed that King's supporters were applying a good deal of pressure. But while acknowledging King's high priority rating, he explained that its needs rating was very low because the school had the benefit of a bequest which yielded a very large income. For this reason he felt assistance should not be given until 'after the needs of the big, strong city schools have been met'. Defending his low placement of King's, Robson pointed out that its annual income from the Futter-Macansh bequest exceeded even the most generous allotment that the Fund could make them. In his view, twenty of the sixty HMC schools had needs (financially and/or for science accommodation) that would not be seriously affected if unassisted by the Fund. Furthermore, Robson warned that if the Fund were to alter its policy and give something to all HMC schools from the present sum, many would get amounts so small that they could not be effectively used. The correct policy for the Fund, he affirmed, was to 'leave low priority schools until later, meanwhile ignoring remarks or inquiries from persons who are interested in a particular school and who do not see the scheme from the national viewpoint'.[63]

In support of his selection procedures, Robson also produced a confidential table (to go to the three councillors previously mentioned), rating all the HMC schools on a five-point scale for each of the three selection variables:

1. Ability to promote the aims of the Fund now and in the future.
2. Need for better laboratories.
3. Need for financial help.

King's, Geelong Grammar, Knox and St Joseph's (Nudgee) were the only four of the sixty-one schools to be given the lowest financial need rating.[64]

It may have been a further response to dissatisfied schools which led the Fund to produce, about this time, a circular entitled 'Principles guiding selection of schools for assistance':

> The considerations kept in mind in extending invitations to apply for assistance have been:
> (a) ability of the school to promote the objects of the Fund,
> (b) relative need to improve the school's existing accommodation for science teaching, and
> (c) relative need of the school for financial help in building laboratories.

The last two considerations do not need explanation. The ability of the school to promote the Fund's objects is held to depend upon

> —the size of the school: a school with a large secondary enrolment is likely to have a large output of qualified pupils,
> —the size of the VI form,
> —the volume of science, particularly at VI and Honours levels,
> —the standard achieved by the school,
> —the number normally passing to the university or to industry,
> —the possibility that good laboratories erected in the school may influence scientific education over a wide area.[65]

In November 1960, as a result of the completion of Robson's report on the Queensland schools in October, the council agreed to add four schools from that State to the sixteen schools already invited to apply.[66] Total contributions promised had now reached £569 980 7s, while contributions actually received had reached £276 090 17s. Nearly a year later, however, the total promised had only increased by £12 000.[67] It was fortunate that the Fund had succeeded in launching committees in the various states by early 1960, for this gave them nearly a year's fund-raising activities before a serious economic slump began to grip Australia. Had the Fund been a year later in establishing these state committees, it may well have been a failure as a national body. At the annual general meeting of the Fund in March 1961 the councillors present resolved that 'approaches for further contributions not be pressed until the economic situation has improved, except where negotiations are in train or chances "favorable" '. However, it was agreed to retain the existing building schedule, and it was reported that the first sixteen schools would be well advanced with their projects by the end of 1961.[68]

The fund-raising climate remained comparatively bleak for the rest of the Fund's existence and henceforth the job, with the exception of the Brisbane committee, was largely one of implementing the building programme. New South Wales did have renewed fund-raising drives in July 1962 and 1963, but with little success.[69]

The Brisbane committee was finally launched under the chairmanship of Sir Reginald Groom, ex-Lord Mayor of Brisbane, with a dinner for industrialists on 10 October 1961.[70] However, Queensland, faced with the task of seeking funds during a period of economic slump, had only managed to raise £7406 from nineteen contributors by July 1963.

Between the end of 1960 and Menzies' federal science laboratories election promise of November 1963, the affairs of the Fund were reduced mainly to those of routine administration of the building programme; meetings overburdened by economic gloom; and the attendance of representatives at school science laboratory 'Openings'. An IF interim report in August 1963 indicated that the Fund had spent, or committed itself to spending, £593 643 in providing new laboratory accommodation at thirty-five schools. Twenty-one projects had been completed and were in use, building was well advanced at six, and planning was proceeding in another eight (see Appendix II, p. 102).[71]

The Contribution of the IF to Menzies' Science Laboratories Scheme

I have explored elsewhere the broad educational, political, economic and social factors contributing to the emergence of the first federal aid for schools scheme—Menzies' federal science laboratories programme—and will not elaborate on them here.[72] Rather, I wish to focus solely on the specific contribution of the IF and its relationship to the Menzies Government prior to and immediately after Menzies' promise—recognizing, of course, that it was only one of a number of major influences on Menzies and his government's policies.

The Menzies election promise of 12 November 1963 to provide a federal science laboratory scheme to government and non-government schools 'without discrimination' in effect signalled the demise of the IF. Robson's assessment of the effect of Menzies' promise was that, short of some unforeseeable circumstances, the Fund was henceforth moribund apart from collecting promised contributions and completing projects in hand. 'No industrial firm in its senses would now fork up for the Fund when the Government has undertaken the job', he asserted.[73] This development poses the intriguing question: 'What was the relationship between Menzies' science laboratories scheme and the Industrial Fund?' Clearly, two separate questions are involved. Once having made up his mind to promise some form of federal aid, to what extent did the IF model influence Menzies' decision to opt specifically for a science laboratories scheme? And, what was the relationship between the Fund and the Government scheme after Menzies' decision was announced?

The answer to the first question is that Menzies' familiarity with the Fund undoubtedly provided him with knowledge of a successful working scheme. Menzies had been exposed to the Fund and its activities in a number of ways over a period of years. In October 1960 a letter drafted by Robson and signed by Sir Edward Knox was sent to Menzies telling him about the Fund. It spoke of the evident stimulus given by the Fund to the thinking of school councils, headmasters, and teachers in the HMC schools, and expressed the hope that this would go even further as buildings were provided. The enthusiasm of the Fund was evident in the hope expressed to Menzies that it would have a big influence on scientific education in secondary schools and that the influence would extend well beyond the schools in which operations were to be undertaken.[74] Three years later, Menzies was to make these hopes a reality, and it may well be that this letter had some small part in setting Menzies thinking about the issues. In his reply, Menzies indicated that he had been aware of the existence of the Fund as early as January 1960 when F. M. Osborne, the Minister for Air, had told him of its operations, and he assured the Fund that it was 'held in the highest esteem by the Government'.[75]

During the course of the next few years Menzies kept in touch with the Fund's progress by attending various HMC schools' science laboratory 'Opening Ceremonies'. Significantly, perhaps, just seven months before his electoral speech in which he made revolutionary promises of federal aid for both secondary science laboratories and scholarships, he opened Sydney Grammar's IF science block and heard its then headmaster, C. O. Healey, chairman of the HMC, make a strong plea for increased scholarships so that independent schools did not become the prerogative of the rich.[76]

Only three weeks before his election promise, Menzies opened Waverley College's new IF science block. When addressing the gathering, Robson apologized to Menzies for having to listen to him speak on the fourth such occasion. Robson made a plea for more funds in order that the Fund might continue its good work rather than cease. It is quite possible that Robson's appeal in this speech was the catalyst for Menzies' federal science scheme decision which was announced several weeks later. Certainly, Menzies was strongly reminded by Robson of the great value of the scheme and of its serious difficulties with raising further funds in the current economic climate. Perhaps this reminder and the pragmatic Menzies' recognition of his government's potential electoral dependence on the national Catholic vote were the factors which largely shaped his decision at this or some subsequent time over the next two weeks. Certainly, according to Robson and others, Menzies rose and in his response, spoke in glowing terms of the Fund's contribution to Australia's scientific development.[77]

Within weeks of Menzies' election promise and successful re-election, his Government was in touch with the IF over ways and means of implementing the new laboratories scheme. Following a request from William McMahon, Minister for Labour and National Service (with whom Trigg was on first-name terms), Trigg had Robson prepare a special memorandum for the Government explaining the Fund's establishment and

E

operations. In December, at a special meeting of the IF Council to discuss the IF's future, Trigg

> . . . informed the meeting that Mr McMahon had been in touch with him and had asked for information about the Fund. Mr McMahon made no secret of the fact that the Prime Minister was very interested in the Fund's work and that the idea for the offer in his policy speech was certainly influenced by the achievements of the Fund. The Minister was given a copy of the Fund's brochure and annual reports and other documents, and also an explanatory memorandum prepared by Mr Robson (a copy of this memorandum is attached for Councillors' information). Subsequently, Mr McMahon asked for and was given two more sets of these papers, one set being understood to be for the Prime Minister. . .[78]

A variety of subsequent comments by public servants, headmasters, politicians and others confirm the significant influence of the Fund in triggering the specifically science-oriented election promise.[79]

Brian Hone, headmaster of Melbourne Church of England Grammar School, in a letter to Trigg in March 1964, said:

> I do congratulate you and Len Robson on the success of your Industrial Fund and the effect it has had on the Menzies Government. I should think that few men could claim to have had such a direct impact on the budget![80]

In February 1964, when opening the Geelong College science laboratories, Menzies is reported to have acknowledged that he had derived his inspiration for the Government science scheme from the Industrial Fund.[81]

At the Fund's special meeting on 20 December 1963 there was general agreement that the experience of the Fund should be placed at the disposal of the Government. In fact, some members urged that the Government should be persuaded of the Fund's suitability to act as the instrument for administering the HMC sector of the non-government schools' federal science grant. Robson had probably already broached the subject with the Government, for he told the meeting he understood that the Government might find it difficult to treat one group of schools differently from others, and noted that the Conference schools were only a portion of the independent schools. Robson further remarked that the Government would find it difficult to arrange financial distribution on the proposed 'population basis' unless it was guided by some general principles which the Fund could help provide. He suggested that some general principles might be: the wisdom of concentrating spending on substantial projects rather than diffused expenditure; the establishment of standard criteria for ratio of science rooms to school size and type; the preparation of flexible 'standard layout' plans; and the compilation of standard equipment lists. Throughout December Robson seems to have had some contact with the Commonwealth Office of Education and its director, 'Jock' Weeden. According to a fairly cryptic and almost illegible memo recording a conversation between these two men on 30 December, Menzies had instructed Weeden and John Gorton, the newly-appointed Minister assisting the Prime Minister in education matters, to study the Industrial Fund's operations carefully and to 'do the right thing' by the Fund.[82]

On the same day, Robson 'temporarily froze' negotiations with four schools which were about to be offered Fund assistance in order to await Government development.[83] What Robson had in mind became clear on 14 January 1964, when he wrote to Gorton on behalf of the Fund indicating the 'minor problems' created for the Fund in collecting outstanding business contributions, and sought a Government guarantee of the outstanding amount as a cover against non-collection. Subsequently it became clear that Robson was angling for the Government to take over these four projects as the first of the Government's independent school schemes and this was hinted at in his last paragraph: 'Again, you may well consider it desirable to have as small overlap as possible between our operations and those under your scheme'.[84]

Robson had probably chosen the date of his suggestion to Gorton fairly carefully, for he had previously told Trigg that he was biding his time for the right moment to raise the question of the Fund's relationship with the Government[85] and he was aware that the Minister had carefully considered this question and that Cabinet would be taking decisions on this and related Government scheme matters that same week. Robson had consultations with Gorton in Sydney on 18 January and, while Gorton was apparently sympathetic, he rejected Robson's suggestion about the four schools.[86] Two days later, Robson wrote to Gorton offering to the Government the full consultative services of the Fund, including his own willingness to go to Canberra for consultation if desired, and also offering advice which Gorton had asked for, but which he had not had time to give on the 18th:

this is a scheme which ought not to be tackled too hurriedly at the cost of pretty thorough investigation and preparation. There is the chance here to do something of great interest and importance in Australia which has not been done on such a big scale, as far as I know, elsewhere. If the effect is to be striking, something more must be done than merely to grant money to enable Education Departments and schools to pursue their own routine ideas. School science is advancing rapidly and, in my experience, a bit more rapidly than many schools realize. If I may say so, the object might be not merely to see that routine laboratory requirements are met, but also to increase the interest of school science work, to raise its standards, and to stimulate initiative and originality.
The possibilities are great if there are provisions and encouragement

for the exercise of imagination. Of course, I understand the desire to get ahead with the job, and I do not think that preliminary planning need delay it significantly.

On 21 January Robson prepared a four-page document for the Government (probably for Gorton), setting out his views on the aims and objects of the Government scheme, on practical matters needing careful consideration and on the process by which the Government might get the scheme started. Many of his important suggestions on procedure and policy were ultimately adopted by the Government: a committee of advice was set up to assist the minister; money was only to be spent on complete projects and so means for determining priorities were devised; finally, no assistance was granted to schools retrospectively.[87]

A month later, Robson was summoned to Canberra for consultations with Gorton and possibly Menzies.[88] About this time it appears that Robson was invited, and accepted the invitation, to become chairman of the federal advisory committee on science laboratories which he had previously proposed.

Between February and July 1964 the Fund re-entered negotiations with the Government about the possibility of the laboratory projects at the four schools previously mentioned being taken over by the Government. Much to the disgust of Robson, after numerous assurances that it would do so, the Government declined to take them over. The Fund was then obliged to re-enter negotiations with the schools and provide them with grants.

During the course of the next few years, the Fund gradually wound up its operations and ultimately lodged £24 000 in residual funds with the Academy of Science in Canberra. The annual income from this Industrial Trust Fund is used at the discretion of the Academy to fund projects which foster the advancement of science in secondary schools in Australia.[89] By the time of its cessation the Fund had achieved the impressive record of having distributed grants totalling £620 643 (raised from 253 industrial and commercial organizations) amongst thirty-seven HMC schools for the construction of high standard science laboratories. It had proved the capacity of industry to work co-operatively on a nation-wide basis for the purpose of establishing examples of first-class science accommodation across the country.

In conclusion, it is clear that the efforts of the Fund were influential in promoting federal government interest and eventual participation in a nation-wide scheme of secondary science laboratory construction in state and independent schools. Furthermore, the Fund had a major role in determining the subsequent shape of the Menzies Government's national science laboratory scheme. Unquestionably, the Government relied heavily on the expertise of the Fund and Robson in particular in planning and implementing its science laboratory building and equipment programme for the independent schools sector. More generally, the study reveals the remarkable strength of 'old school tie' loyalty and linkage between the business élite and the small exclusive group of HMC schools in Australia in the early 1960s.[90]

APPENDIX I

Guest List for Melbourne Industrial Fund Dinner
7 April 1960

Guests	Company Affiliation	Ultimate Company Contribution (£)
D. H. Alexander	Secretary, Australian Paper Mills	12 500
Harold Austin	Associate Editor, *Age*	
M. L. Baillieu	Chairman, North Broken Hill, Ltd.; Managing Director, Broken Hill Associated Smelters; Director other similar companies, also of Associated Pulp and Electrolytic Zinc	10 000
J. W. Barnaby	Secretary, Imperial Chemical Industries	15 000
Sir Walter Bassett	Chairman, Mt Lyell; Member of Provisional Council, Monash University	
K. G. Begg	Chairman and Managing Director, Imperial Chemical Industries	15 000
P. A. Berry	Drug Houses of Australia—representing Mr Grimwade	1 000
T. G. Crane	Managing Director, Monsanto	5 000
M. A. Cumming	Chairman and Managing Director, Commonwealth Fertilizers, etc.; Director, Broken Hill Proprietary; Director, Imperial Chemical Industries	1 000 50 000 15 000
E. E. Dunshea	Director Dunlop, and also Chairman of Council of Carey Grammar School	10 000
R. C. C. Edwards	Editor, Melbourne *Herald*	
J. Chester Guest	Chairman and/or Director North Broken Hill, and a group of associated companies	10 000
G. C. Hill	Chief General Manager, National Bank; Director, General Motors-Holden	5 000 25 000
W. A. Ince	Chairman and/or Director Vacuum Refinery Company, Rheem, Consolidated Zinc, Balm Paints, International Harvester, Monsanto, etc.	5 000 10 000
W. McCullough	Chairman and Director, International Harvester	2 500
Essington Lewis	Retired Chairman B.P. (Australia)	
J. G. W. MacIntyre	Chairman and Managing Director, Ford Motor Company	10 000
M. A. E. Mawby	Deputy Chairman, etc. Consolidated Zinc and Zinc Corporation	10 000

Continued on page 102

Continued from page 101

Guests	Company Affiliation	Ultimate Company Contribution (£)
M. N. Pierson	Director, Vacuum Oil	
Ian Potter	Financier. Director of a number of companies, including Email	25 000
P. J. V. Ramsden	Vice Chairman, Australian Paper Mills; Director other companies	12 500
J. F. Rich	Broken Hill Proprietary Company, Ltd.	50 000
L. C. Robson	Guest from New South Wales	
R. Selby-Smith	Headmaster, Scotch College	
A. W. Stewart	Director in a number of companies in Collins House Base Metal Group	
J. R. C. Taylor	Chairman, Shell	10 000
F. E. Trigg	Guest from New South Wales	
H. D. T. Williamson	General Manager, A.N.Z. Bank	5 000

APPENDIX II

I.F. Laboratory Construction Progress as of 20 August 1963

Completed Projects

The Scots' College	N.S.W.	Sacred Heart College	S.A.
Pulteney Grammar School	S.A.	Barker College	N.S.W.
Melbourne C.E.G.S.	Vic.	Ipswich Grammar School	Qld.
Scotch College	W.A.	Aquinas College	W.A.
Trinity Grammar School	N.S.W.	Toowoomba Grammar School	Qld.
All Saints' College	N.S.W.	Scotch College	S.A.
Canberra Grammar School	A.C.T.	Downlands College	Qld.
Carey Baptist Grammar School	Vic.	Sydney Grammar School	N.S.W.
C.E.G.S., Brisbane	Qld.	Brisbane Boys' College	Qld.
Wesley College	Vic.	Camberwell Grammar School	Vic.
Cranbrook School	N.S.W.		

Total assistance given £368 643

Building in Progress

Waverley College	N.S.W.	Geelong College	Vic.
Sydney C.E.G.S.	N.S.W.	Brighton Grammar School	Vic.
Assumption College	Vic.		

(The above are expected to be complete for term I of 1964)

Scotch College   Vic.

(This scheme is in two stages, to be completed respectively during 1963 and early in 1964)

Progress payment made   £38 006
Balance committed   £71 994

Planning in Progress

Geelong Grammar School	Vic.	Prince Alfred College	S.A.
The King's School	N.S.W.	Brisbane Grammar School	Qld.
Trinity Grammar School	Vic.	St. Joseph's College	N.S.W.
Christ Church Grammar School	W.A.	Newington College	N.S.W.

(These should be completed during 1964)

Amount committed, subject to approval of plans: £115 000

NOTES

1. Most are church schools, independent of government control, and all are conducted by councils responsible to the corporations to which they belong. Their élitism is reflected in HMC policy of occasionally 'admitting' to membership 'schools of like standing which pursue the same ideas' and in their conscious emulation of 'the famous Public Schools of Great Britain'. See C. E. W. Bean, *Here My Son* (Angus and Robertson, Sydney, 1950), p. vii. See also S. Encel, *Equality and Authority: A study of class, status and power in Australia* (Cheshire, Melbourne, 1970), pp. 157-8.

2. I am grateful to the Academy of Science for making the IF records available to me, and to F. E. Trigg for his discussions and assistance. Without them this study could not have been written. All subsequent references are from the Industrial Fund records (hereafter ASIF), unless otherwise indicated.

3. ASIF, 75/12-1, Trigg to Roland Jacobs, 21 April 1960.

4. 'Report on the IFASES' by the UK executive committee, May 1957, p. 1.

5. ASIF, 75/3-1, P. Ashton to Trigg, 29 July 1958, p. 1. 'Report on the IFASES', p. 1.

6. 'Report on the IFASES', p. 1.

7. ASIF, 75/3-1, op. cit., p. 1.

8. Ibid., p. 2.

9. Ibid.

10. 'Report on the IFASES', pp. 16, 29.

11. Definitive statement on the IF for the Australian Academy of Science, prepared by F. E. Trigg, May 1972.

12. Ibid.

13. Ibid.

14. ASIF, 75/1, typed memorandum headed 'What has been done so far', August 1959.

15. Annual Report of IF, 1960, p. 3.

16. Chairman and Managing Director of John Lysaght Australia, educated at Eton College.

17. President of British Tobacco (Australia), educated privately.

18. Deputy Chairman Commonwealth Banking Corporation, 1962, educated at Melbourne Church of England Grammar School.

19. Solicitor and Chairman of Rolls Royce (Australia) and Crane (Australia), educated at Sydney Church of England Grammar School.

20. Advisory consultant to the committee. He was educated at Sydney Grammar.

21. ASIF, 75/1, op. cit.

22. Ibid.

23. Information obtained by the author from W. C. Radford.

24. ASIF, 75/12-1; Trigg's memorandum on dinner correspondence at Australian Club, Melbourne, 3 April 1960.

25. *Provision for science teaching in the non-government schools of Australia* (ACER, Melbourne, August 1958), p. 8.

26. Minutes of executive committee meeting (hereafter Minutes), 4 April 1960.

27. ASIF, 75/1, op. cit., p. 1.

28. ASIF, 75/3-1, op. cit.

29. During his visit to the UK in 1960 on behalf of the Australian IF, Robson spent some time touring schools with Sir Graham Savage (assessor for the IF in the UK), learning his techniques.

30. ASIF, 75/3-1, op. cit., pp. 2, 6.

31. Ibid., p. 6.

32. Minutes, 26 February, 1959.

33. Ibid., 9 July 1959.

34. Ibid., 27 May 1958, 3 November 1959.

35. ASIF, 75/1, op. cit., p. 1.

36. Ibid.

37. Ibid.

38. Ibid.

39. Minutes, 3 November 1959. R. Selby-Smith, headmaster of Scotch College, Melbourne, was also on the committee of advice, and he and Robson became, in effect, chief advisers for Melbourne and Sydney respectively.

40. Ibid., 5 February 1960.

[41] ASIF, 75/4-2, press cuttings. Robson co-ordinated this publicity and even asked Sir Harold Wyndham, the NSW Director-General of Education, to be ready to praise the IF if interviewed.
[42] Ibid., 3, 4, 8, 2 February 1960.
[43] Chairman of BP Kwinana and former chairman of the council of Scotch College, Perth.
[44] Chairman of the SA Brewing Company and an old boy of Geelong College.
[45] ASIF, 75/12-1, Trigg's *aide-mémoire* on dinner at Melbourne Club, 3 April 1960.
[46] ASIF, 75/12-1, Trigg to D. W. Brisbane, 19 April 1960.
[47] ASIF, 75/12-1, Trigg to Robson (undated, approximate date March 1960).
[48] ASIF, 75/12-1, Trigg's *aide-mémoire*, 3 April 1960.
[49] ASIF, 75/12-1, Robson to Trigg, 24 March 1960.
[50] ASIF, 75/12-1, Booth to Trigg, 7 April 1960.
[51] Ibid., p. 7.
[52] Minutes, 5 February 1960.
[53] 2 February 1960.
[54] Minutes, 1 April 1960.
[55] ASIF, 75/3-6, reports on schools (handwritten), 1 April 1960.
[56] Ibid., 4 April 1960.
[57] ASIF, 75/3-4.
[58] NSW: Canberra Grammar, Trinity Grammar, Shore, Cranbrook, Scots College, Barker College, All Saints College, Bathurst.
VIC: Melbourne Grammar, Scotch College, Wesley College, Carey Baptist Grammar, Geelong Grammar.
SA: Pulteney Grammar and one of the Catholic schools.
[59] ASIF, 75/3-6, visits to schools.
[60] Aquinas College (RC), Scotch College.
[61] ASIF, 75/3-5, Circular letters to schools, 12 July 1960.
[62] ASIF, 75/10-1, schools correspondence, 6 December 1960.
[63] ASIF, 75/3-6, further report, 24 August 1960, pp. 4-5. Robson to Carver, 6 December 1960, p. 1.
[64] ASIF, 75/10-1.
[65] ASIF, 75/3-6, attached to 'Note of matters in train', 21 November 1960.
[66] Minutes, 3 November 1960. The schools were Brisbane Church of England Grammar, Ipswich Grammar, Downlands College and Toowoomba Grammar.
[67] Minutes, 11 September 1961.
[68] Minutes, 29 March 1961. Only eight members were in attendance, thus confirming the central importance of the 'inner nucleus' to the Fund's operations.
[69] Minutes, 27 July 1962, 20 November 1962. ASIF, 75/12-1, Trigg to Weir, 1 July 1963. The NSW committee resorted to a Victorian-style dinner for industrialists without much success.
[70] Minutes, 27 February 1962.
[71] ASIF, 75/14-2, chairman's interim report, 20 August 1963.
[72] 'The origins of federal aid to schools: the Commonwealth science laboratories scheme 1963', *Australian Journal of Education*, vol. 21, no. 2, June 1977, pp. 167-78.
[73] ASIF, 75/14-2, Robson to Trigg, 6 December 1963.
[74] ASIF, 75/12-2, 31 October 1960.
[75] ASIF, 75/12-2, 23 November 1960.
[76] *Sydney Morning Herald*, 6 April 1963.
[77] ASIF, 75/3-7, 20 October 1963.
[78] Minutes, 20 December 1963.
[79] ASIF, 75/14-2, Robson to Trigg, 6 December 1963, and Trigg to Booth, 20 December 1963. ASIF, 75/3-7, Robson at the Prince Alfred College science laboratory 'Opening'.
[80] ASIF, 75/14-2, 14 March 1964.
[81] ASIF, 75/14-2, Robson to Trigg, 14 February 1964. Booth to Trigg, 17 February 1964.
[82] ASIF, 75/14-2, Robson to Trigg, 6 December and 30 December 1963. Robson to Brisbane chairman, 16 January 1964.
[83] ASIF, 75/14-2, Robson to headmasters of Christ Church Grammar School, Caulfield Grammar, Newington, and Knox, 30 December, 1963.
[84] Robson to Gorton, 14 January 1964.

[85] ASIF, 75/14-2, Robson to Gorton, 25 December 1963.
[86] ASIF, 75/14-2, Robson to Trigg, 22 January 1964.
[87] Ibid.
[88] ASIF, 75/14-2, Robson to Trigg, 21 February 1964.
[89] ASIF, 75/2, Minutes, 20 March 1968.
[90] The remarkable extent of this linkage is further demonstrated in John Higley, Desley Deacon and Don Smart, *Elites in Australia* (Routledge and Kegan Paul, London, 1979), pp. 85-8.

*This paper was delivered to the Fink Memorial
Seminar at the University of Melbourne in 1983.*

5

MEETING NEEDS: SEVEN YEARS' HARD LABOUR

by K. R. McKINNON

Almost exactly ten years ago I was sitting in a back room office in Port
Moresby, Papua New Guinea, having just moved out of my office as
Director of Education for Papua New Guinea to make way for my eventual successor, a Papua New Guinean. The telephone rang. The call was
from the then Minister of Education, Kim Beazley, inviting me to be
Chairman of a commission to be set up in response to the Karmel Report.
It was to be known as the Schools Commission. Like many others, I had
read and been excited by the vision of the Karmel Report, so I immediately decided that I would very much like to be involved. I took up duty
in Canberra on 24 September 1973, thereby starting seven and a quarter
years of hard labour with the Schools Commission and a decade of
absorbing involvement in Australia's educational problems.

Commission Membership

On 12 December 1972 the newly-elected Prime Minister, Gough Whitlam, established an Interim Committee for the Australian Schools Commission.[1] This committee, chaired by Professor Peter Karmel, reported
in May 1973. It was this report which had brought me to Canberra as
Chairman-designate. As the passage of the Bill for the establishment of
the Commission was delayed until 19 December, an interim Commission
was established, with membership intended for the permanent Commission.[2]

The Minister carried out his announced intention to consult me about
the membership and, of course, consulted his permanent secretary, Ken
Jones. The Commission was to have twelve members, four of whom
would be full time. Apart from myself, the full-time members were Jean
Blackburn, Deputy Chairman of the Interim Committee, Greg Hancock,
also a member of the Interim Committee and formerly from the Department of Education in New South Wales, and David Bennett, who, at that
time, was a stranger to me. In helping select part-time members, I sought
continuity with the membership of the Karmel Committee and a spread
of membership among the states. Members were appointed in their own

right, representative of, but not officially representing, particular organizations.

The Role of the Commission

David Bennett, who had long had a part in the development of Labor's policy of needs, first briefed me on the history of the concept of a Commission and of the hopes people held for it. I recall his telling me that there were many who believed the Commission should be called the 'Needs Commission'. I probably did not fully appreciate the nuances of his briefings, for although I thought I understood the problems the Labor Party had had with devising its policy of support for non-government schools, I regarded the Commission as an historic opportunity to establish at national level an on-going statutory authority responsible for analysis of educational issues and problems, within which funding issues, and especially those affecting non-government schools, should become a relatively minor responsibility. Indeed, Kim Beazley told me that he expected that the Commission would take the funding of education out of the political arena. I saw no reason to doubt that funding problems for non-government schools could be overcome, just as difficult problems had been overcome in establishing a unified education system in Papua New Guinea.

My attitudes were conditioned by my experience in national policy development in Papua New Guinea. I had well-developed views about the possibilities for devolution of responsibility to the school level within the framework of a national vision of education, with values articulated and fostered by the national government. State bureaucracies at that time seemed to me to be myopic and excessively centralized. I had long been an exponent of the power of ideas and felt that the Commission should primarily exist to investigate issues, consult widely and develop and disseminate new thinking to improve schooling. As it happened, most of the Commissioners were vitally interested in educational reform, so the main focus of the Commission quickly became one of concern for the educational dimensions of our terms of reference.

During the passage of its governing Act, the clauses obligating the Commission to report on the needs of schools and allowing it to report on any other matter were not controversial. The Bill, however, contained a clause (S13[4]) enjoining the Commission to have regard to eight particular considerations relating to the provision of primary and secondary education and to increased and equal opportunities for education. The first of these was:

(a) the primary obligation in relation to education, for governments to provide and maintain government school systems that are of the highest standard and are open, without fees or religious tests, to all children.

Part of the compromise avoiding a double dissolution was acceptance of an amendment introducing another sub-clause promoted by non-government parent bodies which asserted:

(b) the prior right of parents to choose whether their children[were] educated at a government school or at a non-government school.

Juxtaposition of these two sub-clauses set up a situation in which government school supporters felt they had justification for their financial claims, because the primary role of the Commission lay in assessing and meeting the needs of government schools. Equally, non-government school supporters claimed that the right to choose would be a hollow right without the means of choice—financial support. They claimed that the sub-clause obligated the Commission not only to meet the needs of existing non-government schools but also to recommend finance for new ones.

Although the sub-clauses had no mandatory financial consequence, their presence established ambiguity about the legislature's intention, leaving the Commission open to charges from both sides of the state-aid dispute of either partisanship or of not carrying out its proper role. The inserted sub-clause was used by Senator John Carrick when the Liberal-Country Party government took office in 1976 as part of the justification for responding to Mrs Slattery's (Australian Parents' Council) representations on behalf of high resource non-government schools. Senator Carrick was already very responsive to these approaches, and the legislative ambiguity bolstered the case.

The initial phase

The Commission came into operation formally on 1 January 1974 and the Interim Commission became the first members of the permanent Commission. They were appointed for varying periods to allow for the possibility of rotation of membership. The authorized expenditure for its first two years was eight hundred million dollars, but it had no staff of its own. A commencing staff of approximately ten people, on loan from the Commonwealth Department of Education, was all that was made available to initiate an array of educational programmes of a complexity, scope and novelty never before attempted at the federal level. At the same time, this small group had to grapple with the multiple problems of establishing a Commission, obtaining space, initiating systems and gaining approval for staffing—all of this in an atmosphere of great expectations among the educational community.

And so commenced seven years of varied and intensive effort. This is not the occasion to chronicle every event in the establishment and life of the Schools Commission during my time as Chairman, but rather to review a few significant issues of continuing importance. I will examine the approach taken by the Commission in four areas: needs, equality, openness and innovation, with particular reference to the values adopted and also with reference to the direct and unexpected effects of implementation processes. I had had some hard lessons in Papua New Guinea about effective and ineffective means of implementing policies, about the ways of energizing and enthusing people to effective action on their own behalf—experience which I was anxious to apply in the Australian setting. Given an active and involved group of commissioners, it was inevitable that the result would be an activist Commission whose activities would create effects just as surely as would any formal actions of government or any financial allocations.

Let me now turn to the four areas mentioned. They are ones which have continuing relevance and they were typical of the policies and programmes developed by the Commission.

Needs

Non-government schools

It is difficult to distinguish the concept of need from that of equality for, as the Karmel Committee pointed out, the standard of schooling children receive should not be dependent upon what their parents are able or willing to contribute directly. The principle of need involves the attempt to assess and quantify what it takes to make the circumstances of schooling equal. For the moment, that definition is sufficient to allow further discussion of how need was given practical expression in funding programmes for both government and non-government schools. The problems and controversies concerning the funding of non-government schools make it logical to start with that aspect even though there have always been similar problems in the recurrent funding of government schools, which I will discuss later.

The needs principle appealed to supporters of the Labor government. It denied any 'as of right' financial support for non-government schools, but acknowledged the reality of their existence, the unlikelihood of their demise, and the financial plight of many of them. But there were two schools of thought about the meaning of the needs concept.

The first meaning, which seems to have been the one that most Labor supporters felt they were supporting, was that any school which had insufficient resources to provide a satisfactory educational programme, after it had raised all of the finance that it could reasonably raise, would be given additional amounts which would vary according to the size of the 'gap'. The assumption was that they would only be given what they *could not* raise, what they *needed*. The second, more encompassing school of thought, comprised those for whom the concept of the rights of young people to an adequate standard of schooling naturally led to a view that governments should ensure that schools had adequate resources. Governments should supply what parents or school authorities did not supply, irrespective of their capacity; students should not suffer from the sins of parents either of omission or commission. A fundamental assumption at the time of the Karmel Committee survey was that schools were pressing themselves as hard as they could, that any shortage of resources was a matter of inability to pay, not unwillingness.

Few of those participating in the early stages of the debate had a clear realization of the disparities between government school resources and those of the poorest non-government schools. Fewer still realized that Catholic schools—which represented approximately 90 per cent of non-government schools—were undergoing a radical change in staffing, with secular teachers replacing religious. Religious orders were suffering the traumas of retirements, large numbers leaving and few recruits. A few religious orders were also directing their efforts away from education into other areas. Ironically, the programmes of the Schools Commission allowed them to do this without serious harm being done to the Church's educational effort. The diminution in the value of voluntary input from religious staff substantially limited the resource-improvement effect of increased grants. Despite rapid increases in the grants, the disparity between the resources of poor non-government schools and those of government schools did not narrow. Supporters of the 'gap' concept of need became dismayed at seemingly limitless needs.

No clauses were ever written into the legislation to ensure that private effort was maintained. Most importantly, the assumption that schools would want to maximize private input was wrong. Catholic schools, for example, had never sought to maximize parental input. They had always attempted to keep school fees low. This was possible in earlier years because parents had tolerated large classes and because there were large numbers of religious staff working for very small allowances. Like other labour-intensive activities, schooling has become relatively more costly, and financial problems have been exacerbated both by diminished voluntary effort and by an influx of immigrant parents accustomed to free or low cost Catholic education. School authorities could only secure the future by having as their concept of need the view that governments should meet all costs above a certain level, to ensure that adherents would not be deterred from sending their children to Catholic schools.

Moreover, Catholic bishops apparently have a canonical responsibility to extend Catholic schooling to adherents without schools, in this case, those in the outer suburbs of cities. The provision of capital and recurrent funds to establish schools in new suburbs was a goal more important even than overcoming the gap in resources in existing schools. Realization of this objective had to result, as it did, in the bill getting larger, not smaller, and with there being no prospect of ever being able to meet needs, except at politically unacceptable cost levels. There has been no hidden intent. On the contrary, it has been my experience that Catholic authorities have been surprised that anybody would be unaware of their long-standing philosophy on the provision of schooling. They have always moved on the pragmatic basis of extending their school system as opportunity arose. They have consistently asked the faithful to share resources, to put the interests of all Catholic children ahead of insistence on their own children's interests. By and large, the faithful have supported those policies, the main new element being the appeal to governments to meet their resource needs.

Governments have had difficulty in grappling with this pragmatic approach. Many of those who supported the needs principle have been opposed to any extension of non-government schools; they have been concerned that, although the needs gap was not being bridged, available resources were being stretched to cover new schools. The important point is that there was no clear political will to define precisely the limits and conditions of funding when the scheme was inaugurated. The responsibility being accepted by government, even in outline, was not defined; the number of students and/or schools to qualify was not limited; no conditions were set for qualification for grants by an individual school. Moreover, in the first stages of programme implementation, adoption of the Karmel proposal to assess and pay grants to systems in aggregated amounts resulted in little knowledge being available about the efforts made by individual schools on their own behalf and no clear understanding of the overall problem.

The problems of the needs concept is further illustrated by a hypothetical example of two non-government schools located in the same homogeneous suburb. One school, without the benefit of voluntary assistance and without a low fee policy, would have been charging substantial fees in 1973 when the needs-based scheme began. Fees in the other school were low, this being deliberate policy. Under a needs-based policy the first school would have received a lower Commonwealth grant than the second. The equity of this situation has always been questionable. This is merely one illustration of the insufficiencies and inequities which are with us today, because no government has wanted the real issues of the needs scheme, particularly the matter of comparability of conditions, to be subjected to public scrutiny and debate.

In many ways, it is inappropriate to call the present recurrent grants scheme a needs scheme. It must be stressed that it does meet real needs for the most part, but it does not do so equitably or fairly. Its benefits are biased; it is overdue for a completely fresh approach, the details of which must await hard government decisions on the size of the non-government sector to be financed, the means of securing equity, and the proper balance between the size of grants and the conditions to attach to them.

I have always accepted the principle of financial support for non-government schools, believing that the passion devoted to this aspect of education policy has been disproportionate. I had been responsible for the development of the Papua New Guinea integrated system, which included a unified teaching service. In that country, in return for full funding, all schools participated in the planning and adhered to national standards of access, openness and accountability. I remember saying to Prime Minister Whitlam early in 1974 that overseas experience would suggest that in the long term there would be no logical resting place for non-government funding short of full funding, finding to my surprise that he agreed and, moreover, that he was unruffled at the prospect. Mr Beazley was the most sympathetic minister the non-government schools could have wished for. He was especially sympathetic to the selfless efforts of teachers working with Aboriginals in remote mission schools, and provided full funding for them; he was never keen to impose restrictive conditions on funding. But conditions of funding were, of course, the point of public controversy. Would there be access, openness and accountability?

Government schools

The Schools Commission had the same problems of definition of need in respect of recurrent grants for government schools. The Karmel Committee found that some states were spending less per student annually than other states and recommended amounts to 'top-up' that expenditure. Again, the underlying rationale was that students needed resources and, if governments did not provide them, the central government should act to ensure that the level of resources was adequate.

The primary objection to this approach was soon voiced. It was claimed that state governments had the revenue capacity to provide adequate resources for each student and if they chose not to do so, despite their apparent constitutional responsibility for education, it was inappropriate for the federal government to impose its will by providing 'tied' grants. It was also claimed that, in providing 'top-up' grants, the federal government was, in effect, rewarding those states which had been most dilatory in providing for their students, since the states spending most got least. The counter-arguments revolved around the responsibility of the national government to provide for all citizens and all children.

Some commentators have suggested that the Schools Commission's role in providing additional resources was at odds with the equalizing role of the Grants Commission. This was not so. The Grants Commission has the role of redressing imbalances in the revenue capacity and the relative costs of providing services in the states. The Schools Commission, on the other hand, has the role of recommending minimum acceptable levels of services for students. Nevertheless, it has to be admitted that while the two roles were distinguishable, they indicated the coexistence of different philosophies of government, the Grants Committee role underlining the sovereignty of the states and their freedom to spend money in accordance with their priorities, and the Schools Commission role ensuring that a certain level of educational services was provided for students. There is a difficult constitutional conundrum for the federal government in considering whether its real role is to respect the constitutional right of states to provide what they deem an appropriate level of educational services, or to take the stance that provision of adequate resources for young people is a national priority.

The needs principle has never been satisfactorily elaborated beyond the initial conceptions. Successive governments have declined to take up the recommendations, made in a series of reports by the Schools Commission, for further development and elucidation of the basic policy. In respect of non-government schools, the Schools Commission suggested several means of overcoming problems. In the early years, it proposed greater definition of maintenance of effort and appropriate clauses in the States Grants Act which would have ensured proper accounting and accountability. In 1975 it also visualized the longer term pattern and suggested that a category of non-government 'supported schools' be established. These would be fully publicly-funded schools operating under equivalent conditions to government schools with regard to openness and public accountability. These suggestions were not taken up. Nor did the publication in 1978 of the Schools Commission's *Some Aspects of School Finance in Australia*, which tried to promote public debate about questions of public policy and about future directions, achieve any real success in moving policy forward.

In the near future the national government will have to take up these issues. At the moment it is locked into a short-term strategy which will reduce the grants to the well-to-do sector over the next two years. The reductions proposed do not address directly the question of whether need as a variable amount is to be added to a base grant for needy schools or whether some high resource schools may eventually be considered ineligible for government grants. The related questions of maximization of private input and the conditions to be attached to grants also remain to be tackled. These problems are also acute at the level of state governments, because public opinion there is even more polarized. The interaction of Labor governments at state and federal level on this issue will be most interesting over the next few years.

Administration of needs

When the Schools Commission was established in January 1974, operational decisions were forced upon it in the first few months in order to get the grants flowing. For the government schools' recurrent grants programme, the money was channelled to states on a quarterly basis, without their being required to produce plans for effective use of the money. There was little flow of information from the states. It wasn't until towards the end of the first year, 1974, that they were willing to provide details of the use of the money and then only the minimum consistent with legal compliance with the States Grants Act.

In later years the Liberal Country Party government tended to make greater demands on the states, requiring them to identify all capital works projects before the release of funds. Yet the attitude of state officials to the Schools Commission was much more favourable in the later years than in the early ones. I can only put the change of attitudes down to early resentment and fear that parochial power bases were being disturbed by outside resources, and a reversal of opinion when it became evident that there were no grounds for concern. Increasingly it was seen that Commission reports provided state officials with the intellectual and administrative justification for implementation of educational advances which many of the officials had been seeking for years.

In the non-government sector the early decision to provide aggregated lump sum grants for Catholic schools was a crucial one. It might have been possible, in the first few months in the life of the Commission, to have demanded individual school accounting, but the lack of staff made this administratively impossible.

With regard to other non-government schools, the decision to involve their representatives in state Planning and Finance Committees responsible for advice on the classification of the schools for grants was also intended to follow through the devolutionary policy of the Karmel Report. The non-Catholic non-government schools opposed the use of an index measuring the resources applied to school programmes as the basis for needs. They had two concepts of need which were used as justification for grants. One was that the mix of students in the school threw up special teaching needs which justified the high expenditure per pupil and which required additional federal government help. The other was that parents were paying excessively high fees and that federal government grants would assist in moderating fee levels.

The Planning and Finance Committees were formed of a mix of non-government people, together with a few disinterested representatives, to ensure that the decisions taken could be publicly justified. The Committees worked rather well. They brought the administration of the recurrent and capital grants programmes closer to the schools. In general the Committees handled requests by schools for special consideration with sensitivity. First-hand information resulting from visits assisted applicant schools to feel that their needs were at least understood. Nevertheless, a large number of the non-Catholic non-government schools continued to believe that grants should flow on a uniform per capita basis and that capital grants should be equally mechanical (and generous), so that in the early years there was continual resistance to this form of administration, and to the questionnaires about individual school resources which were a necessary part of ascertaining the needs of schools. In those early years it was clear that schools were unused to data-based analyses, and tended to rely more on political representation.

By 1977-78 there was a reversion by the Liberal Country Party government to behind-closed-doors discussion of the needs of schools between the Minister and the principal parties. Catholics were not anxious to be separated from other non-government schools lest it be thought that they were getting better treatment. They were officially content with a system in which all schools received a grant and their schools received considerably more. In the period 1977 to 1981 more of the real decisions about the funding of non-government schools were taken by the Minister and the Cabinet itself, with input from the Secretary of the Department of Education, rather than adopting in detail the advice of the Schools Commission. But the Commission was used to legitimize the pattern of increases decided by the Government, since it was the Commission which had documented the gaps in resources. Thus the Commission was placed in an increasingly difficult position from which it has not yet extricated itself and possibly never will. The Government was justifying increased grants by reference to the Schools Commission, but using advice selectively and not implementing the complete proposals which might have made the emerging pattern of grants acceptable to the whole community.

This tendency was particularly evident in relation to the capital programme, where the Commission was instructed to provide funds for new places for growth of non-government schools, although it had indicated the problems inherent in financing whatever growth of new schools was decided upon by school authorities. In the period of increased overall growth in enrolments, the policy of increasing non-government enrolments was not as contentious as it is in the current period of contracting enrolments.

The history of the needs principle is a lesson in problems which arise when an advisory body is set up to advise on what is essentially a political problem. Had the Commission been given the power to act independently the problem might have been capable of resolution, but the sums of money involved alone made that possibility unrealistic. In consequence, however rational the solutions proposed by the 'expert' body, the protagonists are sufficiently powerful, and the issues involved sufficiently important, for the real struggle to be a political one. The mismatch which results in a Commission being used or blamed when convenient and ignored when its advice is inconvenient is perhaps unavoidable. The unrealistic expectations set up when the Schools Commission was created have been diminished by the passage of years.

Equality

The Karmel Committee put equality as one of its key perspectives and the preceding discussion has, of course, been implicitly referring to it. In so far as the needs principle is concerned, the conception used was equality of resources as between schools. That particular conception of equality represents a notion of equity in access to resources and a fairly pragmatic approach to the allocation of general resources.

A second sense of equality was used in the Karmel Report and throughout subsequent Schools Commission reports to justify the provision of resources for the handicapped and slow learners. This was a conception which suggested that people who start unequally in terms of personal resources or in terms of the resources needed to provide the equivalent of those provided to other students, should have the extra resources needed. Equality in this sense means parity of service. This principle is increasingly acknowledged in discussions relating to the handicapped. If physically handicapped people have the 'right' to participate fully in society, they can only exercise that right if there is adjustment of the physical plant of schools and if there are people who can lift, carry and organize so as to provide the handicapped with the same access to facilities that non-handicapped people have.

A less obvious but equivalent notion of equality requires that slow learners be given additional teaching, teaching aides or other assistance sufficient to allow them the opportunity to participate in society. There is nothing new about this approach to equality. Special schools have had resources allocated to meet these needs for decades. Isolated communities are provided with schools even though the cost is much higher per student than in more populous centres. As a nation we have interpreted

equality as meaning parity of service of this kind, stopping short of extension of the principle to profoundly handicapped people, but nevertheless
supporting different levels of expenditure in the name of equality of service.

The formulation of equality in the Karmel Report took the notion a
step further, in terms of the needs of students from deprived
environments—basically a socio-economic criterion. In effect it said that
the richness of experience available to students of more affluent environments justified some weighting of resources to others to ensure that their
in-school experience provided some equivalence. This line of argument
resulted in the Disadvantaged Schools Program° which, with some justification, has been seen as being modelled on the priority area programmes in the United Kingdom, but which, I think, did not argue from
a model of compensation for deprivation so much as from the standpoint
of provision of opportunity to realize full potential.

The Schools Commission took up the theme of equality and sought to
clarify its implications. It did this in two ways, one with special application to individuals, the other with special reference to groups. In relation
to the central intellectual purposes of schooling it sought a more equal
basic achievement, a plateau of competence. It articulated what is an
increasingly widely accepted view, that the penalties of non-
achievement are growing, and that there is need for every student to have
acquired certain minimum skills for successful participation in adult life.
It argued that the basic plateau of competence which all students should
achieve continues to rise, and that schools should have an overwhelming
commitment to the task of ensuring that all students achieve at least minimum competence in basic skills. Because of the varying needs of individual students, the overall resources of schools will need to be increased
sufficiently to allow achievement in these basic competencies.

The Commission also argued for that much misunderstood notion of
equality, 'equality of outcomes'. Critics of the notion of equality of outcomes erected a straw man and then demolished it, arguing both that
it was absurd to expect every individual to achieve equally with every
other individual and that equality of outcomes meant a levelling down
and hence promotion of mediocrity. Neither view could have been read
into Commission reports. The sheer hypocrisy and dishonesty of the arguments opposed to the concept of equality of outcomes amazed me. One
was forced to the conclusion that the commentators had either not read
what the Commission had said or were deliberately distorting it.

What the Commission said remains eminently justifiable, that is, that
it is reasonable to expect that identifiable sub-groups in the total com-

°This spelling has been retained in titles.

munity should ideally be equally represented in the various strata of status, wealth and influence of that community. If, as a group, Aborigines are wholly missing from the ranks of tertiary education professionals and from positions of power and influence, there is a case to answer that the society should be providing better educational opportunities for them. The Commission viewed insufficient representation of migrants, girls and similar groups as prima facie evidence that either the educational programme offered them was inappropriate or that insufficient resources had been devoted to their needs. It further argued that the case for additional assistance would remain strong until such time as there was equality of outcomes in the overall community. The Commission was, of course, alive to the structured inequalities in our wider society and to the impossibility of overcoming them by educational action alone, but took the view that the power of education in these circumstances had never been probed, let alone established.

The Commission's emphasis on equality was the basis for the study of the special needs of several groups. One report resulting from this effort was *Girls, school and society* in 1975, which remains the main study of the education of girls in Australia, although it is now out of date because of rapidly changing circumstances. Access and participation are now more equal, but other fundamental problems in the education of girls remain to be solved.

The notion of equality pursued by the Schools Commission took a fairly wide view of the factors which would promote equality and argued for more democratic participation as a factor. It argued this under such headings as devolution, openness and community involvement, matters which I will explore in more detail later in this paper.

The Commission also argued for more attention to school processes in *Schooling for 15 and 16 year olds* (1980). That report stressed the importance of valuing the whole age group and the need for organizational changes which would bring about fuller opportunities for all students; it argued for attention to educational outcomes which would provide all students with greater power over their own individual circumstances and hence greater opportunities for participation and success in society.

Here again there was explicit recognition of the structured inequalities in the society at large. The Commission did not argue that schooling could overcome those structured inequalities even if the resources of schools were improved. It did argue, however, that as schooling is compulsory and as all young people attend until age 15, schools should certainly be organized and provided with resources to foster equality.

In retrospect, the Commission was not as persistent as it ought to have been in some aspects of the fight for greater equality. In an early report it pointed out the disparity in expenditure between those who leave early and those who go on to tertiary education. It argued for greater expenditure on primary education, pointing out that some of the 'dropping-out' might be avoided if early school failure could be minimized.

Administration of programmes promoting equality

As one would expect from the name, the Disadvantaged Schools Program was directed primarily at redressing the disadvantage which occurs as a consequence of poverty. It was not a programme designed to overcome insufficient family resources, provide family allowances, or amounts to schools in respect of individual students, as states do with book allowances and other similar provisions. The concept of disadvantage was that of a school becoming disadvantaged by a concentration of students from low socio-economic areas, where the parents were unable to provide those extras which add richness to the learning environment. The concept also took account of those students who did not have essential extra-curricular experiences. Thus the objective was to provide a relatively small amount of additional resources, approximately 3 per cent of annual average per student expenditure, to about 10 per cent of all schools declared to be disadvantaged.

The principle of declaration of such schools was adopted to prevent states from dissipating the money widely over all schools. An index of disadvantage was derived from a complex of identifying characteristics clustered around socio-economic criteria. From the beginning there was considerable freedom at the state level to decide which schools were to be included. States were supplied with the data which the Karmel Committee had used in deciding on the scope of the programme, but were free to make adjustments to lists of schools in the light of local knowledge. At the beginning there was little understanding of the programme and, as expected, there was pressure to extend the coverage to more schools. The Commission resisted this trend in order to ensure that the limited funds would be sufficiently concentrated to make an impact.

The Disadvantaged Schools Program was an innovation in Australia. States and schools did not know what to expect. Thus it was possible in the first few months of 1974 to have guidelines for representative state committees and the distribution of the available cash accepted without demur. These guidelines sought the involvement of parents and representatives of teachers' organizations. In Victoria a system of area committees was set up and these proved excellent peer groups for decisions on the distribution of funds to individual schools.

The early months of 1974 were a productive and exciting time in disadvantaged schools. Many teachers who had hitherto been working with great idealism but few resources, felt their concerns were appreciated and, in addition, they would obtain the resources to implement their ideas. A log-jam of frustration was swept away in a flood of energy and enthusiasm, making many of the disadvantaged schools pace-setters in worthwhile educational reform. It must be stressed that the money was marginal, although it was certainly a substantial sum in schools long deprived of ready resources. Few schools received more in one year than the equivalent of the salary of one more staff member, but access to resources whose use they could command made a marked difference to the impact of those resources.

Among the states there were marked differences in administration. In Victoria, effort was made to implement the programme in accordance with the Commission's views. In New South Wales, under a resistant director-general, it took several years for real progress to be made.

Initially there was a reluctance to classify schools as disadvantaged but, when the programme had been in operation for a couple of years, it was considered an advantage to be declared disadvantaged. In the beginning there was a widespread feeling that the name would become a stigma and some states changed the name (e.g., Victoria—Supplementary Grants Program) indicating an unwillingness on the part of the state administrators to face up to the reality of students from particular circumstances having less than equal opportunities in education.

There is no doubt that the impact of the Commission's multi-programme approach, combining the Disadvantaged Schools Program with the Special Education Program, the Teacher Development Program and eventually the Migrant and Multicultural Education Program and other programmes, led to a closer examination of the composition of student bodies and in consequence greater attempts to meet their needs. The cynical would say that this was simply opportunism by some schools. On the whole, the evidence is, I think, that schools became more aware of student needs, more anxious to see schooling as requiring renewal and change if it was to meet the needs of young people.

Even though the grant for each school was relatively small, there were marked disparities between the schools included in the Disadvantaged Schools Program and those which failed to qualify, causing heart-burning at the local level. Theoretically, it should have been possible for state authorities to have adjusted their resources to have gradations minimizing the differences, but this did not prove possible. State education systems had for so long been locked into provision of staff in preference to all other resources, that there were few other redistributable resources within systems. Consequently, when a disadvantaged school was able to equip itself with, say, musical instruments and develop a good musical programme, neighbouring schools not declared disadvantaged felt very envious.

Another problem with the Disadvantaged Schools Program, which will continue to be a problem in the future for those programmes which operate on the basis of capturing the energy and creative abilities of idealists, was the growth of 'submissionitis'. Although not required by the Commission, state groups allocating funds tended to require long detailed submissions before granting even tiny amounts of money to individual schools. The unproductive work pressure this caused in schools was considerable, especially as many of the schools had little experience of the 'grantsmanship' which would ensure professional-type submissions. Where committees were inexperienced and uncertain they tended to demand more detailed submissions, to the consternation of schools. Much diversion of energy was expended which ought more properly to have been applied to the educational programme itself.

The Commission was concerned to be seen to be evaluating programmes. It started to do so as early as the end of 1975, and eventually produced several evaluations, none of which was of much use. The fact that evaluations had been made may have been helpful in convincing federal parliamentarians that the Commission was a responsible body, making good use of the funds and that these should be kept flowing. I doubt it for, as David Cohen has pointed out in the *Harvard Educational Review*, social action programmes like the Disadvantaged Schools Program, indeed the whole array of Schools Commission programmes, rest more on political will than on any expert data. He argues that they will neither start nor stop on anything but political action, with the role of professional experts at best that of mediation. Nevertheless, from the Commission perspective, evaluation was a means of making those involved with a programme conscious of its outcomes.

Unlike American experiments, the Australian Disadvantaged Schools Program was consciously set on the basis that groups could best operate on a loose rein rather than within cast-iron regulations, as none of us felt that we knew beyond doubt what initiatives in particular schools would bring about improvement. We suspected that it might be necessary for a majority of the activities to focus on making students feel good about themselves. It might also be necessary to provide them with enriching experiences outside the classroom before there could be any visible outcome from intensive cognitive projects.

Devolution and Involvement

In the Karmel Report devolution and community involvement were key values. The Commission, in its first report, broadened the general thrust of this cluster of values within the framework of openness of relationships.

Apart from feeling that the centralization of education systems had been overdone and had become fossilized, the Karmel Committee apparently thought that it was desirable for there to be less cleavage between schools and the communities they were set up to serve. There was need for schools to become less isolated, for the basis of educational policy-making to be broadened to include direct community participation. The Committee said that it was neither able nor willing to be prescriptive about the forms which school/community relationships should take, but experimentation should be fostered so as to forge links between school, family, peer group and the society at large.

In broadening the focus, the Commission emphasized not only the way in which society had shaped schools as institutions separate from the life and work of the community, with detrimental effects for the institution and the community, but also the evolution of a pluralist society in Australia, one which, moreover, is undergoing continuous change as a result of external pressures and its own composition. The Commission said that institutions 'if they are not to become museums require continuous reappraisal as social circumstances change and as new possibilities open up'. The Commission questioned the institutional traditions of length of lesson period and classroom organization, raised the possibility and desirability of diversification of curricula and discussed the need for a more open view of the possibilities and functions of schools, all of which would lead to acceptance of the possibility of revised organizational arrangements and functions of institutions.

The Commission was constantly groping for ways to foster better human relationships in education and of matching more adequately the objectives of schools and the life of the community. It saw the school as inescapably part of the local community; by lessening the barriers between school and community, it would be enhancing the educational effectiveness of the formal learning programme. This is not simply a question of the right of the community to be involved in the governance of schooling, which is a sufficient argument in itself for increased devolution. There was a strong argument for devolution based on the need to open up large, unresponsive, overly-bureaucratic education departments.

But there was a further educational rationale. Historians have often pointed to the tradition of Australians relying on government initiatives to solve community problems. This pattern of reliance on government and government regulation had been taken to extremes in education, with the consequence that students throughout their school life are conditioned to accept distant, all pervasive, arbitrary authority. The greater the degree of devolution, the greater the likelihood, first, of there being real adjustment of the school to the needs of students, and secondly, of students learning how to be self-directing.

I had a very special interest in devolution. My experience with decolonization in Papua New Guinea had convinced me of the energizing, empowering effects of people learning to take decisions on their own account, suffering from bad ones, but being liberated intellectually and spiritually through having that power. Australian education systems in the early 1970s were based more on a colonial model than on the needs of a free society in the twentieth century. The trained incompetence of generations of parents had to be overcome as part of the process of developing schools as models of at least partially self-governing communities, communities in which human relationships were sustaining and mutually respectful.

Schools are often not models of the relationships which ought to characterize society. They have too often exhibited relationships in which a substantial proportion of each age group has not found in the school experience enough or even anything that is sustaining and encouraging. It may even be the case that many young people, and particularly girls, have emerged from schools in past generations less confident of their abilities, less ready to participate in adult life than if they had not gone to school at all. The Commission's attitude to relationships, devolution and structures was predicated on the need for schools to provide positively helpful experiences for all students.

In articulating these values the Commission sought to explore the nature of the community with which the school was involved, the types of involvement, the roles of participants, the expansion of the curriculum and organizational settings into the community, and the increase in educational opportunities through such things as recurrent education. On the other hand, it could not solve all of the problems arising from endorsement of these values. For example, an unresolved problem is the proper balance of authority between the centre and the periphery of any system. In the Westminster system of government the state minister is responsible for the policies and the implementation of the government's educational programme and both the proper degree of devolution and the means of achieving that goal are not easily settled. Apart from legal and organizational problems, achievement of the right balance between local initiatives and detached concern for the needs of the society as a whole remains a continuing difficulty.

In some states there are people who argue that each school community should have full control of its own destiny and be wholly responsible for its educational programme. They argue that a fully self-governing school community provides the best setting for students to acquire the skills which give them power over their environment. Others point to the responsibility of governments to ensure not only equality of provisions but the implementation of key values in the curricula and organization of schools. They insist upon all schools providing for all students the best possible exposure to the common culture, the knowledge, skills and ideas which comprise the human heritage. Exponents of this view hold that individual students cannot be left to the shortsightedness or prejudices of particular communities: part of being a citizen is the right of access to the common culture.

If there is to be involvement of the community in the governance of schools, care must be taken to ensure that the rights of minorities do not suffer. This is no easy matter as we shall see in Victoria as the policy of devolution of power to school councils is further implemented. Again, it is unlikely that there will be a formula which works in all circumstances.

At the school level there will be a tendency for the professional staff to resent the involvement of school councils in the development of school policy, especially if their involvement intrudes into detailed school programming and organizational practices. No teacher would want to be told by the school council how to teach reading; but the school council might well be involved in the selection of reading material to ensure, for example, that it is non-sexist.

We have been used to notions of bureaucratic and ministerial power in education. The movement that the Schools Commission has fostered is towards shared power based on mutual respect. The path to acceptance has not been and will not be easy. In Victoria the current strong negative reaction of school principals to the concept of shared responsibility between staff and school council in matters concerning school policy shows how sensitive the power issue is. The problem of establishing mutual trust and respect is a continuing one.

Implementation of openness

As indicated earlier, probably the most effective first steps towards devolution and community involvement were achieved through the Disadvantaged Schools Program in the early stages of its implementation. The insistence of the Commission led to the inclusion of parents on the various committees dispersing grants. The value of the information gained from such participation quickly became apparent. More parents became skilled in the hitherto forbidding arts of making submissions and obtaining grants. From the outset, submissions for grants from schools had to have the involvement of the whole school community.

Similarly, in the programme which started out as the Teacher Development Program and eventually became the Professional Development Program, members of the community were regarded by the Commission as participants in the process of approval of courses and distribution of grants. More importantly, they were regarded as legitimate participants.

Consequently, as initiatives developed to allow visits by people from one state to another to observe particular innovative processes, parents were able to apply and secure places in the programme. Since the parent network, largely informal at first, but increasingly sophisticated, was better at internal communication than most other bodies, there was a successful sharing of information about participation across Australia, and a growing desire to participate.

State departments were not as willing to change their practices quickly. While the parent bodies had an ongoing tradition of delegations to state ministers and a reasonable success rate in their representations, there was no tradition of community participation on departmental committees which made and implemented policies. It says something for the effectiveness of the Commission's initiatives, that by the end of my period as Chairman of the Schools Commission, community participation was much more a routine occurrence. In one state, events had moved so fast that by 1980 it was possible for community organizations to insist that policy changes and senior departmental appointments be not made without the active involvement of representatives of the community.

Even so, one of my regrets about the Schools Commission experience is that I did not push sooner for greater community involvement. I am not sure whether I underestimated the need or overestimated the progress that had already been made. Even at the end of my term, the number of community activists was still fairly small. Since there is always turnover as participants drop out when their children complete their education, with new ones having a hard task to acquire the organizational know-how, this part of the Commission's activities would have justified much more effort. Joan Kirner, as a member of the Commission, was an unflagging advocate of parent participation. She was politely persistent at all times and at every level of activity. I think she would agree, however, that we did not succeed in overcoming the traditional view of the role of parents. This trained incompetence, part of a group of attitudes that Galbraith so aptly calls 'convenient social virtues' led to parents and other members of the community thinking of themselves as 'only parents' or 'only community members'.

One special effort to find a better way of developing the insights and capacities of the community came near the end of my period. The Commission's publication, *Schooling for 15 and 16 year olds*, was intended not only to examine the problems and needs of students in this age group, while offering a vision of a better future, but also to encourage each school to look at what it might do. The report was intentionally written as a non-prescriptive document, in the hope that each community would be able to apply its arguments and evolve new approaches in the local setting. My departure from the Commission coincided with the release of that report, so it wasn't possible to see whether the proposed massive follow-up, requiring effort equal to that used in producing the report, would have been helpful. I am not suggesting that a single initiative would have overcome generations of non-involvement, but it might have built up a worthwhile basic community involvement in the educational aspects of schooling, which could have been further developed with time.

One of the Commission's most successful initiatives to foster open attitudes came through the Innovations Program, which incidentally was another way of involving the community in its own schools. Since innovation was a major concern of the Commission I now turn to a discussion of the programme with that name.

Innovation

Under the deceptively simple title of Fostering Change, the Karmel Committee proposed that there be a six million dollar fund over two years to foster both school-level and system-level innovations in schools. The Innovations Program was based, at least to some extent, on the research and development model characteristic of educational research in the late 1960s and early 1970s. From the outset the programme generated a level of excitement in the educational community well beyond that which might have been expected from such small funding. In May 1974 the Commission advertised nationally, inviting applications from individuals and schools (but not confined to teachers) with ideas for educationally innovatory projects. It was as if a dam had burst. We were deluged with applications to such an extent that we had major processing problems.

Both by preference and in order to cope with this situation, we devolved the appraisal of projects through a system of counsellors who were paid on a sessional basis to work with applicants and intending applicants. Their brief was to help applicants think through the educational aspects of their proposals. We insisted upon the helping, sustaining character of the counsellors' work, as did the half-time convenors we engaged in each state to schedule and organize counsellors.

A state-level appraisal process developed, whereby counsellors reported to a small group of other counsellors; projects were appraised in their own right and against each other. State committees then made recommendations to a National Innovations Committee comprising the state convenors and some others who, in turn, recommended a final list to the Commission.

In retrospect, we were remarkably successful in enlisting some of the most thoughtful, energetic and visionary people in education in Australia as convenors and counsellors for this programme. The time they gave to it was well beyond anything we paid for; they encouraged, cajoled and generally ensured that innovatory teachers got a good hearing for their ideas and, if the projects were worthwhile, some assistance to undertake them.

The research and development model was very hard to resist. It suggests that, as in manufacturing, a good idea once tested can be replicated a thousand times with equal effect. We were constantly asked whether the programme had generated any worthwhile techniques which could be implemented in other schools. But schooling is not like manufacturing: schools have students and staffs with different characteristics; they have different histories. It is frequently necessary to seek a unique approach to problems. Gradually the Commission came to favour a more generalized model of organizational renewal.

The term 'innovation' is also a problem. Often there were doubts about whether particular grants were, in fact, given for innovations in the strict sense, that is, for entirely new educational ideas. Of course, a majority were not. The Commission evolved its own working definition of an innovation as being a project which was innovatory for *that* school in *that* location at *that* time. Schools in different places would be at different stages of development. In essence the test was that the proposed project involved a novel approach, addressing a problem defined as important by that school, with a solution proposed by that school. The emphasis was on self-regarding, critically aware school communities developing responses to problems they had identified as important in the education of their children.

It is important to stress that the self-regarding criterion did not confine participation to professionals. Submissions for grants had to have the support of the school, but grants were available to the people in the community as well as to professionals. The constant rhetoric of the programme was of the need to involve all members of the school community.

The other feature of the programme which made it novel for Australia was that it was a source of funds quite outside the regular patterns of state resources. For the first time, teachers could gain support for their own educational ideas from outside traditional lines of authority and patronage. Two lessons are inherent in this process. One is that individuals working at the local level can do wonders with a few additional dollars protected from diversion to routine expenditure. The second is that funding from a national body for a local idea gives that proposal legitimacy sufficient to have the idea tried and properly appraised. The importance of the latter cannot be overstated. Australian educational penury and the long tradition of centralization had resulted over the years in the stillbirth of myriad good ideas. Support gave recognition and encouragement to those with ideas and the energy to undertake them.

As in any such programme, some projects were funded that the Commission wished had not been supported. But the majority were first class proposals worthy of greater support than we were able to give. The few failures simply emphasize that even with the Innovations Program there were too few growing points in Australian education systems, given the rapidity of social and economic change.

The practice of making grants direct to individuals and schools posed threats to the authority of one or two of the state directors-general. The Commission worked out a process of having a senior officer of the department on the state consultative committee. It also made it clear that it would consult with states and that there was no question of a project going ahead if the state did not sanction it. The Commission insisted, however, that if the state rejected a project it should be clear, if the project was otherwise acceptable, that it was the state that was unwilling to sanction it. In Western Australia, under successive directors-general, the state was very wary about allowing several projects to proceed. In the end, the desire not to be seen as educational reactionaries led to the eventual resolution of most of these problems, sometimes with modifications acceptable to all.

So far I have not said anything about the other element of the Innovations Program, that is, the National and Systems Projects. The Commission reserved some funds to encourage systems to undertake projects which could only be implemented above the school level. Some of these were the Schools Travel and Exchange Scheme; the feasibility of a national cataloguing service for school libraries; an item bank project; a schools' information service; pilot projects in multicultural education, and so on. A major advantage of these was that they brought together, in open educative discussion, some of the top administrators in the state. The relatively unfamiliar heady experience of having resources to apply to worthwhile educational projects led to spirited and fruitful interchanges as well as worthwhile projects.

Implementation of the Innovations Program

I have already commented on the flood of applications for the Innovations Program and the difficulty of setting up systems which would cope with the need for accountability of projects. Issues such as disposal of equipment, auditing and cash flow for projects constantly took up a disproportionate amount of time, causing delays and some frustration among applicants, who for the most part, were people oriented to the classroom and impatient of red tape.

As the pressure of applications increased, the average size of grants tended to decrease. Grants which sustained the salary and other costs of an additional person in a school for any length of time were rare, consequently the grants for the most part paid for additional materials, equipment, excursions and part-time assistance. There was constant debate about whether it was better to have a few good big projects or many more small projects. There was equally constant pressure to spread the funds to ensure that at least some of the projects that consultants had worked on were funded and to respond even in a small way to the eagerness of those at the school level.

From the beginning the Commission was anxious that the programme be not open to attack for waste. We might have been over-careful, but even in retrospect I do not think so. At the time there were far too many conservatives anxious to snipe at any challenge to orthodoxy. One amusing way in which this issue surfaced was via the titles of projects. The processing of a thousand projects demands some economy in titles. I remember one from Tasmania which was called 'Trout fly tying'. When the list was published this one drew derisory flak. It turned out to be a marvellous little project, costing $300, for teaching handicapped children the manual dexterity associated with trout flies and giving them valuable educational outdoor experiences at the same time. Similarly, anything to do with sex education aroused great interest.

I am not intending to imply that all of the problems were with the titling of projects. Many challenges to innovatory projects were direct challenges to the right of a group or groups to introduce new ideas into schools. The most persistent opposition I can recall was directed at projects associated with the equalization of opportunities for girls—non-sexist education as it has come to be called.

The most difficult project I can remember was one associated with Yipirinya in Alice Springs—a continuing saga, so I'm told. The Aboriginals of the area sought assistance to establish an alternative school which would have provided them with what they saw as an appropriate educational programme, one which would respect and sustain tribal culture, while at the same time giving skills associated with modern living in a predominantly English-speaking community. Constant political pressure was applied within the Northern Territory to block operation of the school, yet the students concerned could not have been any worse off than they had been under the existing schooling provisions. Experience in New Guinea suggested they would probably be far better off with a curriculum designed to meet their particular needs.

As might be expected from the foregoing comments, the Commission was particularly anxious about evaluation of projects. The common conception of an evaluation is to see if money has been spent to advantage. The Commission realized that it was relatively easy to establish that point and inaugurated accountancy and audit requirements adequate to that purpose. If the purpose of the projects was primarily educational, however, one would expect there to be some changed practice in schools.

F

For that outcome to be achieved, people involved in the project had to go on to adopt new practices. A system was devised in which grantees were provided with advice and assistance from a team of people with evaluation skills and were asked to develop evaluations of the projects in association with those consultants. The absence of a sense of being judged or given marks allowed evaluations to be honest. Many were willing to admit that the project was not a success, or was only a partial success. Even the successful majority were encouraged to be scrupulously honest about the balance of pluses and minuses. For those projects which received relatively large grants of money, the Commission conducted 'augmented evaluations' which involved outside evaluation assistance. Even here the intent was to keep the focus of the evaluation firmly on the way in which the Innovations Project had contributed and could contribute to better educational practice.

In addition to counselling and evaluation, there was strong emphasis on communication and dissemination of projects. Grantees were asked to write up their project and their own view of its outcome and make these available to others. Directories of projects were developed. A national information retrieval centre, containing descriptions of all projects, was funded in Adelaide. Discussions and conferences with grantees and potential applicants were held in all capital cities.

The educational ideas of the Commission were demonstrated most clearly in the Disadvantaged Schools Program, the Teacher Development Program and, in particular, the Innovations Program. Those programmes successfully identified the Commission as forward-looking and supportive of thoughtful, constructive educational practice. The care with which the array of programmes was implemented and the difficulties grantees had in getting funds made it clear that it was not thought that educational problems are solved simply by the provision of money. In short, the Programs' emphasis on educational practice was an indispensable element in promoting more thoughtful, national understanding of educational problems.

In my view, the most important benefit of the Innovations Program, apart from the supportive atmosphere it generated for new practice, was the developmental effect it had on participants, whether grantees or those associated in a supporting role as counsellors, evaluators and administrators. Even unsuccessful applicants received sympathetic counselling. In the course of projects, grantees were involved in a continuous process of personal development in a supportive and helpful atmosphere which enabled most of them to gain new professional insights.

Regrettably, in the atmosphere of conservatism which has pervaded the last few years, the Innovations Program has been virtually abolished. It was never sufficiently well funded to bring about national reform of school practice, but it did re-establish the respectability of innovation and renewed understanding of the unique role of classroom teachers. The overall effect was certainly greater than the sum of the projects.

Consultation

The Commission's mode of operation was in itself a force for development. For instance, the Commission developed a practice of having every second meeting in a different state and using extra days to visit schools and meet with interest groups. Initially the consultative techniques of the Commission developed in an *ad hoc* way. We invited written submissions, some of which merited further discussion. Soon a regular process developed whereby not only officials but interest groups, particularly non-government authorities, parent groups, teachers' unions and others associated with education had regular access to the Commission.

In addition, the Commission consulted regularly with directors-general of education and other semi-official people such as directors of Catholic education and independent school representatives. The annual, two-day meetings with directors-general were regarded by some as the most interesting of their annual meetings because there was discussion of educational ideas in an atmosphere free from the usual administrative demands. The practice of meeting in this way grew to be an important part of the Commission's annual cycle of activities, indispensable for achieving better understanding. There were also formal visits to each state department to discuss the Commission's programmes with senior state officials.

The Commission was fortunate in securing people of high idealism to work for it. They were very much involved in developing policy as well as implementing programmes. Morale was high and the working atmosphere happy and productive.

Consensus

One of the more interesting features of the early years of the Commission was its ability to achieve consensus among members representing the full diversity of ideas in Australian education. From time to time, the search for consensus and its achievement have been criticized by people who apparently believe that clashes of ideologies are best resolved by those gaining power riding rough-shod over the views of the minority. In education, it seemed to me, children would be the losers by that approach. The time needed to reach consensus seemed to some an inefficient way to conduct meetings but, in my view, the search for consensus and its consistent achievement for about five years was a major factor in establishing the Commission as a potent national educational body. The problem with the Schools Commission ultimately came to be one of interaction with the political process, not one of working through the problems within the Commission, since the Commission was blamed or embraced by the Fraser government according to political advantage, straining beyond acceptable levels the goodwill of Commission members.

Conclusion

How do I sum up the Commission and its work from 1974 to 1981? As a principal player on this part of the national stage I had a biased as well as a privileged perspective, so I will not try to make a definitive or extensive analysis. I feel that over the seven years I was in office the Commission was effective. First, it established a national point of view about education; second, it established the primacy of values in determining educational action; third, it evolved strategies for financial provisions which would have substantial educational effect; fourth, it developed means of implementing programmes which broke new ground and which achieved minimal slippage between programme intention and implementation; and fifth, it developed means by which the multiple currents of thinking in Australian education could be harnessed into a system of interacting advice which gave participants the feeling that the national government would listen and respond to their points of view.

The work of the Commission was respected partly because establishment of a Commission was the right move at the right time, partly because the addition of substantial amounts of money to an historically impoverished education system gave it a new lease of life, and partly because the Commission had intellectual vigour which made it warmly received by the educational community. It was fortunate to have among its members some of the best people in Australian education including, especially, the full-time members Jean Blackburn, David Bennett and Greg Hancock.

Even though it was seven years' hard labour only the first two years of it coincided with a Labor government. Kim Beazley, the idealist, was succeeded as Minister in November 1975 by Senator Carrick, an able, persuasive, patient minister determined to implement Liberal party policies. He, in turn, was succeeded by Wal Fife, who arranged that I would go as I had come. A telephone call a few days before my term ended summoned me to his office to announce that, contrary to his firm assurance before the federal election which had just been concluded, I would be given a final ticket of leave.

Unlike most sentences of seven years' hard labour, I had enjoyed the term. I was ready to move on, but grateful for the intensive education, the camaraderie and the exhilaration; grateful too that the Commission had been able to make a real contribution to Australian education.

NOTES

[1] Membership of the Interim Committee:
    Peter Karmel, *Chairman*
    Jean Blackburn, *Deputy Chairman*
    Greg Hancock
    Edward T. Jackson
    A. W. Jones
    F. M. Martin
    Peter Tannock
    M. E. Thomas
    Alice Whitley
    Wilfred A. White
        J. J. Wilson, *Secretary*
[2] Membership of the Interim Commission:
Full-time
    Ken McKinnon, *Chairman*
    David Bennett
    Jean Blackburn
    Greg Hancock
Part-time
    Ray Costello, *Government teacher unions*
    A. W. Jones, *Director-General*, South Australia
    Joan Kirner, *state school parents*
    Tony McNamara, *non-government school parents*
    F. M. Martin, *Director of Catholic education*, Victoria
    Peter Moyes, *Headmaster of Christ Church Grammar*, Western Australia
    Peter Tannock, University of Western Australia
    Desmond Wood, *Headmaster of special school*, Tasmania
        John Scutt, *Secretary*

6

THE ORIGINS AND FORMATION OF TEACHERS' UNIONS IN NINETEENTH CENTURY AUSTRALIA

by ANDREW SPAULL

Prologue

In 1907, as John Joseph Low waited to speak before the Tasmanian Teachers' Union—which had just forced an official inquiry into the administration of the education department while defending the right of public comment by public service unions—he possibly reflected on the long struggle to bring a teachers' union to the island state. He would have recalled how his father, John James Low, a teacher imported to the colony in 1840 imbued with the principles of a teachers' association from the Teachers' Quarterly Association of London had organized a series of meetings and in 1861 an informal organization to protest against reductions in teachers' salaries. For his efforts he was dismissed from teaching, but returned twelve years later, handing on the principles of teacher organization to his son, who founded the first teachers' association in Tasmania at Latrobe in 1882. John Joseph Low spent the next twenty-five years developing a teachers' union in northern Tasmania. His efforts culminated in the formation of the State School Teachers Association of Tasmania (1902) and the Tasmanian Teachers Union (1905).[1] It was to this union that John Joseph Low moved forward to deliver his presidential report.

Tasmania was the last colony/state to establish a central union of teachers; a union which, like those in the other states, has a direct, continuous link with teachers' unions of today. In many respects the story of the Lows' struggle for teachers' unions in Tasmania is representative of the Australian nineteenth century experience in state education. It covers the dramatic contours of labour history: leadership by dedicated individuals; organizational triumphs and many more failures; teachers' ambivalence towards unionism; sectional antagonism within organizations; official repression to curb teachers' collectivity, and resistance by a few teachers in the face of such threats. All were powerful ingredients which cast light and shade on the uneven paths leading towards the formation of modern teachers' unions. Australia's teachers' unions have attracted the attention of historians and others for many years, but most studies have focused on an individual state or union, without more than a sideways glance elsewhere.[2] This essay is an attempt to explain the origins and emergence of teachers' unions in Australia, which are now on the eve of their centenaries.

A Framework for Comparative Analysis

Few studies of the historical growth of teachers' unions adopted a framework for comparative analysis. Recent overseas studies are concerned with detailing the formation of a particular union in several American cities or examining post-World War II changes in teacher union strategies in different Canadian education systems.[3] Earlier studies in Australia and elsewhere emphasize the natural, autonomous formation and early growth of teachers' unions.[4] Others concentrate on the growth of regional associations of teachers, such as are found in the French teachers' federation, or commence their history beyond formation, or provide superficial discussion of formation, often examining the growth in terms of a dialectic between 'professionalism' and 'trade unionism'.[5] Studies of teacher union growth are also found in political science, sociology (the study of professions) and, more recently, in the 'new' political economy.[6] Such studies are not generally helpful because of their superficial treatment of the early growth of teachers' unions.

Industrial relations analyses of white-collar union growth focus on aggregate movements and commence at a point beyond the unions' formation. One major American study 'measures' the growth of United States teacher unions by analysing social and inter-union competition factors. It is a prime example of the inadequacies of modern American studies of union growth, being conducted without serious regard to the sensibilities of historical argument, or the processes in the formation and later stages of union growth and the 'work history' of teachers.[7] Industrial relations scholarship, however, raises the possibility of applying theories of labour movements to the growth of individual or national teachers' unions. Labour movement theories have been traditionally interested in classifying the social and economic functions of trade union growth, or the strategies of a union movement in a changing political-economic environment. American writers have developed a strong interest in this field which was pioneered by the 'Wisconsin School' of John Commons and Selig Perlman.[8] But it is John Dunlop, a Harvard labour economist, in his discussion on the theories of labour development who suggests a framework for the study of trade union formation and development. His framework is based on four strategic, inter-related factors of growth: 'technological context'; 'market structures'; 'wider community institutions', and 'social ideas and beliefs'. These determine the conditions and circumstances necessary for the emergence and early growth of trade unions.[9] Dunlop's framework in 1947 was unsophisticated, but it has been subsequently refined by others to provide more precision for the factors of growth and their elements. These still retain the essential Dunlop web of inter-relationships in origins, emergence and early growth. Dunlop also believed that the framework could help explain formation and growth in white-collar public service unions and allow comparisons of union growth between countries, the comparative aspect being a feature of industrial relations studies at that time. Finally, he warned that his analytical framework was an abstraction and that we should be aware of the complexities of behaviour in unions. Analysis 'must not leave the impression of the labour organization as primarily rationalistic'.[10]

The framework for this study of Australian teacher unions is derived from Dunlop and subsequent revisions by Joseph Shister and others.[11] It recognizes three strategic factors (each containing separate elements) which are necessary for the formation of teachers' unions.

The three strategic factors of growth are:

The work situation of teachers

This comprises two elements: first, the relative decline in economic rewards (salaries, payments and allowances) in the teachers' labour market; secondly, changes in the work process, whereby teachers become increasingly subordinate to bureaucratic control within the school system and within larger schools. The work process in teaching is freely adapted from the Marxian 'labour process' which proposes that with increased capital concentration large owners expropriate the workers' control of the productive process, and subordinate them to capital, ultimately degrading their labour. Changes in the labour process increase the workers' consciousness of the need for proletarian action which leads to forms of collective resistance, including trade union activity. As Richard Price suggests, the labour process

> is a social process in which the technical characteristics of a particular work environment shape and condition the forms of the struggle for authority and control. It is in the continual search from both sides for a better bargain that the dynamic of the labour process in labour's history can be seen to lie.[12]

In the case of 'middle class' teachers it leads not to absolute proletarianization, but to an increased collective consciousness of the need to resist bureaucratic control either by informal groupings or through trade unionism of the most rudimentary form, defined by the Webbs in 1894 'as a continuous association of wage earners for the purpose of maintaining or improving the conditions of their working lives'.[13] This does not imply that teachers will establish unions which will necessarily integrate with the labour movement through trade union affiliation. As an historian of the Canadian Civil Service Association has noted, white-collar workers 'can acquire a significant number of the attributes of the proletariat condition, without merging with the actual proletariat'.[14] The use of the labour process as an analytical tool in defining part of the work situation of teaching rests on several assumptions. There is an assumption that despite their lower middle class background, state school teachers are salaried workers. There is an assumption that non-manual work, although different from manual work, can be degrading to the worker. This can occur through deskilling and/or increased subordination to managerial control. It is assumed that there are different levels of trade unionism based on levels of worker consciousness, which result from the deterioration, or threats of deterioration, in working conditions.

Union leadership[15]

This is a strategic factor in the emergence of teachers' unions, and an essential factor amongst workers with bourgeois values who do not have class, family or previous occupational intimacy with labour collectivity, and who perform individualized tasks (in the classroom, for example) as well as supervisory tasks for the state. Leadership can be charismatic through an individual or a sectional élite, or institutional, once a teachers' union has consolidated its growth. All union leadership requires the skills and techniques of organization and persuasion: teachers must be brought to see the need for collective organization which makes use of some, though not all, of the methods of trade unions.

A favourable socio-political framework

This is also necessary for white-collar workers, especially in public service occupations, to form a collective organization. There must be a favourable climate of public opinion, as expressed through the press or parliament, supportive of teacher union formation. For example, there should be legal recognition of teachers' unions; employer and/or government approval of unions; and acceptance of the right of teachers' unions to criticize employers and government. Finally, within this favourable socio-political framework there must be a labour movement from which white-collar unions such as teachers' unions can derive support and inspiration.

Thus, to restate this framework within Dunlop's approach to trade union development, three strategic factors—'the work situation of teachers', 'union leadership', and a 'favourable socio-political framework' must co-exist and inter-relate in the emergence (and later, realization) phases of teacher union formation. However, before the emergence of teacher unions can be considered, teachers' earlier attempts at collective organization in Australia should be examined, particularly the nature and character of these forerunners, their relationship to the emergent phase, and the reasons for their demise.

Forerunners—*The* Résistances

The first organizations of teachers appeared in eastern Australia in the mid-1850s. They appeared and died in the larger towns and capital cities between then and the early 1880s. Most were short-lived and unsuccessful in their objectives and appeal to teachers. Hence they offer no direct link with modern teachers' unions. These forerunners have been described as 'ephemeral associations' or 'mutual improvement societies'.[16] Ephemeral they were, but they rarely provided mutual improvement. They were imposed upon teachers by authorities, and then ignored by teachers, or even used by them as a kind of rudimentary trade union. A more appropriate description of these forerunners, therefore, is one that recognized this trade union impulse, the labour resistance, a concept derived from French labour organizations formed in the 1840s.[17] These resistances were essentially defensive organizations protecting standards or conditions already enjoyed by teachers.[18]

The process of resistance is apparent in the rise and collapse of Australia's teachers' associations before the 1880s. Teachers' grievances arose from threats to teachers' working conditions and employment rights, which affected their economic security. This is not to deny that, once formed, certain resistances adopted other objectives related to teachers' improvement. But these were of secondary importance in the formation of resistances, as was indicative in the teachers' lack of support for other objectives. As J. S. Kerr told the Queensland Royal Commission into Education, 1874-75, 'our present association has confined its business to simply one point, namely salaries'; he also asserted that even in the future members would not be interested in educational questions.[19] Similarly, the notion of an educational institute for teachers was rejected by teachers because, as 'Anti-Humbug' wrote to a Sydney newspaper in 1870, such institutes were promoted by and for inspectors, and were therefore inappropriate to teachers' material needs.[20]

Due to the incipient nature of the teacher resistances, and the need on many occasions for anonymity from zealous officials, the existence and interests of these resistances is subject to 'almost archeological' investigation. It is known that teacher resistances flourished in the 1850s and 1870s. Geelong, Victoria, was probably the cradle of teacher unionism, as the town spawned a long but broken thread of teacher associations from 1855 (with the formation of the Geelong Teachers' Association) to the demise of the Geelong Teachers' Union in 1881. Melbourne, Ballarat and later Bendigo joined Geelong in formal protests over salary reductions, security of tenure and inspection in the late 1850s.[21] In Sydney, although a Teachers' Association was formed in 1855 to rebut a School Commissioners' attack on the quality of teaching, it disappeared within a year, having first ventilated teachers' grievances against the method of inspection. Resistances in mining towns of the Hunter and Illawarra districts of New South Wales and the copper towns of Moonta and Burra, South Australia, like those of Ballarat and Bendigo, seemed more durable in the 1860s and 1870s than in the capital cities.[22]

The Queensland Public School Teachers' Association (QPSTA) is typical of the way the resistances operated. It was formed by Brisbane (and Darling Downs) teachers in 1873 because of the loss in tuition fees to teachers following the introduction of 'free' education in 1870. The QPSTA sought compensation for the fees, a general improvement in salaries and civil service classification for teachers. J. S. Harlin, its president, also declared that there had been too much repression of teachers' rights: 'when we became schoolmasters we did not cease to be citizens'.[23] Its principal activity became the collection of a petition on salaries and allowances. At the monthly meetings, agendas were concerned with the difficulties of presenting the petition, problems of fluctuating school attendances, and grievances from country teachers, with only a single session devoted to an instruction issue, 'Orthography in the Schools'. The QPSTA was frustrated by two problems which ultimately led to its demise. Firstly, the Central Board of Education refused to consider its resolutions. This meant that it had to resort to political influence through petitioning and meeting local members of parliament. In this role it was successful, in that it persuaded the government to increase the compensation rate by 25 per cent from July 1874. This success, however, exacerbated the QPSTA's second problem, that of support for the union. The 'victory' over the compensation rate was followed by a sharp decline in support in Brisbane and the disappearance of the Darling Downs branch. Finally, in December 1874 Brisbane teachers disbanded the association. The QPSTA's formation appears as an isolated process, with the same type of history as the resistances of the 1850s in southern colonies or, in Western Australia in 1892, when the Government Teachers' Association was formed in protest against the continuation of certain inequities in the teachers' collection of school fees.[24] Yet the QPSTA's formation has some resemblance to the reappearance of teacher resistances elsewhere in Australia in the same years, 1871-73. Sydney teachers, after several years of public agitation, formed the Teachers' Association of New South Wales in April 1873. It saw itself as a union of teachers, but asserted that it was neither rebellious nor identifiable with recent trade union agitation. Its main focus was on a threatened unfavourable reclassification of teachers, and their overall low salaries. It published the *Journal of Public Education* to counter the official *Australian Journal of Primary Education* and, despite the editors' promise that it would not become a vehicle for abuse of officials, did so, at least in the eyes of the Council of Education and the Legislative Assembly. It paid for its militancy, being censured by parliament and having its officers disciplined.[25] It succumbed to these pressures fifteen months after its formation. In Adelaide between 1871 and 1873 teachers formed protest groups and a vigilance committee on education legislation in anticipation of proposals to bring teachers under closer departmental control. At such meetings in 1873 arguments were raised that agitation would be better channelled through a teachers' union. Indeed, following the establishment of the new education system in 1875, a South Australian Public Teachers' Association was formed in Adelaide (and several country areas) which survived in varying forms for five years.[26]

In Victoria two groups of teachers, head teachers, and men assistants in Melbourne met in January 1873 to protest their loss in working conditions and salaries following the establishment of a colonial teaching service under the control of the new education department. Their grievances were ignored by the minister and dismissed by the *Argus* as 'unwarranted in view of the light working hours involved in teaching'.[27] The two groups combined into a committee of grievances, to which over five hundred teachers submitted particular complaints, or intimated they would have done so, except for the public service restrictions. Over 120 respondents called for some form of organization, and as a result the Victorian Institute of Teachers (VIT) was established in April 1873. Its organizers included popular men assistants, but the head teachers provided the leadership through Ross Cox and Patrick Whyte, head teacher of the Model School. The institute was concerned with restoring conditions to pre-1872 levels, although such an industrial orientation was contrary to the minister's and department's wishes. The assistants group either did not join the Institute or withdrew from it, but continued to press for the restoration of salaries. Both organizations were unsuccessful in their political representations and in their attempts to gain support from other teachers. The VIT continued meeting spasmodically, as if waiting for a leader, who came in the form of John Glennon in 1876.

Was this upsurge in teacher collectivity during the early 1870s merely coincidental? Perhaps the social turbulence of this period (as measured by labour activity and trade union formation) extended to colonial teachers. Bruce Mitchell notes the formation of the Teachers' Association of New South Wales occurring during a period of labour unrest in Sydney.[28]

Perhaps the teacher resistances were the outer perimeter of the social unrest in eastern Australia and therefore an example of what E. J. Hobsbawm refers to as 'explosions' in labour activity produced by economic fluctuations. Such explosions, he speculated, in the context of European modern history, represented qualitative as well as quantitative changes: 'Generally expansions of the [social] movement into new industries, new regions, new classes of the population coincide with a clustering of new organizations, and the adoption of new ideas and policies by both new and existing units'.[29] If some of the fall-out from Australian 'explosions' touched teachers in the 1870s, it is not apparent in their collective behaviour or arguments, unless it was in their rejection of the labels: 'militant', 'rebellious', 'trade unionist'.

A stronger argument, although still speculative, is that the resistances of the early 1870s can be placed within a new educational milieu. The establishment (and early success) of the National Union of Teachers (NUT) in England in the 1870s became known to local 'informed' teachers. This came from personal knowledge in home letters to former 'old country' teachers;[30] from the popularization of NUT activities through replicas of its *Schoolmaster* in the form of the *Australian School Review and Educational Advertiser* (published in Yass) and the *Journal of Primary Education* (Sydney); and from the inter-colonial leapfrogging of ideas on teachers' unionism between various teachers' groups. The NUT, with its central union structure, successful official recognition and successful representations on behalf of teachers offered to Australian teachers beacons of hope, rather than a model for replication.

The resistances of the early 1870s dared not call themselves unions, but the seeds of a central union of teachers were at last planted. They took root in Victoria between 1876 and 1878 when John Glennon, a flamboyant but erratic individualist, who waged a constant battle with the department on personal issues, mobilized teachers' employment grievances into a revival of the VIT, to be called the Victorian Teachers' Institute (VTI). Glennon's own troubles with his employer and those of the VTI were brought to an end by the heavy hand of official sanction. But during several frenetic years he was able to form and sustain a Victorian teachers' organization, vaguely similar in structure to the NUT, start a teachers' journal, *Teacher*, and take a leading part in sustained public agitation by teachers against their employer. Glennon's *Teacher* made 'many attacks on the Education Department, handed out free advice to teachers about their examinations, conducted campaigns against some of the older and unqualified inspectors and generally reported on all matters to do with education in Victoria and elsewhere'.[31] He strayed too far in his attacks on the inspectors and was charged with insubordination. He resigned, though he was later cleared of charges. The VTI collapsed, but Glennon's efforts at organization were encapsulated in the formation of a rival resistance, the Victorian Teachers' Union (VTU). It established a central branch in the Melbourne area, with branches in Geelong, Ballarat and Sandhurst, all calling themselves unions. The Victorian Teachers' Union was formed in true resistance style in July 1878 when there was a massive government drive against public service spending, including reductions in teachers' salaries. Teachers reacted in large, angry groups 'almost amounting to insubordination . . . and the expediency of a general strike, it has been stated, has been seriously discussed', commented the *Age*.[32] A long petition and strong representations from Patrick Whyte and Henry Jones, both active in the earlier VIT, brought some relief to the cuts in assistants' salaries. The Union then slid into dormancy, except for its sponsorship of the new *Victorian Schoolmaster*. The Geelong Teachers' Union, however, remained active until at least 1881. The VTU could not be awakened, despite concerted calls for revival or a fresh start at organization during the course of the Rogers-Templeton Inquiry into the education department (1883-84).[33]

Why were most teacher resistances so short-lived? Why were there no durable links to produce a chain of teacher organizations, as occurred in England before 1870 or New Zealand before 1883?[34] It would seem that Australia's teachers preferred the resistance to the 'suspect' educational or teacher institutes. Further, as can be seen from European labour history, the resistance was formed around single (or narrowly defined) issues; removal of the grievance would cause the collapse of an incipient union, whether the grievances existed for four years or four months. Perhaps the 'removal' of the grievance amongst Australia's teacher resistances occurred as much from repression of the resistance leadership as from other factors. There are examples where the teachers' organization could not survive because it was denied access to the relevant educational and political authority, or was told that its objectives and strategies had moved outside the legitimate domain of a teachers' mutual improvement group. The Teachers' Association of New South Wales continued its campaigns without official recognition until its leaders were threatened with dismissal in 1874. All recanted before the Council of Education, but even so, four teachers[35] were suspended for two to three months (including the president, Frederick Bridges). A similar fate awaited the QPSTA leaders who had criticized the Central Board of Education during their struggle to present a petition of grievances to the minister in 1874. J. S. Kerr and William Cox were advised that they would not be considered for promotion until they explained their actions. Cox resigned as secretary of the QPSTA. William Swanwick was threatened with dismissal unless he withdrew his allegations. He did so, but became the QPSTA's new honorary secretary.[36] The disciplining of the QPSTA leadership appeared to discourage teachers' support for the organization. Indeed a local magistrate asserted that the Central Board's behaviour was designed to break the QPSTA.

> There are, as the Board of Education may be inoffensively assumed to know, many methods of finishing off a dog besides hanging him ... I understand that the Board of Education have amongst, what may be called, their instruments of torture, a dreadful and mysterious book of record in which the shortcomings of national school teachers are inscribed, or 'A Register of Censures'.[37]

This was was not the first or last occasion on which the leaders of teacher resistances, as distinct from individual rebels, were to feel the harsh hand of bureaucratic or political penalty. John James Low, we recall, was dismissed for his organizing attempts on behalf of Tasmanian teachers in 1861. John Glennon was 'forced out' of the Victorian teaching service in 1878 while in 1866 a group of young Sydney teachers who organized a public protest concerning their low salaries were demoted, after being threatened with dismissal. This action was taken by Frederick Bridges, one of the victims of the 1874 suspensions, but now Deputy Chief Inspector of Schools, who believed the teachers had not shown 'proper respect and submission ... This is particularly necessary in the case of teachers, who should set an example of obedience to constituted authority'.[38]

Nevertheless it would be a romantic view of labour struggle to insist that victimization of teachers in Australia was a major impediment to the formation of teachers' organizations. Of more pertinence was the focus of resistance groups on single issues, admittedly a virtue in mobilizing support for a new organization, but an impediment once 'the cry of pain', was forgotten. Geographical distance between groups of teachers, suspicion of city teachers by teachers in remote areas, and the lack of readership of the new teachers' journals which were designed to bridge distances, were also constraints on the life of a teacher resistance. However, another kind of restraint, that of the 'teacher's mind' was the basic impediment to the viability of resistances. The appeal for a grander, more permanent, central union of teachers throughout a colony, strong enough to withstand the political wilderness and bureaucratic opposition to its members, was made by only a few visionaries and those who yearned for the old country's organizations. Such appeals fell largely on deaf or untrained ears. Only a small minority of teachers accepted the resistance; fewer still could see beyond the resistance to the need for a permanent teachers' union. This need would have to be felt by teachers before such unions could appear.

The Emergence of Teachers' Unions 1884-1893

The founding and early growth of teachers' unions in the major Australian colonies, except New South Wales, between 1884 and 1893 is an important stage in the development of teacher unionism in Australia. It was brought about be the convergence and interplay of three basic factors in union growth. These factors were all present in the emergence of individual unions, although the relative strength of particular factors varied between unions. Although the factors are inter-related, the dynamics of growth will be separated below for the purposes of discussion.

Work situation of teachers

The 1880s was a period of marked changes in the work situation of state school teachers. Most of these changes, which had been accumulating during the previous decade and the early part of the 1880s, were deleterious to the economic rewards and working conditions of teachers. By the mid-1880s they had become so serious as to significantly raise teachers' consciousness of the need for collectivity to protect their interests from government and education departments. We have seen that such a teachers' response was not new; the resistances had been testimony to the 'cry of pain', producing sharp, and often short, bursts of organized protest. In contrast, the 1880s marked the beginning of a long period of educational turbulence (1882-98) when the pains reached a chronic disorder that was felt by the entire teaching service in a colony. The 1880s are remembered as a period of sustained growth in state schooling (except in Western Australia where the growth occurred in the 1890s), but a growth so steeped in contradictions and hidden chaos, that it extended and intensified the difficulties already part of the teacher's lot. It was an era of tainted promises, administrative mismanagement, bureaucratic excesses and educational disappointments—the last reflecting the widening gap between educational rhetoric and the real difficulties of providing schools. For convenience, the two major elements in the changing work situation of teachers will be treated separately although, in process, they were inter-related.

The first element was the question of economic rewards for teachers in the form of salaries, payment by result allowances, promotion and other benefits. The 1880s witnessed an elaboration of the two levels in the primary labour market: high salaries for a decreasing number of teachers in the higher ranks of the teaching service (generally city and town head teachers and first class assistants in the larger schools) and low, depressed salaries and related benefits for an increasing majority of teachers. Overall, the market situation for teachers declined during the 1880s relative to that of other white-collar workers and more significantly (as far as teachers were concerned) to that of many manual workers.[39] The only compensation was the relative security of teaching compared to that of manual occupations. In essence, colonial governments were not willing to fund the expansion of public schools. And, even if willing, they were forced to draw on the cheapest forms of teacher labour through the pupil-teacher system, a reserve army of young women, and the system of payment by results.

Four general observations can be made on the decline in economic rewards for teachers. First, although teachers' average salaries improved slightly in the 1880s, compared to those of the 1870s or 1890s, they were subject to fluctuations when colonial treasuries curbed public recurrent expenditures in short periods of economic downturn by reducing capitation fees, numbers on staff or merit rank, the number of promotions (by raising pass-rates in teacher examinations) and the late payment of allowances, or payment below the normal rate. How much of this was due to political direction or to public service economies is difficult to assess, but teachers believed that their economic rewards were subject to the whim of governmental or departmental economy measures.[40] This attitude, in conjunction with the view that the most vunerable teachers in the hierarchical system were being exploited as cheap labour, became prevalent amongst teachers. And with good reason when women teachers' salaries as a ratio to men's salaries declined from around 80 per cent of male salary to between 65 and 75 per cent during the 1880s. While women teachers did not demand equal pay for equal work until the first decade of the twentieth century, they did agitate and organize for restoration to the earlier ratios in the 1880s. Moreover, many young teachers in country areas were not given horse allowances for their part-time schools, or they had to pay high rents for teacher houses, some of which were in a shocking state of neglect. There was also the injustice of non-payment or token payment of teachers' wives who taught in their husbands' schools as infant teachers or sewing mistresses. In Queensland, for instance, they received a lower salary than a final-year pupil-teacher.[41] Secondly, salaries for many senior teachers in urban areas did not move with the cost of living in the boom conditions of the 1880s. Not only was there a relative decline in incomes, but often teachers' salaries did not meet the life style of Melbourne or Brisbane, where salaries were eroded by high rents, land speculation, and the high cost of manufactured goods, trade and professional services. The 1880s boom also created anxieties about retirement or disabilities. As a result the teachers' unions of the 1880s pressed for pension schemes. Thirdly, women teachers, especially single women who could not leave the larger city schools because of family commitments such as aged parents, or who were boarding in city accommodation, found themselves almost on fixed incomes. Others could not transfer to larger schools because there were ceilings on the number of senior assistants and restrictions on women as head teachers in such schools. Nevertheless, women teachers in this period began to staff the smaller remote schools. For many it was an opportunity to work, or to be paid at a higher level, but with it went loneliness, cultural deprivation (especially for those from town and city) and arduous, even debilitating work.[42] Finally, teachers' incomes could be supplemented by other work such as tutoring or newspaper scribing; but in the 1880s second 'public' incomes were discouraged as teachers came under tighter public service controls.[43] Women teachers in small Victorian schools who also served as postmistresses complained that the small allowance did not recompense them for their loss of school vacations.[44]

Teachers responded to their decline in economic rewards in different ways. Many resigned and entered the more lucrative fields of business and commerce, private school teaching, or other branches of public service, all of which were expanding in a period of scarce non-manual labour.[45] In Victoria over two hundred teachers resigned from the education department following the new classification of teachers in 1885.[46] Others suffered their economic grievances in humiliating silence or with a smouldering resentment which they carried into their classrooms. A few teachers resisted as individuals and fought injustices in classification, promotion or pensions in the highest courts of the land, even in the Privy Council, sometimes with material support from colleagues.[47] Others resisted by advocating or supporting teacher unions.

The changing work process in teaching affected teachers not only in their classrooms, but also as employees in a large and expanding state education system that was highly centralized in power and increasingly centralized in bureaucratic control. It is this increased centralization, which commences around 1880 and continues for the next fifteen years, that provides the key to understanding the work process and its effects on teacher collectivity. To explain this increased centralization we must return to the preceding twenty-five years.

During this period (c. 1850–c. 1875) two major developments occurred which affected educational changes and teachers.[48] The first was the emergence of state education as the dominant mode of schooling in the colonies. Its educational and funding implications produced material changes in the role of teachers. They became identifiable as teachers, and not as a mixture of occupations (cleric-teacher; farmer's wife-teacher) and moved from loosely linked individual instructors to members of a teaching service. They became conscious of their changed role and concerned about their material needs which at times were so threatened that some formed collective organizations (hence the resistances). The second change, towards the end of this twenty-five-year period, and fusing with the rise of a state education system, was the beginning of the centralization of state education systems. Centralization of an education system occurs when the educational administration is accorded the leading part in the system, and through it the governing and/or ruling group directs policy. Centralization of education required rational, administrative coordination. This was achieved by imposing a bureaucratic hierarchy upon teachers. Their ability to negotiate within the system was constrained both by public service restrictions and departmental monitoring of any collective organization such as occurred in the 1870s.

The 1880s witnessed an escalation of the centralizing of the colonial school systems. It was this escalation which increased the subordination of teachers to bureaucratic control. Subordination permeated the school system, but was especially severe on pupil-teachers, women and young assistants. Increasing control was seen to be necessary by the departmental officials as a means of coping with the increased scale and complexity of the state education system, a system staffed by poorly-trained teachers and a system now so entrenched in the public life that the so-called 'liberal' political and financial investment in universal, free education had to be safeguarded, while inefficiencies were concealed from public scrutiny. Built into increased centralization were the emasculation of teachers' proprietary or professional interests in the schools, and an increasing bureaucratic mistrust of teachers to perform their duties. Education departments attempted to impose higher standards of educational and administrative efficiency—largely by remote control—resulting in further routinization of school and departmental organization and practice.[49] Moreover, the avenues for the preparation of teachers and the improvement of teaching skills, rather than being expanded by increased access to training colleges or formal secondary schooling (as was occurring in other countries and in New South Wales) were denied to teachers or prospective teachers.

Thus,

> the word 'schoolmaster' with its connotations of authority and independence gave way in departmental usage to the humbler term, 'schoolteacher'. To be a state-school teacher meant to be a defectively educated member of society's lower orders: *not* to have received a secondary education was almost a prerequisite for being a teacher.[50]

The subordination of the teacher was also affected by the 'success' of state elementary schooling. It had proved popular—as measured by school enrolments, but not necessarily by attendances. Natural population growth, immigration of families and young adults, urbanization in the capital cities, closer settlement in agriculture, new frontiers in grazing and mining, rising expectations in the cities and larger towns, accompanied and contributed to the prosperity and sustained growth of the 1880s. These forces of growth made new demands on schooling, which could not be met by the normal resources available for popular schooling. Thus, despite public rhetoric, the political will to meet the challenges was lacking, or resulted merely in the construction of a few elegant school buildings in urban areas. Moreover, the demography of the school population produced disequilibrium, and teacher supply could not be corrected without resort to, or continuation of, gross expediencies in the recruitment, training and remuneration of teachers. Such burdens fell most heavily on the slim shoulders of youth, young adults and women, but they touched the entire teaching service.

Men in senior positions disputed the loss of their right to appoint teachers or to select pupil-teachers, and complained that their staffing was disrupted by the greater needs of the service. They also felt that their status, economic rewards and professional opinion were dragged down towards a lower, common denominator, that of the assistants and rural headteachers.[51] Curriculum revision in the 1880s, imposed from above, also tested the efficiency and adaptability of teachers and, whether by payment by results or by promotion, affected the rewards and the promotability of teachers. Amongst younger teachers who had entered the training colleges or gained additional literary qualifications elsewhere there was growing disenchantment that the mechanics of a seniority system ensured a long wait in smaller remote schools, or under school heads who did not have additional qualifications and in some cases had gained their positions or promotions by political patronage (at least until the early 1880s in Victoria and South Australia) or through favouritism from head office. It is not surprising that young male graduates of training colleges in Melbourne, Adelaide and Sydney and the Central School in Brisbane were in the forefront of moves towards teachers' unions. Their sense of injustice was undoubtedly assisted by the relatively liberal thinking of their senior instructors, men such as J. S. Kerr in Brisbane, F. J. Gladman in Melbourne and J. R. Madley in Adelaide. C. R. Long started a Trained (ex-trainee) Teachers' Association in Melbourne in 1883, intended to become in his words 'the vanguard for the professional advancement of all teachers'.[52] Yet it failed because of its élitist, craft union appearance in the 'new unionism' era. Women teachers who held relatively senior positions also bore professional and economic frustrations at being denied the highest positions in larger schools (these being the preserve of men) as well as the indignity of being told by officials or male colleagues that their appointment to positions in charge of junior and men teachers was injudicious. They released this frustration by supporting or even forming unions.[53]

And during the 1880s there appeared to be a stronger tendency towards departmental control of the social behaviour of teachers. Public service regulation, the 'secular' clauses of the education acts, even 'superiority' of the new state school systems over older ones, meant that teachers' behaviour was more closely scrutinized. Concomitant with an increased emphasis on moral education in the schools of the 1880s was the expectation that example should be exacted from the teachers.

> The respectable right living teacher, characteristic of the New South Wales public school from the beginning, impressed upon his pupils 'the principles of morality, truth, justice and patriotism' and taught them to 'avoid idleness, profanity and falehood' whether or not he knew that the Public Instruction Act (1880 and 1886) required him to do so.[54]

Thus drinking, gambling, and profane habits, indebtedness, falsification of records, even tardiness in school record-keeping, became more serious offences.

While the education department leadership professed and even believed that a centralized school system was one of the highest forms of educational efficiency, the school systems actually deteriorated due to bureaucratic and clerical mismanagement. Under the weight of growth within the systems, unsupported by political will or financial resources, the teachers (if not the pupils) became the victims.

Inspectors and the methods and purpose of inspection were the main source of complaints at various official inquiries.[55] To a 'loss of professional encouragement' were added real and imagined grievances about secret reports, wrong examination advice, unfair examination of pupils or teachers, inflexibility of mind or capricious treatment of teachers, and obdurate arrogance in some senior inspectors. C. R. Long recalled that one inspector had taken exception to his work and ambitions because of nothing more than his defective eyesight and albino appearance.[56] In South Australia an astonished Commission of Inquiry (1882) on questioning an inspector as to why he sometimes failed pupils in writing even though they were more competent than others in the class who had passed, received a reply: 'I think in their training there ought to be a certain amount of suppression and repression'.[57] The inspectors also came to be seen by teachers as something akin to medieval tax collectors, frontier bank managers or pawnbrokers, because, in one form or another of payment or advancement by results, the inspectors controlled their livelihood. During the 1880s the uneasiness which had existed between inspector and teacher in previous decades grew into total mistrust. C. R. Turney, in his 'The rise and decline of an Australian inspectorate', notes that by the 1880s the New South Wales inspector, rather than criticize the pernicious influence of a form of payment by results, believed in its efficacy and opposed revisions to it. 'Mark mania was the disease of the day.'[58] John Murphy, a founder of the State School

Teachers' Union of Victoria (SSTUV) said of inspectors in 1886, 'Are teachers the only body in the community who cannot be trusted to do their work honestly and fairly, without such a prying, inquisitorial ordeal having to be submitted to?'[59] Other teachers thought of the inspector as a 'pedagogical detective'.[60] Yet the process of inspection subordinating the teacher through payment by results is elegantly explained by a modern biographer of Victorian teachers:

> Payment by results helped the Department to accustom its employees to its ways. It degraded the teacher in his own eyes and squashed any nascent professional pride by treating him as if he were unwilling to work unless enticed by a bribe. Conceived in mistrust, the system bred mistrust, yet by a cruel paradox, the more teachers disliked and distrusted the Department, the more like it they became. Resentfully they studied the regulations which controlled their financial and professional future; sullenly they conformed, often paying the Department the supreme compliment of judging themselves by its criterion: success in obtaining results.[61]

To these institutional devices in bureaucratic control of teachers must be added the personality traits of the inspectors and senior administrators. They too had to bear the burden of the educational turbulence and, for some, the abusive comment of their brother officers. But no plea of mitigating circumstances could excuse 'the Martinetism and assumption of superiority which up to a very few years back characterized Department officials in many other states', wrote the *Australasian Schoolmaster* in July 1902. The South Australian inquiry exposed teachers' genuine fears of certain inspectors and the high-handedness of the Inspector-General, J. A. Hartley. Nearly a decade later an observer was to write that teachers and others feared his love of autocratic power, and detested

> his impetuosity, his overbearing ways, his want of generosity in giving credit to his officers for disinterested work, his claiming originality for reforms which have been in operation for years in other countries, and his want of tact in obtaining the best work from the assortment of minds over which he has had to rule.[62]

In Queensland 'the Almighty Siamese twins' of the Department of Public Instruction, John Anderson, Under Secretary for Education, 1878-1904, and David Ewart, General Inspector, 1878-1904, so subordinated teachers (whom Ewart called 'the instruments who carried out the system') that by the late 1880s teacher resentment had reached a point 'very little short of rebellion', reported an official inquiry in 1888.[63]

Changes in the work process of teaching, combined with the economic difficulties of large numbers of teachers, were important in raising teacher consciousness on collectivity. Their response brought teachers into a trade union ambit, albeit as a white-collar teachers' union separate from the trade union movement *per se*, but at least in a frame of mind that was more receptive to the notion of a central union of teachers strong enough to counter centralized bureaucratic control. These two strands of thinking can be found in the emergent teachers' unions of the 1884-1892 period. The West Moreton Teachers' Association (WMTA) and East Moreton Teachers' Association (EMTA) in Queensland were formed because of teachers' concern about economic and working conditions and promotion by inspection, and the arbitrariness of 'staff rank' determined by the inspector-general. Ultimately this led to the demand for teachers to be placed under a classification and appeal committee.[64] Like South Australian teachers, Queensland teachers had in mind the Committee of Classifiers in Victoria, which was established in 1883 after years of procrastination. Ironically the first decisions of the Committee of Classifiers provoked a wave of resentment against lower than expected classifications of men and women teachers, and was instrumental in the formation of the Victorian Lady Teachers' Association (VLTA) and other unions, sectional and country, which were to form the SSTUV. This incident then led to a log of grievances on the economic rewards of teaching, especially for assistant teachers, payment by results and methods of inspection.[65]

South Australia's teachers' response to the work situation is a good example of the measured steps towards a central union. Teachers' associations in country districts and a Head Teachers' association in Adelaide were formed in response to the new curriculum of 1885. The curriculum required adjustments to the organization, planning and methods of instruction with an increasing dependency on the inspectors' prescriptions and assessment. The education department encouraged these associations; inspectors were active in the country associations, while senior head teachers contributed to the new *Education Gazette* in the name of teachers' associations. Following this 'takeover' of the associations, teachers withdrew, the country associations collapsed, and the South Australian Teachers' Association (SATA) became dormant in 1886. The associations were quickly revived by teachers, when they encountered difficulties in implementing courses. The new syllabus wanted to raise standards and this required additional preparation by teachers. For a time results were lower and teachers' incomes were affected, as were their chances of promotion. This spread to concern over the inspector's role in the new curriculum and in the assessment of teachers, including the use of secret reports and fines for late school returns. The need was felt for a more liberal classification of schools for promotion, and ultimately came the demand that teachers be included in a civil service board

'so that their position would be better defined, their promotion more certain and their status as teachers more fully recognized'. Parallel with this
localized agitation were attempts for a bridging of country and Adelaide
teachers' associations through a central union. These attempts were
initially successful in the reorganization of the SATA as a colonial-wide
union in 1887. However, it was in essence a union of delegates meeting
at an annual conference, while the management of SATA remained in
the hands of Adelaide head teachers.[66]

Union leadership

If teachers' unions were to emerge and become permanent organizations,
then it was crucial that a leadership of teachers be present to guide them
through these formative years. It may be unfashionable currently in
labour history to consider charismatic or sectional leadership as a strategic variable of formation. In dealing with nineteenth century state
school teachers of lower middle class origins, bourgeois values and
inherent conservatism or, at best, confusion about collective organization, a leadership presence was necessary to carry them past this political, even cultural barrier. Leadership of teachers became a necessary
condition in the emergence of teachers' unionism, to harness and direct
the teachers' collectivity derived from changes in their work situation,
and to capitalize on the emergent favourable socio-political climate for
white-collar and public service unionism. It was also necessary that leadership exist to encourage a central union rather than disparate sections.
It required organizing skills, dedication and patience to reach teachers
in non-metropolitan areas, but in this the railway and other improved
communications were helpful. It required leadership to be informed,
indeed worldly in public affairs, and related matters; here the influence
of the training college or model school on its small band of graduates
was to become important, as was knowledge of the NUT, other British
teacher unions and, once the process had started, other colonial teachers'
unions. Finally, and at times above all else, individual leaders needed to
be fearless (or foolhardy) to withstand the frustration of disapproval by
employers, teacher indifference or reaction, and the past lessons of
official reprisals against insubordinate teachers.

It may be that leadership of a union came from a vanguard of head
teachers. Were this the case, such leadership would probably have been
concealed to avoid the taint of 'Head Teachers' organization'. The taint
was evident in South Australian and Victorian formations and even
Queensland, where the guiding hand of imported British teachers may
be discerned.[67] A different type of importation occurred in Western Australia in the 1890s, when the leadership in the formation of the Western
Australian Teachers' Union (WATU) was provided by head teachers who

had immigrated to the gold boom colony from Victoria, New South Wales and even England as a result of the economic depression 'at home'. They wanted a teachers' union like those they had belonged to but, in establishing a Western Australian union, they had to overcome the suspicions of local teachers by insisting on a formula of one local teacher to one 'import' in executive positions.[68]

None of the teacher union leaders of the 1880s was trade unionist by ideological commitment. Few apart from Patrick Whyte and Henry Cox, the first president of the SSTUV, or J. S. Kerr in Queensland, and John Low and Thomas Alexander in Tasmania were leaders of the earlier resistances. None of the new leaders used their union experience as stepping stones for career advancement because in the 1880s such stones had a precarious angle which could lead to personal disaster. Admittedly a second rung of leadership, such as that of C. R. Long and Frank Tate in Victoria, progressed to the higher echelons of the department but not on the 'backs of the union'. (This situation was to change in some states in the twentieth century.) Some of the leaders at a central and local branch level made political capital from their involvement. Anthony St Ledger, the organizational wizard in the Queensland Teachers' Union's formation, was to take his place in the Senate of the Australian Commonwealth as an anti-socialist member (1913), while local branch leaders entered the Queensland Parliament.[69] In Tasmania, admittedly at the end of the period under review, the former leader of the 'rebellious' clique of training college students became its president.[70] From that vantage point he entered politics, becoming a Labor Premier and ultimately Prime Minister Joseph Lyons of Australia—at the head of a conservative government.

In the period 1884-92 the union leadership factor as manifested in the organizational work of individuals was pronounced in Queensland, Victoria and Tasmania, but less obvious in the formation of the South Australian Public Teachers' Association. Victoria spawned one leader in the formation of the SSTUV, John Murphy.

John Murphy started as a pupil-teacher in 1869 and after years in the bush was accepted at the Training Institute in 1882, the oldest of F. J. Gladman's graduates. That year he taught at Richmond Central School and became part of a lively, critical group of young male teachers. Murphy was the most active, at first in processing the wrongs and anomalies imposed on himself and other assistants as a result of the new classified roll. His persistence and arguments (he wanted to study law, but studied for an Arts degree instead) met with success, and he was publicly congratulated for his efforts on behalf of junior teachers. Encouraged, he revived the idea of a teachers' union, to which Tate and Long gave enthusiastic support; they founded the Melbourne District

Teachers' Association (MDTA) in 1885.[71] He also joined and became active in the Male Assistant Teachers' Association (MATA) formed in the same year. He persuaded teachers not to affiliate with the Public Service Association, also formed in 1885. Instead he advocated and mounted the campaign for a central union comprised of sectional and country associations. It was on his initiative that the Melbourne District Teachers' Association proposed a conference of teacher representatives which established the SSTUV at Easter 1886, with Murphy as treasurer. An activist in every way, he continued honorary work in the Australian Natives Association, the Celtic Club and later the Henry George League. Yet union activities dominated his interests and he held office not only in the SSTUV (as either treasurer or secretary) but also in the MDTA and MATA. This was a recipe for divided loyalties. He was forced to take sides on the issue of the paramountcy of the SSTUV to represent teachers in dealing with the government. In despair he watched his MATA disaffiliate from the SSTUV over the issue in 1889. Almost as though suffering a personal defeat, he retired from office and disappeared from public view in union matters in 1891.[72] Yet he had made his mark. Of all the Victorian teachers of this period, Murphy was important in reviving an organization for teachers, giving it new industrial and political direction along with early success, such as improvements in the formula for payment by results. He had preached and practised the tenets of a strong, central union of teachers, but these went unheeded by men and women with tunnel vision.

In Tasmania the leaders of the Tasmanian State School Teachers' Association (TSSTA), John Low, Thomas Alexander and J. N. Clemons are remembered for their patience in dealing with teachers in rural northern Tasmania and conservative Launceston. Their virtue was rewarded a decade later when they convened the TSSTA Congress— which became the first all-Tasmanian teachers' union.

Patience was not one of Anthony St Ledger's known virtues. But he compensated with other personal attributes with which he drew Queensland teachers into a union ambit, and then almost single-handedly devised a suitable vehicle for expression, the QTU. It had spectacular success in its foundation years, becoming the then strongest (and oldest surviving) teachers' union in Australia. Yet it is the manner in which St Ledger manipulated teachers' grievances and his reading of a changing political situation which makes him the most impressive of the union leaders.

Anthony St Ledger was an assistant at J. S. Kerr's Central Boys' School. He joined the East Moreton Teachers' Association (EMTA) in 1887 and was immediately appointed its honorary secretary. St Ledger was then 25 years old, English born but Queensland bred, intelligent, erudite and ambitious. The product of a Catholic schooling in Ipswich, he had gained first place in the first government grammar school scholarships in 1873. He had been a pupil-teacher in both Roman Catholic and state schools, joining the latter in 1884 and rising quickly through the ranks. St Ledger, as EMTA secretary, wrote to other teachers' communities about the new teachers' associations, hoping that they might establish their own associations which could then be linked by a central union. While St Ledger was canvassing teachers, the Queensland government established a Civil Service Commission to investigate the efficiency of government departments, including the Department of Public Instruction. St Ledger approached Felix Unmack, the Commission's Chairman (and 'Liberal' MLA for Toowong, the seat where the 'Liberal' St Ledger lived) to extend the inquiry by seeking rank and file teachers' opinions on the administrative control of teachers. The commission agreed and a circular was sent to certificated teachers in April 1888. This form of inquiry was not new; it had been used by the Royal Commission into Education, 1874-75, and at inquiries in Victoria and South Australia.[73] St Ledger sent a second round of letters to teachers asking them to meet locally, to co-ordinate replies to the survey, nominate teachers to give evidence at the Commission, and reconsider the question of a teachers' union.

The Civil Service Commission became the rallying point for the existing associations at their large monthly meetings; it was 'the topic of the day'. St Ledger, who co-ordinated the teachers' evidence at the Commission, was also kept busy drafting rules for a central teachers' union, to be composed of affiliated local associations, and arranging an inaugural conference. These details reached teachers in August, again with excellent timing, because the *First Report* of the Civil Service Commission had just been published. It condemned the departmental administration and the senior officers, and praised the role of the teachers' association at the inquiry.[74]

Heartened by public recognition and scenting justice, teachers could see more clearly the desirability of a central teachers' union, not only to maintain this single voice for teachers, but to participate in the reforms they assumed would follow as a consequence of the inquiry. It was in this spirit that seven associations from throughout Quensland met at Brisbane in January 1889 to establish the QTU. St Ledger was elected honorary secretary, with moves to make it a paid position being deferred. Later that year he resigned to practise law (having been admitted to the Bar in 1888). He maintained contact with the union and in 1895 he founded, edited and managed the union's *Queensland Education Journal*.[75] For the next six years he was the strident critic of the education department, causing Inspector General Ewart to minute: '[his] vision of the Department and its operations is a cross between that of a peeping Tom and a hostile spy; and his spirit and attitude are a compound of a retail grocer and a resurrectionist'.[76] No other union leader provoked such acerbic attention as this from a colonial education department; a testimony surely to St Ledger's effectiveness in championing the teachers' cause.

A favourable socio-political framework

The 1880s were also important for the emergence of an overall socio-political climate which favoured the efforts of teachers to organize. This climate was extremely supportive in eastern Australia, and especially in South Australia. Political elements such as increased electoral volatility and the presence of a liberal philosophy amongst elected leaders provided informal support for the emergence and early growth of teachers' unions. Unlike earlier years, there was no political censure of teachers' organizing activities and there were ministers, like C. H. Pearson in Victoria, who believed in the positive role of a teachers' union in an education system, encouraging its participation, although not necessarily bending to its demands.[77] He and other ministers at least listened to teachers' representatives which meant that education department officials, even Queensland's 'almighty Siamese Twins' could not ignore them. Moreover, reformist policies in colonial governments were directed towards improvement in government administration and civil service reform: often these were preceded by official inquiries which provided opportunities for teachers to air grievances, and for leaders among their ranks to foster teacher meetings. There were also other political reforms which by implication encouraged teacher union formation. Voting rights, for example, were first granted to some South Australian women in 1885 and women were admitted to the University of Adelaide in 1880. Emerging organizations with a potential for large female membership had to be acknowledged.

Another element of support came from newspapers in capital cities and large towns, which often followed the 'dailies'' opinion on public issues. Press support for teacher unionism was evident in several forms. Most were critical of education department administration and sympathetic to teachers' problems. There was guarded support for the idea of teachers' unionism, provided the unions did not become militant or self-interested: teachers were, after all, public servants. In each colony there was a leading newspaper which expressed support, even championed the teachers' cause;[78] others at least reported their efforts extensively, sometimes borrowing comment and arguments from the *Australasian School-master*, the unofficial organ of teacher unionism in Victoria and elsewhere. Newspaper politics, however, influenced a paper's attitude to teachers' claims. Thus in Melbourne the *Age* was highly supportive of the teachers' union, whereas the *Argus* remained cynical or hostile. The role of the press not only provided a positive climate; it also informed teachers, especially those in 'up country' schools, on educational, union and public service questions. This role reached its height in the 1880s and, as Geoffrey Blainey argues, 'In an era of self-improvement, [newspapers] were a powerful educational influence and might well have achieved in the average year, half as much as all the schools and colleges achieved: the purpose of most daily newspapers and their readers was serious'.[79]

The most important and most tangible element in a favourable socio-political climate, however, came from the labour movement itself. It flourished in eastern Australia in the 1880s, and later in Tasmania and Western Australia, which may partly account for the later development of teacher unionism in those colonies in the 1890s, rather than the 1880s. The growth of the trade union movement throughout eastern Australia in the 1880s did not go unnoticed. The symbolic character of the Trade Union Acts; the formation of local Trades and Labour Councils; the staging of the Inter-colonial Trade Union Congresses, for example, the fourth held in Brisbane in March 1888; the existence of Eight Hour and Early Closing movements; and the popularity of mutual improvement societies, Mechanics Institutes and parliamentary clubs provided an important socio-political influence on the formation of teachers' unions. Furthermore, as R. M. Martin has argued, Australia's 'New Unionism' of the 1880s should include white-collar unionism: 'a related development which has gone unremarked, while less dramatic in its immediate consequences, its implications were no less significant'.[80] The growth of white-collar unionism was influenced by the growth and strength of trade unionism; the growth of a metropolitan economy which accompanied both trade and urbanization; the concentration of business ownership and the extent of centralized public enterprise. In eastern Australia during the 1880s a favourable configuration emerged which provided the stimulus for the organization of white-collar employees: public servants, telegraphists, journalists, marine engineers, shop assistants, clerks, musicians, draughtsmen, railway and harbour officers, school teachers, articled clerks and, in Queensland, even policemen. These emerged in the mid and late 1880s. The impact of trade unionism, including white-collar unionism, was subtle but occasionally it was directly acknowledged, as, for example, at a meeting to establish a teachers' union at Gympie, Queensland, in August 1888. J. A. McLeod, who was to become its first president, declared:

On several past occasions the idea of instituting here a Teachers' Association was mooted . . . But we never arrived at the dignity of a duly constituted body. And so it may have been owing to this, or perhaps the paucity of our numbers, together with the idea that no tangible advantage was likely then to be gained, that our meeting fell through ... But now our numbers are larger—it is as if the hour has arrived ... These are the days of unions and organizations, and ours when properly constituted will lead to a united voice for teachers and a respect that could never be compelled by any company of separate units, however numerous. We hope that when its history comes to be written it will not be summed up as the proverbial 'Flash in the Pan'.[81]

There was no stigma attached to teachers joining or calling their organizations unions. Similarly teachers who joined—still the minority of teachers—had little of the ambivalence towards most trade union methods, or the labour movement in general, as they had shown in the 1870s, or would show after the great strikes of the 1890s.[82] Neither did they deny the presence of the labour movement in Australian society, or that teachers were moved by the same or similar motives as other workers.[83] At conference dinners the teachers' unions would toast 'organized labour' or 'kindred associations': one president asserted that although 'it had been cast in their teeth, that they were union men, [he] did not mind that they were there for the advancement of education'.[84] But on questions of labour affiliation, observance of the movement's rituals and industrial disputation, teacher unions believed that such strategies were inappropriate for their purposes.

It could not be found in May First or Labour Day processions ... Not that we should be disgraced if we did, but it is outside of our place, we do not wish to enter politics. Neither shall we ever go on strike, as one hot blooded brother urged ... We are the men placed in charge of the new State Education engine. It is our duty to make that machine do its proper work ... it will require cleaning ... its motion must be regulated and repairs will be necessary. When the men think either of those should be attended to, they must report to their foreman, who examines the machine to see if the job pointed out should be taken in hand. Well the teachers are the engineers, and the foreman, the department[85]

wrote the QTU secretary in 1895, admittedly after the great strikes, yet it seems an accurate, if quaint, insight into teachers' perceptions of their particular brand of trade unionism.

So far there has not been any discussion of the largest body of colonial teachers, those in New South Wales. Why did a permanent teachers' union fail to emerge there in the 1884-92 period? What significant factor or factors were absent in New South Wales? Teachers' unions were formed in 1884 and informal organizations existed between 1884 and

1886 and around 1890, concerned about teachers' relative disadvantage in salaries following the introduction of the Civil Service Act, 1883. It is apparent that teachers wanted some type of union to handle grievances. The early 1880s were conducive to union formation, but when the Minister for Public Instruction refused to meet with the New South Wales Teachers' Union formed in 1884 (although he did meet a teacher deputation on the same grievances the following year), and two of its senior leaders were promoted to inspectors, the union collapsed after four months.[86] In 1886, the year of the ex-Training College graduates' demotions, about a quarter of the colony's teachers petitioned parliament on the deterioration of salaries and conditions. In 1890 the Minister told teachers he had no objections to a teachers' union, providing it did not engage in 'unseemly conflict with the Department' and avoided 'forming a union of an aggressive character'.[87] Yet no union was founded until 1895 and the New South Wales Public School Teachers' Association was not formed until 1898.

Mitchell was forced to consider this puzzle in his history of New South Wales teachers' organizations. He saw it not so much a puzzle, as 'remarkable' that teachers' unions had existed at all between the 1850s and 1890s.[88] His response obscured teacher union developments elsewhere in Australia. What should have been seen as remarkable is that teachers in New South Wales, Australia's oldest colony, only established a viable union at the same time as teachers in the youngest of the self-governing colonies—Western Australia. Mitchell attributes the absence of a New South Wales teachers' union to a combination of problems.[89] There were public service restrictions placed on teachers which curbed their inclination for organization. Such was the 1883 clause that 'Teachers of all ranks are required to abstain from public discussions on political or religious topics and from public controversy upon the merit of the system of education'. Similar restrictions, however, operated in other colonies. There were also physical difficulties in New South Wales and internal segmentation of the teaching force which impeded unionism. Yet this is the very fabric of early teacher unionism in Australia, of unions coming to terms with distance and division; and if it could be attempted in Queensland, why not in New South Wales? Mitchell also suggests that as teachers' incomes were static in the 1880s—in real terms they declined—they were not cause for grievance. Yet his study acknowledges that the 1883-86 grievances were directly related to salaries. And from my earlier discussion of the work process, drawn in part from his and other studies on New South Wales teachers, there was real subordination of the teacher to the state education system. That Inspector Brodribb from Victoria could not detect any major grievances by New South Wales teachers in 1888 gives no satisfaction, as he was making the point more in support of his long running battle against the 'troublesome' Victorian teachers.[90] Finally, Mitchell raises the spectre of suppression of teacher-organizers, whether in its mildest form of 1884 or severest form of 1886. There is no doubt that teachers were influenced by such events but, as seen earlier, official suppression was a hurdle, not a barrier, which had to be negotiated by teachers in establishing unions. The under secretary of the department, William Wilkins, had ruled with an iron hand, but he had retired in January 1884. His successors and other senior officers were not as autocratic, nor as successful in moulding a minister's attitudes to teachers' unions.

The press, parliament and strength of local trade unionism provided an appropriate climate for support. However, there was also Sir Henry Parkes to contend with. It was Parkes who had introduced the censure against the Teachers' Association in 1874; it was Parkes, of colonial politics, who crushed the Newcastle miners' strike of 1888. His attitudes and his presence in New South Wales politics may have deterred teachers. But he could not have influenced the official disapproval of the Teachers' Union in 1884 as he had left parliament and was overseas. Perhaps in the later 1880s there was a less liberal climate in New South Wales, as personified by Parkes and his cabinet, than in other colonies, but it is difficult to detect and did not seem to impair the formation of other white-collar unions. There may be reasons peculiar to New South Wales teachers, which explain its pattern of teacher union development. Within our framework, the absent factor in formation during the 1880s appears to be lack of union leadership. We recall that the New South Wales Teachers' Union had collapsed in 1884 when it was 'beheaded' by its leaders becoming inspectors.[91] In 1886 the potential leadership appeared to be too junior to warrant wider support, and no group or individual leader emerged to fill the vacuums created after 1884 or 1886. Samuel Bent, an activist in 1884, became an inspector in 1886 and only on resigning from that post in 1891 did he start to work for a teachers' union. William Matthews, who had organized a teachers' association in the Hunter Valley in 1864, and had been the secretary of the ill-fated Teachers' Association of New South Wales (he was suspended with Bridges and others), was prominent in the early 1880s. It was on his initiative that teachers met and formed the Teachers' Union in 1884. However, his continuing financial difficulties and failing health forced him into the background for the remainder of the decade. Thomas Callaghan who was prominent in this same union was teaching at Newcastle in the 1880s and therefore not well placed to help launch a union in a centralized school system based in Sydney.[92] The absence of identifiable leaders is liable to be dismissed as a simplistic answer to the puzzle, but hopefully it offers more plausibility than existing arguments, and at least provides grounds for further research into the 'exceptionality' of New South Wales.

Epilogue

The emergence of teachers' unions between 1884 and 1892 is important in the history of teacher union development in Australia because the unions formed the first continuous links with today's unions. They were not in themselves the foundations of modern teacher unions, but part of the foundations, the strongest part being established in the later phase of formation between 1916 and 1926. During the emergent phase (1884-92) the teachers' unions attracted varying degrees of support from teachers: over 30 per cent of eligible members in Queensland and Victoria, but less than 10 per cent in South Australia.[93]

The 1880s as a period of educational growth and turbulence, set against a general background of political and trade union development, favoured the emergence and early growth of teachers' unions. But this period was followed by two episodic events, the 1890s strikes and the depression which, in different ways, tested the basic viability of these teachers' unions. Both influenced teachers' attitudes to collective organization in the short term, making it difficult to build or retain members.

The strikes exposed the basic antagonism between organized labour and capital and the state, and demonstrated to many the tenuous qualities of the 'working man's paradise' or 'the classless society'. The teachers' unions, engaged in their own struggle with employers over public economies in education, appeared to alter their position on organized labour.[94] And, as if to semaphore their shift towards stronger middle class identification, the SSTUV introduced an educational congress in 1894. The congress, coinciding with the union's annual general meeting, became a public educators' forum or rallying point for the professional aspects of teaching and a public relations exercise in union-employer relations. These congresses were emulated by teachers' unions in South Australia, New South Wales and Tasmania, and eventually became small springboards for the development of local education reform movements.

Meanwhile, in the real world of teachers' material conditions, the teachers' unions were powerless to prevent the introduction of drastic economies in the school systems. Some policies like retrenchments and salary reductions turned sections of teachers against each other. This situation opened breaches in the uneasy relations of different sections within central unions. As a result women teachers, assistants, and teachers in rural or small country schools left the original central unions, or refused to join, or operated as caucuses or sections independently and, in some cases, in defiance of a central union's authority. Again the unions were powerless to prevent this disunity, their resources and experience being

G

minimal in those years. Sectionalism, fragmentation and disunity were, and are, the occupational condition of teaching, based as it is on hierarchical and gender relations. Moreover the geographical dispersal of teachers in Australia's large and centralized systems provided constant tensions between city and country teachers. The possibility of all these tensions undermining a central teachers' union was freely admitted even in the 1880s. 'I am afraid the idea of unionism is still in embryo amongst us', lamented an SSTUV president, 'teachers are so dogmatic that anything like fusion of them into a homogeneous mass is impossible'.[95] In New South Wales a teacher drew attention to nine divisions of teachers, whose past experience 'proves that any attempt to combine such opposing elements in one association must result in failure'.[96] Teacher unions in the 1890s accepted their predicament, but as the depression exacted further tolls, there were renewed efforts to bolster teacher unionism so that it would not collapse or become badly fragmented. In South Australia, New South Wales and Tasmania new forms of central organizations were gradually introduced either to existing unions or to new unions. These culminated in the South Australian Public Teachers' Association, 1896, the New South Wales Public School Teachers' Association, 1898 and the TSSTA, 1902. In Queensland there were attempts to persuade women teachers and Brisbane men assistants to return to the fold. In Victoria there was some co-operation between the separate unions, SSTUV, and the MATA but it was short-lived, and the Victorians fell into further fragmentation in the early 1900s. It was, and still is, the worst example of union fragmentation. But fragmentation, internal disunity and even ideological differences became prevalent in all states, except Queensland, before World War I.[97]

It was to take a new level of consciousness brought about by a decline in the material conditions of teachers during that war, and the direct intervention of the state in extending to state school teachers the protective arm of a compulsory arbitration system[98] before a single union of teachers could be achieved or restored. This occurred in all states between 1916 and 1926.[99] By then John Murphy, John Low, even Anthony St Ledger, and their dreams of a strong central teachers' union, were forgotten.

TABLE

The Formative Stages in the Growth of Teachers Unions in Australia

	Emergent Phase			Realization Phase	1984
Victoria	Lady Teachers Association (1884-VLTA) — Melbourne District Teachers Ass. (1885-MDTA) — Male Assistants Teachers Assoc. (1885-MATA) — Country Dist. Teachers Assns. (1885 & 1886)	State School Teachers Union of Victoria (1886)		Victorian Teachers Union (1926)	VTU (Primary Teachers only)
South Australia	Adelaide Teachers Ass. (ATA-1885) — Country Teachers Ass. (1887)	S.A. Teachers Association— (1887)	S.A. Public Teachers Association (1895)	S.A. Public Teachers Union (1925-51) Women Teachers Guild (1935-51)	S.A. Institute of Teachers
Queensland	West Moreton Teachers Ass. (WMTA-1886) — East Moreton Teachers Ass. (EMTA-1887) — Marlborough Teachers Ass. (1887-1888) — Country Teachers Assns. (1888)	Queensland Teachers Union (1889)		Queesland Teachers Union (1916)	QTU
Tasmania	State School Teachers Ass. (1892-Nth Tasmanian only) — Hobart Teachers Guild (1898)	TSSTA (1902)		Tasmanian Teachers Union (1925)	TTF
Western Australia	Goldfields Teachers Ass. (1896) — Perth and Fremantle Teachers Ass. (1896-97)	W.A. Teachers Union (1898)		State School Teachers Union of W.A. (1920)	SSTUWA
N.S.W.	Country Teachers Assns. (1892-) — N.S.W. Public School Teachers Institute (1895) — Assistant Teachers Union (1896)	N.S.W. Public School Teachers Association (1898)		N.S.W. Teachers Federation (1919)	NSWTF

NOTES

[1] C. R. Paice, 'Teacher Associations in Tasmania 1882-1902', *Tasmanian Journal of Education*, vol. 9, no. 1 (1975), pp. 69-73; and J. J. Low, 'Historical Retrospect on the TSSTA', *Australasian Schoolmaster* (hereafter *AS*), July 1902, pp. 6-8.

[2] G. S. Harman, *The Politics of Education: a bibliographical guide* (University of Queensland Press, St Lucia, 1974), pp. 98-9; A. D. Spaull (ed.), *Australian Teachers: from colonial schoolmasters to militant professionals* (Macmillan, Melbourne, 1977), parts III and IV.

[3] W. J. Urban, *Why Teachers Organized* (Wayne State University Press, Detroit, 1982); J. Harp and G. Betcherman, 'Contradictory Class Locations and Class Action: teachers' organizations in Ontario and Quebec', *Canadian Journal of Sociology*, vol. 5, no. 2 (1980), pp. 145-62.

[4] The best are: Bruce Mitchell, *Teachers, Education and Politics: a history of organizations of public school teachers in New South Wales* (University of Queensland Press, St Lucia, 1975); J. E. Clarke, The American Federation of Teachers: origins and history 1870-1952 (Ph.D., Cornell University, 1966).

[5] Roger Martin, *Les Instituteurs de l'entre-deux guerres: idéologies et action syndicale* (du Rhône) (Presses Universités de Lyon, 1982); P. H. J. H. Gosden, *The Evolution of a Profession* (Basil Blackwell, London, 1972); J. B. Roald, Pursuit of Teachers' Status: Canadian teachers' organizations 1915-1955 (D.Ed., University of British Columbia, 1970); W. J. C. McDonald, Some Aspects of the Unionism and Professionalism of Teachers in the VTU (M. Ed., Monash University, 1978).

[6] R. A. Manzer, 'Selective Inducements and the Development of Pressure Groups: Canadian teachers' associations', *Canadian Journal of Political Science*, vol. 2, no. 1 (1969), pp. 103-17; Jenny Ozga and Martin Lawn, *Teachers, Professionalism and Class: a study of organized teachers* (Falmer Press, London, 1981); A. Vickary, The Doctrinal and Strategic Problems of SAIT (M.A., University of Adelaide, 1982).

[7] W. J. Moore, 'An Analysis of Teacher Union Growth', *Industrial Relations*, vol. 17, no. 2 (1978), pp. 204-15; but see Rosemary Crompton, 'Approaches to the Study of White Collar Unionism', *Sociology*, vol. 10, no. 4 (1976), pp. 407-25.

[8] J. Barbash, 'Labor Movement Theory and the Institutional Setting', *Monthly Labor Review*, vol. 104, no. 9 (1981), pp. 34-7.

[9] John T. Dunlop, 'The Development of Labor Organizations: a theoretical framework' in R. Lester and J. Shister (eds), *Insights into Labor Issues* (Macmillan, New York, 1948), pp. 163-93.

[10] Ibid., p. 193.

[11] J. Shister, 'The Logic of Union Growth', *Journal of Political Economy*, vol. 51, October 1953, pp. 414-20; Albert Blum, 'Why Unions Grow', *Labor History*, vol. 9, Winter 1968, pp. 39-72; V. Lombardi and J. Grimes, 'A Primer for a Theory of White Collar Unionization', *Monthly Labor Review*, vol. 90, May 1967, pp. 46-9; W. Moore and R. Marshall, 'Growth of Teachers' Organizations: a conceptual framework', *Journal of Collective Negotiations*, vol. 2, Summer 1973, pp. 271-97.

[12] Richard Price, 'The Labour Process and Labour History', *Social History*, vol. 8, no. 1 (1983), p. 62; see also M. Burawoy, 'Towards a Marxist Theory of the Labor Process, Braverman and Beyond', *Politics and Society*, vol. 8, no. 2 (1978), pp. 247-312.

[13] Sidney and Beatrice Webb, *The History of Trade Unionism 1666-1920* (Workers' Educational Association, London, 1920), p. 1.

[14] Anthony Thompson, 'The Large and Generous View: the debate on labour affiliation in the Canadian civil service 1918-1928', *Labour/Le Travailleur*, vol. 2, no. 2 (1977), p. 135.

[15] Shister, op. cit., pp. 420-2.

[16] C. H. Currey, 'Australia', in I. L. Kandel (ed.), *Educational Yearbook of the International Institute of Teachers' Colleges 1935* (Columbia University Press, New York, 1935), p. 28; Bruce Mitchell, A History of Public School Teachers' Organizations in New South Wales 1855-1945 (Ph.D., Australian National University, 1969), p. 9. (Note: the first chapter of this thesis is published in an article, 'Improving Teachers', *Journal of Australian Studies*, no. 11, November 1982.)

[17] H. B. Davis, 'The Theory of Union Growth', *Quarterly Journal of Economics*, vol. 55, August 1941, pp. 612-14.

18 Dunlop, op. cit., wrote: 'no working community is ever completely organized; some danger to the stability of the informal group frequently serves the immediate occasion for formalizing an organization' (p. 177).

19 Queensland, *Report of the Royal Commission on the Educational Institutions* (1875), minutes of evidence, p. 32.

20 Jean Ely, The development of centralized education administration in New South Wales 1848-1880 (Ph.D., University of Tasmania, 1973), p. 285. N.B. *The Victorian Schoolmaster*, writing of the New South Wales Teachers' Institute's formation: 'Hitherto in forming an association teachers have had in view chiefly the improvement of their social position and in this very few reasonable people would blame them', November 1877, p. 54.

21 McDonald, op. cit., pp. 1-3; *Ballarat Star*, 9 December 1855; *Bendigo Advertiser*, 17 November 1857.

22 Mitchell, op. cit., 1969, p. 10; B. K. Hyams, State School Teachers in South Australia 1847-1950 (Ph.D., Flinders University, 1972), pp. 314-16.

23 *Courier*, 10 February 1874, and A. D. Spaull, 'The Growth of Teacher Unionism in Queensland 1873-1916' (unpublished paper, 1983).

24 'Noah Little', History of the State School Teachers' Union, *WA Teachers Journal*, vol. 15, no. 7 (1925), pp. 174-5.

25 Mitchell, op. cit., 1969, pp. 34-9; Ely, op. cit., pp. 288-95.

26 Hyams, op. cit., pp. 311-22.

27 Ralph Biddington, Policies in Primary Teacher Training in Victoria 1850-1950 (Ph.D., University of Melbourne, 1978), p. 174.

28 Mitchell, op. cit., 1969, p. 36.

29 E. J. Hobsbawm, 'Economic Fluctuations and Some Social Movements since 1800', *Economic History Review* (2nd series), vol. 5, no. 1 (1952), p. 2.

30 For example, 80% of 'trained' head teachers surveyed in Queensland in 1874 had been teachers in UK, including 37% in England. The NUT was formed in 1870; the Educational Institute, Scotland (1848), Irish National Teachers' Association (1868). Queensland, *Report of Royal Commission*, op. cit., p. 178; see also *Australian School Review and Educational Advertiser*, vol. 1, no. 2 (1874), p. 120.

31 Biddington, op. cit., p. 192.

32 Ibid., p. 197, and Education Department of Victoria, special case no. 655A (PROV).

33 *Geelong Advertiser*, 2 August 1878, 18 August 1880; *Victorian Schoolmaster*, August 1879, p. 15; *AS*, August, October 1883, September 1884.

34 NB. The present New Zealand Educational Institute was formed in 1883 (taking the same name as the Educational Institute of Scotland). It was formed from local associations at Otago (estab. 1864), Wellington (1873), Auckland (1875) and Canterbury-Nelson (1882).

35 Mitchell, op. cit., 1969, pp. 40-4.

36 Petition to Col. Sec. and related matters of QPSTA, April 1874, EDU/A599, Queensland State Archives.

37 *Courier*, 17 July 1874.

38 Mitchell, op. cit., 1969, p. 61.

39 Information on teachers' salaries is taken from L. Blake (ed.), *Vision and Realisation*, vol. 1 (Education Department, Victoria, Melbourne, 1972), pp. 279-90. Susan Duke, The Education of State School Teachers in Victoria 1873-1901; with Some Reference to New South Wales and South Australia (M.Ed., University of Melbourne, 1976), pp. 142-6. J. R. Lawry, Some Aspects of Education in Queensland 1859-1904 (Ph.D., Monash University, 1968), pp. 385-8, 677; G. E. Saunders, Public Education in South Australia in the Nineteenth Century (M.A., University of Adelaide, 1964), pp. 193-204; Mitchell, op. cit., 1969, pp. 52-6; John Ramsland, 'Living and Working Conditions for Teachers in a New South Wales Country District 1850-1900', *Papers of 10th annual conference ANZHES* (Newcastle University, 1980), pp. 10-16. For general wage movements and economic fluctuations see W. A. Sinclair, *The Process of Economic Development in Australia* (Cheshire, Melbourne, 1976), pp. 126-61; N. G. Butlin, *Australian Domestic Product, Investment and Foreign Borrowings 1861-1938/39* (Cambridge University Press, 1962), ch. 14 (Victorian teachers' salaries) and ch. 23 (Price indexes).

40 Queensland, *Report of the Civil Service Commission, 1888* (hereafter CSC), pp. 237-9;

Saunders, op. cit., p. 202; Low, op. cit., p. 6; *AS*, May 1886, pp. 356-7.

[41] Queensland, *CSC*, op. cit., p. 240. Education Department of Victoria, special case no. 864, VLTA (PROV). Kate Ashford, The status of women teachers in Victoria 1888-1914 (M.Ed., Monash University, 1981), pp. 198-202; Noeline Williamson, 'The Natural Destiny': the education of girls in NSW 1848-1912 (Ph.D., Newcastle University, 1983), pp. 346-55.

[42] For women teachers' working conditions see: Noeline Williamson, 'The Employment of Female Teachers in NSW Small Bush Schools 1880-1890', *Labour History*, vol. 43 (1982), pp. 1-12; Duke, op. cit., pp. 149-52; Ashford, op. cit., pp. 121-3, 193-6; Queensland, *CSC*, op. cit., pp. 207-11, 239-40.

[43] Mitchell, op. cit., 1969, p. 67.

[44] Ashford, op. cit., p. 138.

[45] Sinclair, op. cit., pp. 155-7.

[46] Duke, op. cit., p. 43. Queensland resignation rate was 14% p.a., 1882-1887, 'due to the prevailing want of the system and the inconsiderate and harsh treatment to which teachers are subjected', *CSC*, op. cit., p. 15.

[47] R. J. W. Selleck, 'Mary Helena Stark, the Troubles of a Nineteenth Century State School Teacher', *Melbourne Studies in Education* (hereafter *MSE*), *1982* (Melbourne University Press, 1983), pp. 141-60, and Duke, op. cit., pp. 159-70, deals with other special cases, including court cases of Victorian teachers on questions of pensions, classification, etc.

[48] This analysis is based on Margaret Archer's theory of the development of state education systems in *Social Origins of Educational Systems* (Sage, London, 1979), pp. 143-216. In its application to Australia I have relied on A. G. Austin, *Australian Education 1788-1900* (Pitman, Carlton, 3rd edition, 1972), pp. 112-72.

[49] Indicators of growth in education departments during the 1880s were (excluding Tasmania established 1885 and WA 1893): Total number of teachers, including pupil-teachers, etc., nearly doubled between 1880 and 1891 in Victoria, increased by 80% in NSW, 72% in SA and 63% in Queensland. Pupil-teachers (the majority female) as a percentage of all teachers peaked in 1886 from 25% in NSW, to 44% in Queensland. Pupils per teacher in large schools (100+ enrolments) rose to an average of 1:40 from 1:32, except Queensland, 1:28. School attendance as percentage of school enrolments increased from 59% to 71%. The education departments' responses to this overall growth is drawn from A. G. Austin and R. J. W. Selleck, *The Australian Government School 1830-1914* (Pitman, Carlton, 1975), although the commentary and documents in the chapter, 'Disappointment', covers the period 1870-1900; Lawry, op. cit., pp. 366-85; Saunders, op. cit., pp. 174-206; Blake (ed.), op. cit., pp. 279-303.

[50] R. J. W. Selleck, 'State Education and Culture', *Australian Journal of Education*, vol. 26, no. 1 (1982), p. 7.

[51] Victoria, *Report of Royal Commission on the Administration, Organization and General Condition of Education* (1882-84), minutes of evidence, pp. 114-51, 124-7; South Australia, *Report of Commission on the Working of the Education Acts* (1882-83), *Progress Report*, pp. 106-8, 237-8; *Final Report*, p. xi, par. 29; Queensland, *CSC*, op. cit., p. 15, par. 52-3, p. 17, par. 66.

[52] *AS*, July, p. 5, and September 1883, p. 43; criticism of Long's proposal, August 1883, p. 30.

[53] The VLTA was formed in late 1884 following a meeting of women teachers dissatisfied with reductions in their salaries and loss of promotion opportunities following the introduction of the Public Service Act, 1883. (See effects in *AS*, October 1884, p. 43, November 1884, p. 71, February 1885, p. 125.) It was a small union, but was significant in the aspirations of women teachers over the next thirty years. It affiliated with the SSTUV in 1886, but left the central union in 1902. In 1917 it joined with sixth class assistants to form the Women Teachers' Association, which became the women's branch of the VTU in 1926. The women's branch continued until 1976. The VLTA was Australia's first 'permanent' teachers' union. See Judith Biddington, The role of women in the Victorian education department 1872-1925 (M.Ed., University of Melbourne, 1977), pp. 191-242.

[54] S. G. Firth, 'Social Values in the New South Wales Primary School 1880-1914: an analysis of school texts', *MSE*, *1970* (Melbourne University Press, 1970), p. 124. Victoria, *Report of Royal Commission* (1882-84), *First Report*, p. 26.

[55] See reports of these inquiries at n. 51. Victoria, op. cit., pp. 219-20; South Australia, op.

cit., *Final Report*, pp. ix-xi, 108; Queensland, op. cit., pp. 240-2.
56 'The Recollections of Charles Richard Long', *MSE 1963* (Melbourne University Press, 1964), p. 269.
57 Austin, op. cit., p. 252.
58 C. Turney, 'The Rise and Decline of an Australian Inspectorate', *MSE 1970* (Melbourne University Press, 1970), p. 202.
59 AS, February 1886, p. 309.
60 Turney, op. cit., p. 203 (quoting C. B. Newling); H. Young (VTU president), 'The Last Twenty-five Years—a Retrospect', AS, May 1897, p. 225.
61 R. J. W. Selleck, *Frank Tate: a biography* (Melbourne University Press, 1982), p. 36.
62 W. Catton Grasby, 'Our Public Schools' (1891), in Austin and Selleck, op. cit., p. 122.
63 Queensland, CSC, op. cit., p. 15, par. 55-6. The best account of the two men is M. G. Sullivan, Education and the Labour Movement in Queensland, 1890-1910 (M.A., University of Queensland, 1971).
64 The formation of the QTU is from A. D. Spaull, 'The Growth of Teachers' Unionism in Queensland'.
65 McDonald, op. cit., pp. 8-12.
66 Hyams, op. cit., pp. 323-38.
67 J. J. Dempsey, 'The evolution of the Queensland primary school teacher', *Proceedings of Australasian Association for the Advancement of Science, 1909*, (Brisbane, 1909), p. 736. N.B. Between 1876 and 1889, 161 teachers were brought to Queensland from UK, Lawry, op. cit., p. 609.
68 'Noah Little', op. cit., p. 175.
69 C. W. Reinhold, 1904-1907; Peter Airey, 1901-1909, both ALP; James Tolmie, 1901-26, 'Liberal'.
70 P. R. Hart, 'J. A. Lyons, Tasmanian Labor leader', *Labour History*, no. 7 (1965), p. 34.
71 McDonald, op. cit., pp. 9-12, and AS, February 1886, p. 315, April 1886, p. 348.
72 This account is from R. J. W. Selleck, 'John Murphy' in Selleck and M. G. Sullivan (eds), *Not So Eminent Victorians* (Melbourne University Press, forthcoming). The book includes the careers of Patrick Whyte, John Glennon and Clara Weekes.
73 Surveys of teachers had also been used by: Victoria, *Royal Commission into Operation of the System of Public Education* (1867); Victoria, *Royal Commission* (1882-84), op. cit.
74 Queensland, CSC, op. cit., p. 15, par. 54; for acknowledgement of work of teachers and associations, ibid., p. 13, par. 45, and *Queensland Parliamentary Debates*, 55, 1888, p. 819 (Unmack). St Ledger's role in the inquiry and QTU is from Spaull, op. cit., 1983.
75 *Queensland Education Journal* (hereafter *QEJ*) became *Queensland Teachers' Journal*, 1924+.
76 D. Ewart to J. Anderson, minute, 28 April 1896, EDU/A 262, Queensland State Archives.
77 Duke, op. cit., pp. 178-85.
78 These newspapers were: *Age* (Melbourne); *South Australian Register*; *Queensland Times* (Ipswich); *Telegraph* (Brisbane); *Sydney Morning Herald*, Launceston *Examiner*; also *Geelong Advertiser*, which had called for a teachers' union as early as 14 June 1854. The Melbourne *Argus*'s opposition to strong teacher unionism can be seen in its editorial on the SSTUV, 12 October 1886.
79 Geoffrey Blainey, *A Land Half Won* (Macmillan, Melbourne, 1980), p. 235.
80 R. M. Martin, *Whitecollar Unions in Australia* (Australian Institute of Political Science, Melbourne, 1965), p. 2. See also K. F. Walker, 'White collar trade unions in Australia', in A. Sturmthal (ed.), *White Collar Trade Unions* (University of Illinois Press, Urbana, 1966), pp. 1-15; G. E. Caiden, *Public Employment Arbitration in Australia* (University of Michigan, Ann Arbor, 1971).
81 *Gympie Times*, 20 October 1888.
82 *QEJ*, September 1895, p. 5; December 1895, p. 3. N.B. The SSTUV was formed during the prolonged stevedoring dispute in 1886, the QTU just after the bitter Miners' Strike at Newcastle 1888. These unions appeared unconcerned at effects of industrial turbulence on members.
83 Spaull, op. cit., 1983. N.B., teachers' unions in mining towns like Sandhurst, Kalgoorlie and Charters Towers were more visible in their central unions and seemed to attract a higher membership of teachers than elsewhere.
84 *Courier*, 12 January 1889.

[85] *QEJ*, April 1895, pp. 23-5.

[86] Mitchell, op. cit., 1969, p. 55.

[87] Ibid., p. 64. The New South Wales Public School Teachers' Institute was established in 1895, mainly as a Head Teachers' group. In 1896-97 an Assistants' union was formed. In 1898 the Institute decided to form a 'general union', which became the New South Wales Public School Teachers' Association.

[88] Ibid., p. 64. Mitchell used 'remarkable' from a teacher's comment of the period.

[89] Ibid., p. 65-82.

[90] Brodribb's attitude to Victorian teachers can be seen in *AS*, April 1881, p. 152.

[91] *Freeman's Journal*, 7 February 1885, in Mitchell, op. cit., p. 55.

[92] For Callaghan, see *Australian Dictionary of Biography*, vol. 7, p. 527; for Matthews, *Australian Dictionary of Biography*, vol. 5, pp. 227-8.

[93] N.B. After its formation the SSTUV had an estimated 1700 members or 56% of eligible teachers, but pupil-teachers may have also belonged to country associations. The QTU had 1199 members in 1891 or 32% of eligible teachers, but it excluded pupil-teachers (until 1916).

[94] See n. 82; and Clemon's address to the TSSTA Congress, *AS*, July 1902, p. 5.

[95] *AS*, April 1888, p. 149.

[96] Mitchell, op. cit., 1969, p. 77.

[97] In 1911 the New South Wales Teachers' Union was formed. It affiliated with the TLC and Labor Party and survived as a separate union until 1916.

[98] A. D. Spaull, 'The influence of the compulsory arbitration system on the development of teacher unionism in Australia' (paper to American Education Research Association Annual Conference, Montreal, 1983).

[99] In all states, except Victoria and Tasmania, this was achieved by the state industrial arbitration system or government legislation, which insisted on the 'compulsory arbitration' principle of dealing with only one union of employees in each 'industry'. Victoria and Tasmania had a wages board system; therefore, no such principles applied. For other reasons teachers' unions in both states sought access to the Commonwealth Arbitration Court. To gain the required registration as an industrial union state branches formed the Federal State School Teachers' Union of Australia. Thus Victoria's six unions merged to become the Victorian Teachers' Union in 1926. However, the High Court ruled in 1929 that there could not be a federal award for teachers arising from an industrial dispute, as teaching was not an 'industry', as defined by the Arbitration Act. Victorian teachers were left with the VTU—until major 'breakaways' from it occurred by secondary teachers (1948) and technical teachers (1967). Nine unions had been approved by the Teachers' Tribunal (estab. 1946) before its abolition in 1982. In 1984 the VTU, VSTA and TTUV were moving slowly towards some type of confederation.

7

THE CONTEXT OF THE REORGANIZATION OF TERTIARY EDUCATION IN AUSTRALIA— A NATIONAL PERSPECTIVE[1]

by PETER KARMEL

The purpose of this paper is to examine the historical context of the changes in the organization of tertiary education in Australia that occurred in 1981-82. I am conscious that, having been personally involved in the development of tertiary education over the whole period, I may not be sufficiently distanced from what has been happening to make fully objective judgements. However, this paper is intended to offer some insights into what has been happening.

The Genesis of the Present System

The Committee on the Future of Tertiary Education in Australia was the genesis of the present system of tertiary education. This committee, chaired by Sir Leslie Martin, was appointed in August 1961 to consider 'the pattern of tertiary education in relation to the needs and resources of Australia' and to make recommendations to the Australian Universities Commission 'on the future development of tertiary education'. At that date, the term 'tertiary education' corresponded to what today we call 'higher education'.

The Martin Committee was established in the context of an accelerating growth of universities and a concern whether their continued expansion was the most appropriate way of responding to the expanding demand for higher education. There appear to have been three factors behind the committee's establishment. First, there was the question whether the range of courses available in universities was adequate to the needs of young people seeking higher education:

> Australian universities have grown up according to a uniform and traditional pattern, and it is unrealistic to imagine that they alone can provide the variety of education needed by young people with a varying range of abilities and a broad array of educational objectives. The

Committee believes that much of the pressure on young people by parents, relatives, friends and teachers in urging them to undertake university courses, together with their own desire to do so, is due to the lack of other tertiary institutions of comparable status in the eyes of the community. The known needs of the community for young people trained for a wide range of occupations have led the Committee to recommend the expansion, improvement and establishment of appropriate institutions to provide a wider diversity of tertiary education.[2]

Secondly, there was concern at high failure rates in universities, particularly among part-time students.[3] Thirdly, there was the matter of costs. Continued rapid expansion of universities would be expensive. It was expected that expenditure per student in non-university institutions would be lower than in universities.[4]

A great many recommendations emerged from the Martin Committee when its main volume was completed in August 1964. Those of importance for the present discussion were:

(1) There should be a greater diversity of tertiary educational institutions. This could be achieved by the development of three distinct categories of major tertiary institutions:

  (a) Universities;
  (b) Institutes of Colleges;
  (c) Boards of Teacher Education.[5]

The constituent organizations of the Institutes of Colleges might include technical colleges, agricultural colleges, specialist institutions and such new tertiary institutions as might be recommended.[6] However, technical colleges, and particularly the Victorian system of technical colleges, were to be the foundation on which the new sector of tertiary education was to be built.[7] The Boards of Teacher Education would relate to the teachers colleges in the same way as the Institutes of Colleges would relate to their constituent organizations.[8]

(2) The distinction between university and college work was made in the following terms:

> The objective of the education provided by a technical college is to equip men and women for the practical world in industry and commerce, teaching them the way in which manufacturing and business are carried on and the fundamental rules which govern their successful operation. The university course, on the other hand, tends to emphasize the development of knowledge and the importance of research; in so doing it imparts much information which is valuable to the practical man but which is often incidental to the main objective. Both types

of education are required by the community, and in increasing amounts, but it is important that students receive the kind of education best suited to their innate abilities and purposes in life. At present, certain pressures tend to overtax the academic ability of a considerable segment of the student population which could be better provided for in institutions offering courses of different orientation and less exacting academically.[9]

Part-time study at universities was to be discouraged. External studies should not be a university function. Universities should not offer sub-graduate diplomas.[10] The Institutes of Colleges should offer three-year, or equivalent part-time, post-matriculation courses leading to a diploma. In due course, selected institutions might be encouraged to offer post-diploma courses leading to a degree in technology to be awarded by an appropriate body.[11] Boards of Teacher Education might at a later stage also be authorized to grant professional degrees.[12]

(3) The Australian Universities Commission should be enlarged and renamed the Australian Tertiary Education Commission and charged with the specific responsibility of ensuring a balanced development of all forms of tertiary education in Australia.[13]

The Commonwealth Government accepted the main thrust of the Martin Report. In his Ministerial Statement on the Report, the then Prime Minister (Sir Robert Menzies) indicated that his Government accepted the broad concept of developing 'advanced education in virtually new types of colleges'.[14] However, financial support would be confined to assistance for strengthening, expanding and introducing diploma courses:

> We have noted the Committee's suggestion that at some time in the future the new Institutes of Colleges that it envisages may build on present proposals in order to provide post-diploma courses leading to degrees. But the support now pledged by the Commonwealth will not go beyond supporting the basic concept of the Committee as to new type colleges with a variety of advanced courses leading on completion to a diploma.[15]

The Prime Minister emphasized that the new institutions should resist the temptation to copy the educational processes and curricula of universities.

The Government's endorsement of the concept of Institutes of Colleges did not extend to that of Boards of Teacher Education. The Prime Minister indicated clearly that the Commonwealth was not prepared to enter that field. Nor was the Government willing to endorse the Committee's views on part-time and external studies in universities (so eliminating what was, in the Committee's mind, an important distinction between universities and colleges), or the establishment of a tertiary education commission. In lieu of the latter, it established a special advisory body on advanced education.

The Period 1965 to 1975

The term 'colleges of advanced education' is not to be found in the Martin Report, although it was used in the *First Report* of the Commonwealth Advisory Committee on Advanced Education.[16] The words 'advanced education' were used in the Prime Minister's statement. Senator J. G. Gorton (as he then was), as Minister in Charge of Commonwealth Activities in Education and Research, first used the term 'college of advanced education' in May 1965 in his concluding address in the Senate debate on the presentation of the Martin Report.[17] Funds for colleges of advanced education flowed from 1965 for capital purposes, and from 1967 for recurrent purposes. By the end of the second triennium (1972), there were 43 colleges of advanced education, in which 53 500 students were enrolled. Over the same period the universities continued to expand rapidly, student numbers rising from 83 300 in 1965 to 128 100 in 1972.

In February 1972 the Senate Standing Committee on Education, Science and the Arts reported on the Commonwealth's role in teacher education. It recommended that teachers colleges be granted financial assistance for recurrent and capital expenditure under terms and conditions similar to those for colleges of advanced education. It also recommended that existing teacher training institutions, when not associated with a university, should, as far as possible, be incorporated into colleges of advanced education, and that new institutions should be planned as part of multi-purpose institutions; single-purpose teachers colleges should be removed from the direct control of state departments of education.[18]

As pointed out above, the Commonwealth's response to the Martin Report had precluded the admission of teachers colleges into the Commonwealth-supported system of tertiary education. The Commonwealth had remained opposed to support for single-purpose teachers colleges, although some multi-purpose CAEs had established courses in education with Commonwealth support. After consultation with state Ministers for Education, the Commonwealth Government decided to accept from 1 July 1973 the recommendation of the Senate Standing Committee that teachers colleges become part of the advanced education sector. The Commonwealth indicated that the new arrangements would apply to teachers colleges which were being developed as self-governing institutions under the supervision of state co-ordinating bodies, and that it continued to favour the development of teacher education in multi-purpose institutions wherever possible.[19] At that time there were 39 state teachers colleges and pre-school teachers colleges, enrolling over 32 500 students.[20] It is important to note that the Martin Committee had envisaged teacher education as a separate sector from universities and colleges of advanced education. The Commonwealth Government's decision of August 1972 to admit the teachers colleges to the advanced education system radically changed the nature of the advanced education sector.

The Martin Committee had intended that the quality and status of the technical colleges and similar institutions should be raised to the point where they would become genuine alternative avenues for higher education in Australia. However, there were to be clear distinctions between the two sectors. The universities were to move in the direction of full-time internal study, more graduate work, an academic orientation and a concern with scholarship and research. The colleges were to be practically oriented to industry and commerce, flexible in their teaching methods and admission arrangements, and essentially diploma-granting institutions. These clear distinctions did not survive for long. The Commonwealth Advisory Committee on Advanced Education, and subsequently the Australian Commission on Advanced Education, while resisting pressure both from institutions and from state authorities, gave way slowly but surely in such matters as the granting of bachelors' degrees, the provision of masters' degrees, support for applied research, and the provision of liberal arts courses.

When the Commonwealth Advisory Committee was established in 1965, its terms of reference reflected the Prime Minister's injunction on degrees and included a prohibition on the funding of degree courses.[21] This prohibition continued for several years. In July 1968 the Commonwealth Government appointed a Committee of Inquiry into Awards in Colleges of Advanced Education. This Committee reported in June 1969 and recommended the adoption of common nomenclature for awards in advanced education, including the award of bachelors' degrees for the completion of certain courses in advanced education.[22] Later that year the Minister for Education indicated that the Commonwealth would be prepared to provide financial assistance for degree courses in colleges of advanced education where the standard of those courses had been endorsed by a national consultative body.[23] The establishment of the Australian Council for Awards in Advanced Education followed in 1971. Accordingly, the prohibition on the funding of degree courses disappeared from the terms of reference of the Australian Commission on Advanced Education which succeeded the Commonwealth Advisory Committee late in 1971.[24]

The consequences of these moves was that the effect of the original injunction on degrees was minimal. The first degrees in CAEs had been granted in 1968, when the Victoria Institute of Colleges had awarded degrees to graduates of the Victorian College of Pharmacy. Several years later the Commission on Advanced Education was indicating concern with the tendency to convert diploma into degree courses;[25] indeed, by 1972, 13 out of 43 colleges were offering degrees and 28 per cent of enrolments were in degree courses. From the early 1970s degree courses burgeoned, so that by 1978 more than one-half of enrolments in CAEs were at degree level.

In the *First Report* (1966) of the Commonwealth Advisory Committee, the Committee had stated that too much emphasis should not be placed on entry standards;[26] by 1976 the Commission was stating that students commencing courses of advanced education should either have completed a full secondary education or demonstrated that they had a high probability of successfully completing a tertiary course.[27]

In its *Third Report* (1972), the Commission was already expressing concern that the original intention of a strong emphasis on practical application was tending to be changed by academic pressures.[28] Three years later the Commission was noting the expansion of liberal studies courses and was reaffirming that priority should be given to courses with a specific vocational bias.[29]

As far as research was concerned, the Commonwealth Advisory Committee in its *First Report* argued that, while some members of staff could be expected to devote a measure of their time to investigations having a direct application to industry, there was comparatively little scope for research in the colleges;[30] by 1972 the Commission discussed research in some detail, endorsed the interest of college academics in applied research, and indicated that colleges should provide a small measure of both time and space for these activities.[31]

The difficulty of defining the respective missions of universities and colleges was enhanced when the teachers colleges were admitted to the advanced education sector. In 1974, 41 per cent of enrolments in advanced education were in teacher education, compared with 7 per cent in 1972. In fact, by 1974 the balance of full-time and part-time enrolments was rather similar in both university and advanced education sectors, while the proportion of enrolments in courses with a scientific or technological orientation was greater in universities than in CAEs. Advanced education still had a major vocational orientation, although there were a number of courses which were not strictly vocational. It could, of course, be argued that the non-vocational element of many university courses is also comparatively small; indeed, professional bodies influence many university courses in much the same way as they do CAE courses.

At the end of 1973 the Universities Commission drew attention to a certain blurring of the distinction between universities and colleges, and commented as follows:

> Since the inception of the college concept, the colleges have had a role in providing education which is both complementary and alternative to that offered by universities. The college role is *complementary* to the extent that it offers courses which differ in content from those offered by universities (more specifically, vocational courses in a greater variety of fields) and courses at levels less demanding academically than those of university degree standard. The college role is *alternative* to the extent that it offers genuine tertiary education in geographical areas which could not reasonably be expected to support a university (in particular, in country towns) and to the extent that it provides courses in disciplines (for example, engineering) which offer students real alternatives to university courses in those disciplines. Under these circumstances, it is to be expected that the functions of colleges will overlap those of universities and that there will be blurring in the distinction between them, particularly between the larger metropolitan colleges and the universities. The blurring does not itself represent a confusion of purpose, although any attempt on the part of colleges to model themselves on universities might well destroy the basic objectives of college development.[32]

The Commission went on to say that, while it was difficult to define universities and colleges in generic terms, the two sectors could be characterized by differences in a number of attributes. It listed ten, and pointed out that 'although a particular college may not differ from a particular university in respect of each of the above factors, taken as a whole they enable a broad distinction to be drawn between universities and colleges'.[33]

By 1975 a great deal of diversification had taken place in both the university and advanced education sectors. The 'uniform and traditional pattern' of Australian universities, referred to by the Martin Committee,[34] had been modified: universities such as Macquarie University, Flinders University and Griffith University had been established with different organizational structures; strong graduate schools had developed in some disciplines in some institutions; some universities had liberalized entry requirements; course orientations had changed; faculty patterns varied among institutions. Greater diversification had occurred within and among colleges. The Williams Committee classified colleges into five groups reflecting this diversification, namely:

- central institutes of technology (large metropolitan institutions with a great diversity of studies);
- regional colleges (institutions with a considerable range of studies serving a local region);

- smaller metropolitan multi-purpose colleges;
- colleges predominantly engaged in teacher education;
- specialized small institutions.[35]

From 1972 to 1975 the colleges underwent extraordinary growth from 81 000 enrolments to 125 000, an increase of 54 per cent in the space of one triennium. On the other hand, the growth of the universities began to slacken: by 1975 the college enrolment had expanded to 85 per cent of the university enrolment.

As a result of this growth, and the assumption from the beginning of 1974 of full funding for universities and CAEs instead of shared commonwealth/state funding, increasing concern began to be expressed about possible duplication of courses. In May 1975 the Whitlam Government announced its intention of combining the Universities Commission and the Commission on Advanced Education into a single tertiary education commission for higher education. This decision was given greater impetus when, in the middle of 1975, the four independent Commissions (schools and TAFE as well as universities and CAEs) produced financial recommendations for the 1976-78 triennium which, in aggregate, the Government considered to be well beyond its budgetary capacity. Universities and colleges had now clearly become competitors for students and funds. Furthermore, the two higher education Commissions were operating on different planning assumptions—the student projections of the Commission on Advanced Education were well in excess of those of the Universities Commission.[36]

A report was prepared by a working party comprising the Secretary of the Department of Education and the Chairmen of the two Commissions.[37] The report recommended that a single tertiary education commission, with two statutory councils, be established, and also proposed a two-stage procedure to ensure that the new commission operated within basic parameters laid down by the Government. Legislation to establish a tertiary education commission was before the Senate on the day that the Government fell in November 1975.

The Period 1976 to 1980

The pressures for co-ordination noted in the last section, together with the financial constraints which became evident in 1975, produced increasing concern about unnecessary duplication both within and between the two sectors. Moreover, the establishment of institutions and courses had been predicated on an extrapolation of growth in student numbers that now seemed unlikely to be realized; many institutions were faced with small levels of enrolment, and in some fields there appeared to be too many courses.

This situation led to comprehensive inquiries into post-secondary education in four states: Western Australia (1976), Tasmania (1976), Victoria (1978) and South Australia (1979).[38] In addition, an investigation was made into the co-ordination of CAEs in the Sydney inner metropolitan area in 1977.[39] The four comprehensive inquiries recommended the establishment of co-ordinating machinery across the three sectors of post-secondary education (university, advanced education, and technical and further education (TAFE)). All of the above reports, other than the Victorian one, advocated the consolidation of colleges. The Victorian Committee stated that there were several institutions about whose present state and future prospects it had serious doubts, and that, if proposals for development of TAFE-type courses in these institutions proved to be impractical, then the question of their continued existence should be carefully examined by the proposed Victorian Post-Secondary Education Commission.

The Tertiary Education Commission was established in the middle of 1977. Technical and further education, in which the Commonwealth had been taking an increasing interest since the report of the Australian Committee on Technical and Further Education had been completed in 1974,[40] was included within a revised definition of tertiary education. Thus, the new Commission had the responsibility of co-ordinating three sectors of tertiary education—universities, CAEs (comprising higher education) and TAFE. This ensured that the Commonwealth authorities would be paying more attention to the interfaces of the sectors and to achieving rationalization and avoiding unnecessary duplication. The first major report of the TEC was produced in February 1978.[41] This was published only eight months after the establishment of the Commission, during which period a report for the year 1978 had also been produced. The report did not go into intersectoral matters in any great detail; this was to come in 1981.[42] However, in August 1978, the Commission discussed reductions in enrolments in teacher education at some length, drew attention to warnings that had been issued in earlier reports in respect of the need to reduce staff in teacher education, and stated clearly that 'In some cases, particularly in the college sector, reductions in the numbers and size of institutions may be necessary'.[43]

In September 1976 the Commonwealth Government appointed a committee of inquiry into education and training, chaired by Professor B. R. Williams. One of the terms of reference was to consider and advise on 'the overall pattern of institutions and courses including their objectives'. The Williams Committee reported in February 1979.[44] The Report contained no recommendations for major structural changes in tertiary education, although there were many recommendations in relation to the operations of the institutions and to the relative rates of growth of the sectors. The

Committee noted that, while it believed that enrolments in advanced education would rise over the next twenty years, prospects for growth might be affected by the expected decline in enrolments in pre-service teacher education.[45] The Committee also took the view that small institutions were not necessarily expensive, and did not advocate the closure or amalgamation of any institutions (other than the integration of the activities of the two universities in Western Australia).[46]

In his statement on the Williams Report, the Minister for Education noted that the Committee had not recommended major structural change, but had advocated development within the existing sectors of tertiary education through the process of evolutionary adjustments. The Minister said that 'the overall judgement of the Committee is that the education system is properly constituted to respond to the needs of individuals and the community'. The Government accepted this judgement, and that the future development of the system should be within the present sectors. The Government also accepted that growth in universities should be stabilized and that this should be associated with a greater concentration on postgraduate work and research, and indicated its intention to give priority to the development of the TAFE sector. In respect of advanced education, the Government was more cautious, indicating that, 'the Tertiary Education Commission will advise the Government on the particular fields where future growth, *if any*, might occur'[47] (my italics).

The Year of the Razor

Volume 1 of the Commission's *Report for 1982-84 Triennium*, published in February 1981, was the first major report in which the Commission had an opportunity to consider in detail long-term developments and policies, although warnings of the need for consolidation and rationalization had been issued earlier. The Commission's views on consolidation within the advanced education sector are set out at length in Chapter 5 of Volume 1.[48]

Three main factors provided the context in which the Commission formed its views. First, it was clear that there had been and should continue to be a substantial decline in pre-service teacher education enrolments, and a somewhat lesser one in total teacher education enrolments. Table 1 sets out data on these enrolments. Pre-service enrolments would decline by nearly 30 per cent between 1978 and 1984, and total enrolments by nearly 20 per cent. This decline would impinge with particular severity on single-purpose teachers colleges.

An expansion of enrolments in the technologies and business studies in advanced education was planned to occur concurrently with the decline in teacher education enrolments. This was because demand for such graduates remained high, and many students who would otherwise have enrolled in teacher education were expected to seek enrolment in these fields. This is illustrated in Table 2.

The second factor was the Commission's view that comparatively little growth in enrolments in higher education would be occurring during the 1980s, partly as a result of changes in student preferences and partly because of the clear priority being accorded by the Government to technical and further education.

Thirdly, recurrent funds for higher education had been stabilized over the 1979-81 triennium, and it would have been unrealistic to assume any major change in their availability. This suggested that little expansion in higher education as a whole was feasible and that reductions in resources devoted to teacher education would have to be made.

TABLE 1

Total Students (EFTS) in Teacher Education Courses In Universities and CAEs[49]

(Actual 1978 to 1980, Estimated 1981 to 1984)

	Pre-service	Total
	'000	'000
1978	44.0	64.0
1979	40.5	60.5
1980	36.6	57.1
1981	33.9	54.6
1982	32.0	52.5
1983	31.5	51.9
1984	31.8	52.1

TABLE 2

Estimated Changes in Student Load (EFTS) by Types of Courses in Advanced Education, 1979, 1981 and 1984[50]

	Teacher Education	Science-based	Commerce Social Sciences/ Humanities-based
	'000	'000	'000
1979	49.7	30.1	39.6
1981	45.0	31.9	43.4
1984	42.0	34.9	44.5

Against this background, the Commission proposed the following policy objectives in relation to higher education for the 1982-84 triennium:

• Resources should be reallocated from teacher education to other activities by 1984. Funding for 1984 for CAEs involved in teacher education should reflect their decreased teaching responsibilities; funding for those institutions which were expanding their effort in the technologies and business studies should be increased;
• Institutions predominantly concerned with teacher education should be consolidated into larger units by their incorporation into multi-

purpose or multi-campus CAEs or by integration with neighbouring universities.[51]

As far as the reallocation of resources was concerned, the Commission pointed out that it had three options:

• The existing level of resources devoted to teacher education could be maintained against the need for future expansion;
• Surplus resources in teacher education institutions could be used to permit the diversification of their offerings into fields related to teacher education;
• Resources could be released by the decreased effort in teacher education and reallocated to support other activities, particularly the planned increase in advanced education enrolments in technologies and business studies.

The Commission argued that the maintenance of excess capacity in teacher education could not be justified, and that it would need to seek additional resources for this first option. The second option would involve expansion in general studies courses, the demand for which was not evident. The Commission therefore preferred the third option, which would allow the expansion of courses in demand without requiring significant increases in resources.[52] The decision to reallocate resources from teacher education to the technologies and business studies implied a reduction of activities in those colleges for which teacher education was the major activity. The consolidation of those institutions into larger units was a natural corollary.

In the matter of consolidation, the Commission gave three reasons in favour:

• Larger institutions would be able to exercise greater flexibility in the management of their resources, especially in situations of change or decline in workloads;
• A greater range and improved quality of educational choices could be offered students in larger institutions;
• Economies of scale should result from the establishment of larger institutions, although significant economies were unlikely in the short to medium term.[53]

The Commission was aware of the reluctance of governments to support changes which would affect the future of whole institutions. It had already noted this in its *Statement to Joint Parliamentary Committee of Public Accounts:*

there is usually resistance to measures aimed at major structural changes. The closure of an institution or a substantial reduction in its range of offerings or size almost always evokes substantial opposition because of such factors as the role of the institution in the local community, the threat to the security of employment of staff, and political commitments of governments or local politicians. Resistance to proposals that are threatening to individual institutions ... certainly inhibits moves towards rationalisation. Nevertheless ... adjustments towards a more rational distribution of resources are continually taking place, but they do so within limits imposed by the *realpolitik*.[54]

The Commission did not propose the closure of any institutions, but it proposed mergers through which some institutions would lose their identity. Accordingly, it recommended to the Commonwealth Government that 'the Commonwealth Government support the ... policy relating to rationalisation and reallocation of resources',[55] and it warned the Government that, if this policy were followed, the Commission would be recommending grants to institutions in 1984 which would be consonant with their planned size (i.e., a good deal lower than 1981 grants), 'notwithstanding that these recommendations may evoke strong criticism in some quarters'.[56]

In April 1981 the Prime Minister made a statement to Parliament arising from the Review of Commonwealth Functions which had been undertaken in order to 'streamline and fine down' Commonwealth operations. In this, he said:

> At the tertiary level the Government has been concerned at the proliferation of separate institutions and proposes immediate action to reverse this trend and to provide for more efficient use of resources. Arising from the recommendations of the Tertiary Education Commission, the Government will promote a major rationalisation and reallocation of resources in higher education. This will involve consolidation into larger units of 30 existing colleges of advanced education, for which teacher education is the main activity, by their incorporation into multi-purpose or multi-campus colleges with a single governing body or by integration with neighbouring universities.[57]

The decisions of the so-called Razor Gang in respect of consolidation of CAEs were based on the recommendations of the Commonwealth Tertiary Education Commission, but in no way did the Commission receive instructions from the Government. The decisions implied a more rapid movement towards consolidation: the Government decided that the consolidations should take place by the end of 1981 (although in some cases this was extended to the end of 1982), while the Commission had envisaged that the consolidations would be completed by 1984. Moreover, the Commission had recommended additional funds in 1983 and 1984 for the advanced education sector 'in order to provide adequate resources for

expansion of enrolments in the technologies and business studies . . . while
resources are being released from teacher education programs'.[58] Funds
were provided, but they were not additional to the 1981 level of funding.

In its report, the Commission had illustrated, by way of a table, the
extent of the reductions in intakes in pre-service teacher education in
30 CAEs 'for which teacher education was the major activity'.[59] The
Commission had also recommended that institutions 'which are predominantly concerned with teacher education' be consolidated into larger
units.[60] The table referred to above constituted the list used in the Prime
Minister's statement to define the CAEs that were to be subject to consolidation. It is of interest to note, in passing, that of the 30 colleges 24
were among the original 39 teachers colleges that were admitted to the
advanced education sector in 1973. While a high proportion of these
CAEs had been referred to in the Commission's report as candidates for
consolidation, the Government's decision was more wholesale than had
been set out there.

However, in its progress report on consolidation issued in the middle
of 1981, the Commission reaffirmed its support for consolidation in the
following terms:

> The Commission reaffirms its support for consolidation . . ., notwith-
> standing the particular arguments brought forward by State authori-
> ties in relation to individual institutions. The Commission recognises
> that savings will be difficult to achieve in the early stages of consoli-
> dation.[61]

Implications

To what extent do the decisions of 1981 constitute a 'reorganisation' of
tertiary education in Australia? In its planning for the 1982-84 triennium,
the Commission saw as its main task accommodating the provision of
teacher education courses to the sharp change in the demand for teacher
education graduates. Its recommendations relating to the reallocation of
resources and the consolidation of institutions for which teacher education was the major activity have been largely implemented. They certainly constitute a reorganization of that part of advanced education concerned with teacher education. However, the Commission did not see
itself as restructuring tertiary education as a whole. Moreover, as pointed
out above, the Commonwealth Government is on record as supporting
the Williams Committee recommendations that did not propose major
structural change.

The formation of larger CAEs by merging a number of smaller colleges
under one management hardly constitutes a restructuring of the *system*,
even though it involves major changes to institutions, to the size distribution of CAEs, and to the provision of teacher education courses. The

recent mergers are a continuation of the evolutionary trend in the advanced education sector which has been visible from the early days of advanced education. Since 1965 almost one hundred advanced education institutions have been funded by the Commonwealth at one time or another. The greatest number of CAEs in existence at any one time was 82 in 1976. Prior to the consolidations required by the Review of Commonwealth Functions, there were 68 CAEs; by 1983 the number had been reduced to 45 institutions.[62] The decision to admit the single-purpose teachers colleges to the advanced education sector in 1973 increased the number of CAEs from 42 to 80. To a large extent the 1981 consolidations can be seen as a major modification of this decision.

However, there is still the question of whether the clarity of the sectoral divisions in tertiary education has been affected by the consolidations. In other words, are the events of 1981 the beginning of the end for the binary system? Such effects must relate to the university/college mergers rather than to the consolidations based on merging a number of colleges. In considering this issue a number of points should be noted.

First, there are six universities into which CAEs have been or were intended to be merged. In two of them the merging had already taken place before 1981 (Deakin University in 1975 and University of Tasmania in 1980), and a third was already engaged in this process (University of Wollongong). The possibility of a merger of the University of New England with Armidale College of Advanced Education had been raised as long ago as 1973 in the Cohen Report,[63] and considerable progress had been made before the New South Wales Government decided that the University and the College should remain separate institutions.[64] The possibility of a merger in Townsville had also been raised in the Cohen Report,[65] and referred to in the *Sixth Report* of the Universities Commission.[66] The possibility of university/college mergers in relation to regions with populations too small to support more than one institution of higher education has been discussed since 1973:[67] the development of Deakin University and recent changes in the University of Tasmania are examples.

Secondly, as has already been pointed out, the sharpness of the distinctions drawn by the Martin Committee between universities and colleges of advanced education has always been somewhat theoretical. Blurring occurred as soon as advanced education became established as a formal sector of tertiary education. The blurring has come from both sides of the divide between universities and CAEs. The universities have themselves developed greater flexibility in their entry requirements, and they have moved into some areas in which CAEs had already staked a claim. Although all withdrew from sub-degree work as proposed by the Martin Committee, the university/college mergers will result in some return to this level of academic activity. On the other side, CAEs have moved into degree work to the point that degree work is now the major part of their activities; and some have aggressively pursued the establishment of masters' degrees and the development of research activities.

I doubt if existing distinctions between university bachelor degrees and advanced education bachelor degrees (UG1s) can be maintained in the six universities which have or were intended to have advanced education components; indeed, I doubt the significance of most of these distinctions anyway. Differences in the nature of bachelors' degrees exist among universities and among CAEs. Whether there is a clear distinction between university bachelors and CAE bachelors is a question that I cannot answer, but, at least, there is not supposed to be a distinction between their academic standards.

Four universities are now offering sub-degree diploma courses. These are identifiable, and involve an academic activity of a different kind and with different purposes from those undertaken by the other fifteen universities. Although sub-graduate work may represent a significant minority of the work undertaken by some of the four universities, in aggregate it is likely to amount to only a very small proportion of university enrolments—in 1983, a total of about 1300 students out of 348 000 students in higher education. I do not see this as having a radical effect on either the university or advanced education sectors.

Thirdly, as has also been pointed out earlier, it has never been possible to devise generic definitions to distinguish between universities and CAEs. As recently as 1979 the Tertiary Education Commission set out its views on the typical characteristics reflecting differences in the purposes and functions of colleges compared with universities. In its *Statement to Joint Parliamentary Committee of Public Accounts* it listed fifteen characteristics.[68] These individual characteristics are not black or white. It is simply not possible to predicate a set of conditions which are necessary and sufficient to define a university or a CAE. Collectively, universities are more of this kind and colleges are more of that kind, in respect of a great list of variables. All we can do is to make 'on average' statements. But the heterogeneity of the two sectors together is greater than that of the two sectors taken apart.

Fourthly, since 1977 we have had not a *binary* but a *trinary* tertiary education system. In this, fuzziness occurs on both borders of the advanced education sector. Between universities and CAEs there are border disputes relating to masters' degrees and research; between CAEs and TAFE institutions there are similar disputes on the relationship between associate diploma courses (UG3s) and middle-level certificate courses. Moreover, a limited number of bisectoral institutions exist: there are universities with advanced education components; CAEs with TAFE components; TAFE colleges with advanced education components; community colleges with advanced education and TAFE components. There is no absolute tidiness but, notwithstanding this, the three sectoral divisions remain clear enough.

Conclusion

In my view, we now have a trinary system as entrenched as it, or the former binary system, has ever been. That is to say, formally entrenched but not absolutely rigid. Compared with 1981, some universities have enrolments in sub-graduate diplomas, which, ironically, is a return to pre-Martin days. In 1957 some 19 per cent of university enrolments were in sub-graduate diplomas or certificates; by the 1973-75 triennium such enrolments had virtually disappeared. In 1983 the proportion was less than ½ per cent.

There are distinctions between the sectors that make them readily recognizable in the aggregate. But, for higher education, they are largely differences of degree. These differences are less now than they were in the early days of advanced education. While they will probably moderate further in the future, they are likely to remain sufficient to distinguish the sectors for a long time ahead.

There are also, of course, considerable differences among institutions within sectors. Within advanced education, the range of academic activities within colleges varies a great deal—the large multi-purpose polytechnics being quite different from the small specialized institutions or from the larger newly consolidated institutions. Similarly, universities differ substantially in the range of their faculties. They also differ in their research capabilities, as an examination of the reports of the Australian Research Grants Committee readily shows.

The Commission is likely to continue to support the sectoral division between universities and CAEs on the grounds that diversity of institutions is desirable and the sectoral divide helps to combat the tendency towards increasing homogenization. Given this, some border warfare will continue.

The development of multi-level institutions on a large scale would affect the present trinary system. However, some multi-level institutions have existed since the first days of CAEs, and the recent establishment of community colleges and the merging of some CAEs with universities has been on a comparatively small scale. Thus, I do not see the structure of tertiary education as being affected in any fundamental way by the recent consolidations.

My conclusion is that 'reorganisation' is too strong a term for the events of 1981, and that what has happened is a major readjustment of the resources in higher education devoted to teacher education to meet the changed circumstances of the 1980s. This readjustment will strengthen advanced education in general and a number of institutions (including some universities) in particular to meet the challenges of the 1980s. There will be fewer institutions, but many of them will command considerably more resources than formerly, will have stronger managements and a better capacity to meet emerging demands. Wasteful competitiveness among a larger number of small institutions will be reduced, and advanced education will not be so dominated by the requirements of teacher education. I see the changes that are taking place neither as revolutionary nor as disastrous, but as a further maturing of the Australian system of tertiary education that has been evolving over the past quarter of a century.

NOTES

[1] This paper was delivered at a conference entitled 'The Reorganisation of Tertiary Education in Australia' convened in Toowoomba in July 1982 by the Darling Downs Institute of Advanced Education and the Tertiary Education Authority of South Australia. It was subsequently published with other conference papers in *The Reorganisation of Tertiary Education in Australia* by DDIAE and TEASA and has since been revised for inclusion in the present volume. I am indebted to Mr Lance Hennessy for criticism and advice in its preparation. Opinions expressed in it are, of course, my own.

[2] Committee on the Future of Tertiary Education in Australia (Sir Leslie Martin, Chairman), *Tertiary Education in Australia*, vol. 1, Commonwealth of Australia, August 1964, paragraph 2.61.

[3] Ibid., paragraphs 3.121-3.143.

[4] Ibid., paragraph 8.9.

[5] Ibid., recommendation 6(ii).

[6] Ibid., recommendation 6(iv).

[7] Ibid., paragraphs 6.62 to 6.75.

[8] Ibid., recommendation 6(vi).

[9] Ibid., paragraph 5.137.

[10] Ibid., recommendations 3(xviii), 3(xix), 3(xxi).

[11] Ibid., recommendation 5(iii) and paragraph 5.83.

[12] Ibid., paragraph 4.77.

[13] Ibid., recommendation 6(viii).

[14] Sir Robert Menzies (Prime Minister), 'Tertiary Education in Australia', House of Representatives, *Hansard*, 24 March 1965, pp. 269-70.

[15] Ibid.

[16] Commonwealth Advisory Committee on Advanced Education, *First Report*, 'Colleges of Advanced Education 1967-69', Commonwealth of Australia, June 1966, paragraph 1.5.

[17] Senator J. G. Gorton, Senate, *Hansard*, 11 May 1965, p. 721.

[18] Senate Standing Committee on Education, Science and the Arts (Senator G. S. Davidson, Chairman), *Report on the Commonwealth's Role in Teacher Education*, Canberra, February 1972.

[19] Mr J. M. Fraser (Minister for Education and Science), 'Commonwealth Education Program for 1972-73', House of Representatives, *Hansard*, 17 August 1972, p. 378.

[20] See Special Committee on Teacher Education (Dr S. W. Cohen, Chairman), *Teacher Education 1973-75*, Australian Government Publishing Service, Canberra, 1973.

[21] Commonwealth Advisory Committee on Advanced Education, op. cit., appendix B, p. 57.

[22] Commonwealth Committee of Inquiry (Mr F. M. Wiltshire, Chairman), *Academic*

Awards in Advanced Education, Commonwealth of Australia, June 1969, paragraphs 5.15 and 7.17.
[23] Mr J. M. Fraser (Minister for Education and Science), 'Education', House of Representatives, *Hansard*, 17 September 1969, p. 1440.
[24] Australian Commission on Advanced Education, *Third Report 1973-75*, A.G.P.S., Canberra, 1972, appendix A, p. 115.
[25] Ibid., paragraph 8.7.
[26] Commonwealth Advisory Committee on Advanced Education, op. cit., paragraph 2.34.
[27] Australian Commission on Advanced Education, *Report 1977-1979: Recommendations for 1977*, A.G.P.S., Canberra, 1976, paragraph 2.3.
[28] Australian Commission on Advanced Education, *Third Report*, paragraph 1.8.
[29] Australian Commission on Advanced Education, *Fourth Report 1976-1978*, A.G.P.S., Canberra, 1975, paragraph 3.32.
[30] Commonwealth Advisory Committee on Advanced Education, op. cit., paragraph 2.40.
[31] Australian Commission on Advanced Education, *Third Report*, paragraphs 9.54-9.61.
[32] Australian Universities Commission, *Report on the Proposal of the Government of Victoria for a Fourth University in Geelong, Ballarat and Bendigo*, A.G.P.S., Canberra, 1974, paragraph 3.3.
[33] Ibid., paragraph 3.4.
[34] Martin, op. cit., paragraph 2.61.
[35] Committee of Inquiry into Education and Training (Professor B. R. Williams, Chairman), *Education, Training and Employment*, A.G.P.S., Canberra, February 1979, vol. 1, paragraphs 6.27-6.40.
[36] Australian Universities Commission, *Sixth Report*, A.G.P.S., Canberra, 1975, paragraphs 5.9-5.30.
[37] *Report of the Panel to Advise on Arrangements for Amalgamating the Universities Commission and the Commission on Advanced Education* (Mr K. N. Jones, Convener), Canberra, August 1975.
[38] Committee on Post-Secondary Education (Professor P. H. Partridge, Chairman), *Post-Secondary Education in Western Australia*, Perth, January 1976; Committee on Post-Secondary Education in Tasmania (Emeritus Professor P. H. Karmel, Chairman), *Post-Secondary Education in Tasmania*, A.G.P.S., Canberra, February 1976; The Post-Secondary Education Committee of Inquiry, Victoria (Emeritus Professor P. H. Partridge, Chairman), *Report*, Melbourne, March 1978; Committee of Inquiry into Post-Secondary Education in South Australia (Dr D. S. Anderson, Chairman), *Post-Secondary Education in South Australia*, Adelaide, January 1979.
[39] The Committee Established by the Higher Education Board to Review the Future Development of Colleges of Advanced Education in the Inner City Areas of Sydney (Emeritus Professor G. J. Butland, Chairman), *Report*, Sydney, April 1977.
[40] Australian Committee on Technical and Further Education (Mr M. Kangan, Chairman), *TAFE in Australia*, Report on Needs in Technical and Further Education, vol. 1, A.G.P.S., Canberra, 1975.
[41] Tertiary Education Commission, *Report for 1979-81 Triennium*, A.G.P.S., Canberra, 1978, vol. 1.
[42] Tertiary Education Commission, *Report for 1982-84 Triennium*, 'Recommendations on Guidelines', A.G.P.S., Canberra, 1981, vol. 1, part 1.
[43] Tertiary Education Commission, *Report for 1979-81 Triennium*, 'Recommendations for 1979', Canberra, August 1978, vol. 2, paragraphs 3.21 to 3.31.
[44] Williams, op. cit., vol. 1.
[45] Ibid., paragraph R17.16.
[46] Ibid., paragraphs R6.24 and R5.33.
[47] Senator J. Carrick (Minister for Education), 'Report of the Committee of Inquiry into Education and Training', Senate, *Hansard*, 22 November 1979, pp. 2782-2788.
[48] Tertiary Education Commission, *Report for 1982-84 Triennium*, vol. 1, part 1, pp. 137-65.
[49] Ibid., Tables 4.10 and 4.13.
[50] Ibid., Table 5.3.
[51] Ibid., paragraphs 5.30 and 5.78.

[52] Ibid., paragraphs 5.19-5.29.

[53] Ibid., paragraphs 5.42-5.45.

[54] Tertiary Education Commission, *Statement to Joint Parliamentary Committee of Public Accounts: Inquiry into Funding of Tertiary Education*, Canberra, September 1979, paragraph 2.70.

[55] Tertiary Education Commission, *Report for 1982-84 Triennium*, vol. 1, part 1, paragraph 5.78.

[56] Ibid., paragraph 5.80.

[57] Mr J. M. Fraser (Prime Minister), 'Review of Commonwealth Functions', House of Representatives, *Hansard*, 30 April 1981, pp. 1830-53.

[58] Tertiary Education Commission, *Report for 1982-84 Triennium*, vol. 1, part 1, paragraph 5.78.

[59] Ibid., Table 5.1.

[60] Ibid., paragraph 5.78.

[61] Commonwealth Tertiary Education Commission, *Progress Report on Consolidation in Advanced Education*, Canberra, July 1981, paragraph 5.

[62] Of the 30 colleges which were to be consolidated, four have retained their separate identities; of these, two were to have merged with the University of New England and the University of Newcastle respectively.

[63] Cohen, op. cit., paragraph 7.9.

[64] Australian Universities Commission, *Sixth Report*, paragraph 3.90.

[65] Cohen, op. cit., paragraph 7.34.

[66] Australian Universities Commission, *Sixth Report*, paragraph 3.96.

[67] See ibid., chapter 8; and Karmel, op. cit., chapter 7.

[68] Paragraph 1.39.

8

SEX, SCHOOLS AND EMERGING
OCCUPATIONAL INTERESTS

by F. D. NAYLOR

The salience of interests as determinants of vocational aspiration, occupational choice and job satisfaction has been a serious part of the theoretical underpinning of vocational research for many years. The conceptual role of 'interests' in the many theories of careers and occupational choice occurs primarily as an aspect of motivation.[1] In some theories they are more clearly or primarily motivational, though in all theories they tend to have that character. Thereby they serve to energize and activate occupational behaviour, to define its goals and objectives, and to maintain persistence and consistency in performance.

The origins of interests are obscure, which is not to say that firm views about those origins are not held or expressed.[2] The motivational aspect suggests affective and dynamic components that might be stylistic rather than defined in terms of particular content. Thus, an orientation of breadth versus depth of interest might relate to more general orientations to the world (extroversion versus introversion), to preferred strategies of dealing with the world (e.g. attention to detail), and to persistence in achieving mastery (e.g. time on task).[3]

The acquisition of these personal dynamics might be a function of some combination of native endowment and early experience. The relative weight to be given to these might vary according to other facets of a theorist's or researcher's value-commitments, but it seems agreed that the style is a recognizable and identifiable part of the personality by mid-adolescence.[4] From this point elaboration of the style rather than basic change in it seems to be the hallmark of its further development.

Interests are more commonly thought of in terms of their content. Interests have objects: one is interested *in* rather than merely interested. Characterization of interests purely in terms of content would be incomplete, however. The notions of frequency and intensity of interests, in addition to the object of an interest, are necessary to a comprehensive understanding of their nature, and the ways in which they vary between and within individuals. In fact it is with this variation that theoretical

189

accounts of interest are basically concerned. The differences between people are a major source of this variation in the measurement of interests, and theories are concerned to describe the psychological characteristics of this variation.

Occupational Interests

The uses of interest measurement in career guidance and vocational research have their origins in a tradition of 'matching men with jobs' that goes back to the work of Parsons in 1909.[5] His approach has provided an implicit basis for many guidance practices, and the development of interest measures. E. K. Strong began the development of the Strong Vocational Interest Blank (SVIB)[6] at Stanford University in the 1920s, publishing his first article on interest measurement in 1926.[7] Over a half-century later the SVIB became the merged form of the Strong-Campbell Interest Inventory (SCII)[8] and inspired the development of the Career Assessment Inventory (CAI).[9]

Strong's work was based on the proposition that men in different jobs have different interests, and the SVIB was developed with the aim of identifying those interests. His approach was manifestly empirical, seeking to establish those expressed preferences that distinguished an occupational group from men in general. Its longevity is testimony to its usefulness in guidance.

The adequacy of a strictly empirical or 'dust-bowl'[10] approach to defining the interests of particular groups is questionable both in terms of practical limitations and theoretical understanding. The *Dictionary of Occupational Titles (DOT)*[11] contains entries for over 12 000 occupations, and presumably it would be possible in principle to define a unique interest profile for each of those occupations. In practice, however, the difficulties would be formidable if not insurmountable, and the results would be a mass of data not organized or accounted for in any theoretical sense. Theories of occupational interests attempt to explain existing data, and to predict what future data should look like. In other words they are attempts to achieve a general understanding of all occupational interest data using as few concepts, propositions and hypotheses as are consistent with the data. An adequate theory of occupational interests should enable us to make well-informed guesses (hypotheses) about what the interest profiles of particular occupations look like.

In measurement, interests commonly are inferred from expressed preferences, these in turn being indicated by responses to inventory items. Analyses of data derived from many and diverse inventories showed that the configurations of item scales were similar in all inventories.[12] This implied that they might be similarly interpretable psychologically, and such an interpretation is put forward in Holland's theory of careers.

Holland's theory

Holland first outlined his theory of vocational choices in 1959,[13] and by 1973[14] it had, after revision and supplementation, become a very significant contribution to occupational psychology. The theory proposes that the world of work and persons can be described in terms of a six-category typology: Realistic, Investigative, Artistic, Social, Enterprising, Conventional (RIASEC). These categories represent the key concepts in the theory, and they can be used to classify and understand occupations or persons. It is useful to think of each category as an interest theme that runs through or is characteristic of an occupation or person. Thus we can speak of Realistic occupations and mean that they are characterized by Realistic interest themes. We can speak of Enterprising persons and mean that their interests are characteristically Enterprising. Note that characteristically does not imply exclusively: people and occupations might not fit neatly into one RIASEC theme.

The resemblance of persons to the types is indicated in their *personality pattern* which is expressed in a three-letter code derived from the six interest themes. Persons in particular occupations tend to have typical codes. Thus primary teachers, for example, tend to have the code SAE, which means that their interests are Social, Artistic and Enterprising, in that order. Their working environments support and reinforce these interests because of the kinds of people primary teachers tend to be and the kinds of work in which they are involved. Holland believes that this interaction of persons and environments is what characterizes the world of work.

The qualities of persons and environments that are indicated by each of the six interest themes are outlined briefly below. A full account is contained in Holland's book.[15]

REALISTIC: Realistic environments are characterized by manual and technical demands that stimulate the use of machines and tools in the interests of technical competence and achievement. People in these environments (Realistic types) tend to see the world in straightforward terms without complications. The environment rewards those who hold conventional values and prize material possessions. Realistic types tend to see themselves as competent in activities involving manual and technical skills.

INVESTIGATIVE: Investigative environments are constituted by demands for intellectual and scientific investigation of natural and social phenomena. Investigative types see themselves as scholarly, and able in mathematics and the sciences. They see the world as complex and abstract, and they approach it critically and with curiosity. The environment tends to reward rational and analytic behaviour. The people in it place a high value on scientific activity.

ARTISTIC: Artistic environments foster creative activities in all the art forms. Artistic types regard themselves as creative and original, sensitive to aesthetic qualities, and see the world in complex and abstract ways. The environment rewards ambiguous and free activities and emotional, imaginative and introspective behaviour.

SOCIAL: Social environments are characteristic of the helping professions such as teaching and nursing. People in these environments are susceptible to social and humanitarian influences and like close interaction with others. They see themselves as tactful, responsible, helpful and understanding, and they value social and ethical activities.

ENTERPRISING: The salient features of the Enterprising environment are organizational goals and economic gain. Enterprising types tend to engage in the persuasive kinds of activities that foster these outcomes. They see themselves as good leaders, competent in interpersonal skills. They like wealth and power and are very susceptible to social and materialistic influences.

CONVENTIONAL: The Conventional environment is characterized by structure and order. The organization of data and materials according to systematic plans is a central focus of activity in this environment. Conventional people subscribe to organizational values and respect money, position and power. They see themselves as conforming and orderly, and as clerically and numerically competent.

These types of environments and persons are notional rather than empirical, although that is not to say that pure types might not exist. Holland's secondary concept of *personality pattern* expresses the ways in which the six typological concepts might be organized within the personality. An individual personality might therefore be described by rank-ordering the types of interest preferences expressed. This ordering represents the relative dominance of particular interest themes in the personality, in the manner of the primary teachers described previously. The three-letter code imputed here to primary teachers implies a rank-ordering of the first three interest themes that are characteristic of those teachers and their work. In principle, every occupation is capable of being coded,[16] and Holland and his co-workers have recently published a complete coding of the occupations listed in the *DOT*.[17] This enables individuals to match their own profile of interests with those of particular occupational groups. In this way, so the theory goes, a person's interests and satisfactions in work are optimized.

The relations between interest themes can be spatially represented by a hexagon. Themes adjacent on the hexagon are more similar than nonadjacent themes, and the relation between themes diagonally opposite on the hexagon is random. These relations are illustrated in Figure 1. Thus we are able to say that an Enterprising person (i.e. a person whose highest score on a RIASEC interest inventory is on the E theme) is likely also to have some Social and Conventional interests because these are adjacent to Enterprising on the hexagon.[18] We are not able to make any predictions about that person's level of Investigative interests because that theme is diagonally opposite Enterprising on the hexagon and is therefore not correlated with it. This hexagonal model of the relations among the themes has some empirical support, but it is not unequivocal.[19] However, the ambiguities that exist do not seriously compromise the usefulness of the six themes to our understanding of the world of work, and, more than any other approach, Holland's is a comprehensive formulation with considerable predictive power.[20]

Holland has also developed inventories to measure each of the six interest themes. These are the Vocational Preference Inventory (VPI)[21] and the Self Directed Search (SDS).[22] The scores on each theme measured by the VPI are derived from expressed preferences for occupations. These are also included in the SDS, but in addition the SDS measures expressed interests in particular activities, estimates of competence in particular areas, and self-estimates of skills and abilities. The aim of each inventory is to achieve a comprehensive assessment of those attributes

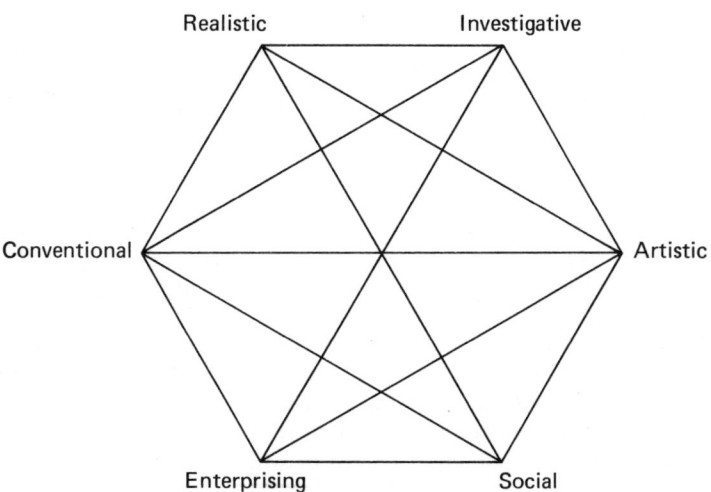

Figure 1.   Hollands hexagonal model of RIASEC interest themes

H

that indicate types, and the three highest scores within the six themes constitute a summary code of one's interests. This is the three-letter code analogous to that referred to previously for primary teachers. For the inventory taker it summarizes the dominant themes among the expressed interest patterns. The codes are assumed to be sufficiently stable over long time-periods to indicate the kinds of occupational environments in which an individual will optimize and maximize work adjustment and satisfaction.[23]

Holland's theory contains some significant secondary concepts which will not be elaborated here.[24] They are important, however, in understanding the full import of the theory as a comprehensive account of the world of work and the kinds of people who inhabit it. The full account of the theory is indispensable to a complete understanding of its implications for occupational psychology, and for those who wish to apply it in education and industry.

The concept of RIASEC types has implications for academic performance. Although interests appear to be substantially independent of aptitudes and abilities, there is a hierarchy of relationship with academic performance that makes a lot of intuitive sense. Educational achievement and aspiration follow a similar pattern. Other things being equal the order is as follows: Investigative, Social, Artistic, Conventional, Enterprising and Realistic. Students perform best when they are of a similar type to the teachers, i.e. where they share common interests.[25]

The Present Study

The role and importance of interests in education are quite explicit in Holland's theory. Given their motivational significance, and their salience in job satisfaction, how they emerge in the educational process is a very important issue. It is important in several senses. First, it is important that education should provide an environment that complements developing and emerging interests so that their motivational impact is maximized. Secondly, it is important that those educational structures and organizations that influence, positively or negatively, the development of interests should be identified so that their effects can be monitored and their implications understood. Thirdly, the limits of schooling in fostering and developing interests need to be determined and appreciated. There is no reason to accept that schools can or should foster every aspect of human development.

The study to be reported here is a descriptive account of the expressed occupational interests of some groups of students in Year 10 secondary school in Australia.[26] More details of the actual groups will be provided below. There is compelling evidence that the Holland model of interests is very useful in career education and vocational guidance in Australian settings.[27] The proposed use of Holland codes as part of the description of Australian occupations in *Australian Standard Classification of Occupations (ASCO)*[28] underlines the practical significance of the theory. Some recently completed research on Australian occupational groups, deemed to be representative of Holland interest themes, indicated that over 70 per cent of group membership could be correctly identified by the use of appropriate interest inventories (the SCII and the VPI).[29] This is a very impressive rate of identification in relation both to the reliability and validity of the inventories and the predictive power of the theory. The results also suggest that Holland codes might make a very useful contribution to *ASCO*.

How, then, might the classification be applied in school settings, and what information might it yield? There seems to be an obvious use for the theory and its associated measurement devices in vocational guidance, and this has already been explored.[30] It might also be a stimulus to the organization of instruction and learning in ways that maximally exploit interests. Holland proposes several ideas here, but a thoroughgoing attempt at application seems not yet to have been reported. Clearly, however, it can yield a great deal of information about the patterns and distributions of interests both within and between schools and school systems. This information has implications both for individual schools and particular systems in the formation and implementation of educational policy. More will be said about these implications when the results of the study are discussed. In the meantime it is important to refer to those features of the study which affect and limit the interpretations which can be placed on the results.

Some reservations
The data to be reported below are not in any sense derived from random samples of known populations, although the number of respondents is quite large.[31] The data were collected from many sources[32] as the opportunity arose and, to that extent, they might be biased by any or all of the factors that influenced their availability. For this reason the data will be treated as two populations, one constituted primarily of independent school students in Year 10 and the other of government school students.

In general, the validity of inferences from samples to populations depends on the truth of the assumption that the sample is randomly drawn from the population. Its truth depends on the sampling procedure, and in so far as a sample is not randomly drawn the truth of the assumption is violated. In these circumstances it is not clear that we can validly assert anything about the characteristics of the population from which the sample was drawn. Nonetheless we frequently do treat empirical data as if they were sample data, even though we know that the justification for so doing is formally tenuous. Sometimes we do this because there is no alternative way of proceeding; data are so difficult to collect that we might be grateful for whatever empirical evidence bears on the question of concern. But we should not be so impressed by our data that we deceive ourselves or others about the significance of our results. The extent to which general trends are revealed by purportedly sample data remains a technical question.

The groups

1. Students from independent schools. The RIASEC data on these students were collected in 1980-82. The students were from 33 independent schools in Victoria, Tasmania, Queensland and South Australia. The schools included single-sex and co-educational schools and Catholic and non-Catholic schools. Data were contributed by 2115 females and 1884 males.

2. Students from government schools. The RIASEC data on these students were collected in 1976 in the first year of the Melbourne Careers Project.[33] The students were from four high and two technical schools in Victoria. One technical school was an all-male school. Altogether 406 females and 501 males contributed data to the project.

The instruments

The Career Assessment Inventory (CAI) was administered to all the students from the independent schools. The first edition of this interest inventory was published in 1976, and further editions in 1978 and 1981.[34] The data reported here are derived from the 1978 edition. The CAI is modelled on the Strong-Campbell Interest Inventory (SCII),[35] combining both rational and empirical features. The empirical aspects of the inventory are based on those items that discriminate members of particular occupations from people in general. This indicates to the test-takers how similar their expressed patterns of likes and dislikes are to those expressed by workers in particular occupations. The occupations, unlike those in the SCII, do not require high levels of education for training or entry. The inventory is particularly useful at Year 10 where options of leaving school or choosing new subjects are generally exercised.[36]

The Vocational Preference Inventory (VPI)[37] was administered to all the students from the government schools. The inventory is based on expressing preferences for or against working in a particular occupation. From these preferences are derived scores for each RIASEC theme. It is possible to derive scores for other variables, but for the purposes of this report those other scores were ignored. The VPI is basically a rationally constructed scale using occupational titles to which one of the RIASEC themes is attributed as the primary or major interest theme shared by members of the occupation. From the responses to the inventory, occupational codes expressed in interest themes are inferred.

Numerical representation of the results
The interest measures were treated descriptively because of the sampling deficiencies mentioned earlier, and no inferences were made about the characteristics of Year 10 students in general. Such a descriptive treatment is possible in a number of ways. Ideally, the best representation would be one not restricted to specialists in measurement, and one which communicated readily to interested readers some of the more salient features of the results. The method chosen is based on discriminant analysis and lends itself readily to a graphical representation. In addition, it enables us to estimate how much of the variation in all the interest measures is attributable to particular interest themes. This gives us some indication of the importance of particular themes as descriptions of the differences among particular groups.

In both the groups tested there are several potential sources of variation in interest scores. These include the individuals in the groups, the schools they attend, their sex, and errors of measurement arising from the characteristics of the inventories. These characteristics include reliability and validity in particular.

In the data from government schools, the results reflect primarily the sources of variation in interests due to individual schools divided into sexes. There were six schools in this group. Four of them were co-educational high schools and one was a co-educational technical school. The remaining school was a boys' technical school. The schools had been chosen in an attempt to represent school types and the socio-economic background of students in metropolitan Melbourne. The schools were in no sense randomly selected, nor was there any formal attempt to achieve true representation.[38] The schools were selected from what was available as an intuitively appropriate mixture. On this account the data were not collapsed beyond schools. That is, each school was considered in its own right and not as part of the context of some further group, such as co-educational high schools. There seemed no grounds, and certainly no formal or statistical grounds, for believing that these schools would be typical of co-educational high schools in general. Manifestly, the technical schools could not be regarded as typical or representative. The data as represented therefore mainly reflect the influences on variation due to sex and school.

The data from independent schools did lend themselves to more consolidated groupings. The groupings are intuitive, but seem rationally defensible. They were based mainly on the premise that nearly 4000 students from 33 schools might be sufficient to allow us to look at some descriptive relations between types of school. Whether such relations are reliable, in the sense of being stable and enduring, cannot be inferred from these results. But they do provide a basis for making empirical predictions. An eightfold classification of the students was developed based on their sex and the types of school they attended. Students were grouped

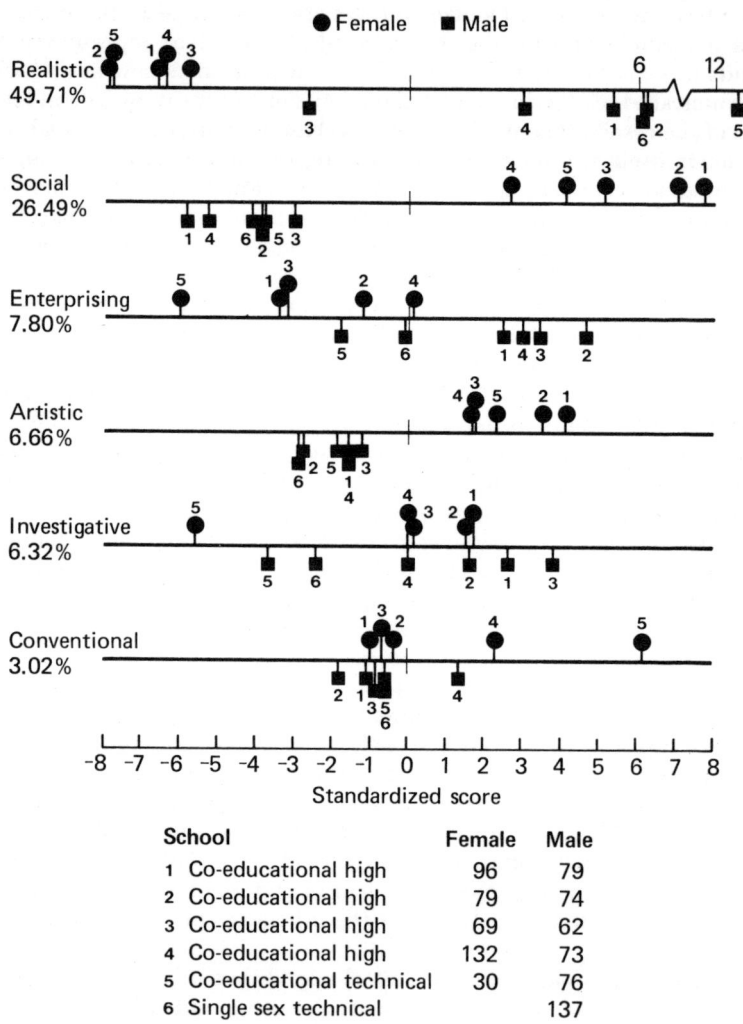

Figure 2.　Plots of Government school results

as male or female, attending a co-educational or single-sex school, and attending a Catholic or non-Catholic school. With these groupings, in no category were there fewer than 185 students, and the largest category, that of Catholic females in single-sex schools, held 1335 students.

The results

The results for government school students are shown in Figure 2, and those for independent school students in Figure 3. (p. 203). Each line of results represents a 0–10 standardized measurement scale (i.e. a scale with a mean equal to zero, and a standard deviation equal to 10). As indicated at the foot of the Figure, the range of standardized scores that can be represented on each line is from –8 to +8. The six interest themes are ordered according to the percentage of total variance (amount of variation) accounted for by each particular interest theme. In each line of the figures, the female groups are represented by circles above the line while the male groups are represented by squares below.

1. Government schools

(a) Realistic interests. The data concerning government schools, derived from responses to the VPI of 501 males and 406 females, indicate that 49.71 per cent of the total variance in interests is attributable to the school and sex differences in Realistic interests. It will be recalled that jobs related to these interests tend to be demanding of physical skills and competences, and that the work environments characteristically tend to be dominated by males and masculine values. Inspection of the first standardized dimension reveals some very large differences in average Realistic interests according to both school and sex, but the sex difference does not need to be qualified by the school attended, or vice versa. That is, females are clearly distinguished from males in Realistic interests, even though there is a huge range of differences between males according to school. This range goes from –2.6 (males in school 3) to 12.7 (males in school 5), a difference of over 15 standardized score points. The female range, on the other hand, goes from –5.8 (females in school 3) to –7.9 (females in school 2). These results suggest that in these schools there is much less variation in the Realistic interests of Year 10 females than in those of Year 10 males. In addition to this apparent sex difference in variability, it is also apparent that the males on average express stronger preferences for Realistic activities and occupations than do females. These expressed preferences are consistent with stereotypes concerning sex-role differences between males and females.[39]

(b) Social interests. Differences in Social interests account for 26.49 per cent of the total variance. Again there are on average manifest sex differences between expressed preferences for Social occupations, with females' interests being greater than those of males. The range of female averages within schools (2.7 to 7.7) is slightly greater than that for males (–3.0 to –5.7).

Realistic and Social interests together account for over 75 per cent of the total variance in interests among these schools. In these results it is clear that these interests also reflect the pervasiveness of sex or sex-role differences in expressed occupational preferences. A further analysis of the data in terms of these differences will be reported below.

(c) Enterprising interests. Differences in Enterprising interests account for 7.80 per cent of the total variance. Again, sex differences are present, though there is some overlap. The ranges of school means are similar (–1.8 to 4.6 for males, and 0.3 to –6.0 for females), but in general the males appear on average to express more Enterprising preferences than do the females.

(d) Artistic Interests. These account for 6.66 per cent of the total variance. Sex differences again appear to be present with the females on average expressing more Artistic interests than the males. The range for males (–1.3 to –2.9) is slightly less than that for the females (1.6 to 4.1), but these differences are probably not important.

(e) Investigative Interests. The amount of variance accounted for by Investigative interests is 6.32 per cent. Here there is considerable overlap between the sexes that suggests the absence of any salient sex differences. This is an interesting result in the context of current concerns about girls' performances in mathematics and science. In so far as interests relate to attitudes, and there is sex-typing in those attitudes regarding mathematics and science, one might have expected sex differences to be manifested more clearly in Investigative interests.[40] On the other hand there is substantial evidence of greatly increased participation by girls in mathematics education.[41] One aspect of these results that is worth remarking upon is the possibility of a systematic difference between school types. The lowest averages are for the technical schools (schools 5 and 6), with the mean for females in a co-educational technical school being the lowest of all.

(f) Conventional Interests. These interests account for only 3.02 per cent of the total variance. In the co-educational high schools (schools 1, 2, 3 and 4) the levels of Conventional interest of males and females appear very similar. The highest Conventional interests belong to the girls from the co-educational technical school, whereas those of the boys from the same school appear to be much more like those of the other males.

The above brief descriptive summary of the results from the six government schools suggests a number of conclusions and speculations. First there appear to be sex differences in a number of the interest themes that are more important than, or over-ride the influences of, the schools themselves. There may be an exception to this in the Investigative theme where in general the students from the technical schools express a lower level of interest. The girls from the co-educational technical school (school 5) on average shared the lowest Realistic interests, while the boys from the same school had the highest Realistic interests. In fact, the average for those boys is beyond the 88th centile for the group as a whole.

The girls from the co-educational technical school on average also had the lowest Enterprising and Artistic interests, and the highest Conventional interests. Whether those results are merely random variations from the group as a whole, or from the female group, it is not possible to say. It is a result, however, that suggests the need for replication in other analogous groups. If it represents some kind of reliable tendency it then appears that technical schools might reinforce a highly particular area of female interests possibly at the expense of others. However, it would not be reasonable to come to that conclusion from the available data.

The results outlined above indicate that sex differences in interest themes appear to be important, particularly in the Realistic, Social, Enterprising and Artistic themes, and a more detailed analysis of these differences was conducted. All the students were divided into male and female groups. A discriminant analysis[42] was carried out to establish that combination of the interest themes which provided maximum discrimination between males and females. The pertinent results are shown in Table 1. The significant F ratios indicate that males and females are maximally discriminated by a combination of Realistic, Social, Artistic and Enterprising themes. The correlations suggest that these discriminating variables can be ordered as Realistic and Enterprising versus Social and Artistic, and the males tend towards the former pair while the females tend towards the latter. The Investigative and Conventional themes do not make a significant contribution to the discrimination between males and females in this group. An appropriate combination

TABLE 1

Discriminant Analysis: Government Schools

Theme	Standardized Coefficient	Correlation	F(1,905)	Significance
Realistic	−.82	−.63	237.50	<.001
Investigative	.01	.02	0.17	.680
Artistic	.31	.29	49.15	<.001
Social	.66	.52	162.70	<.001
Enterprising	−.39	−.12	8.98	<.003
Conventional	.26	−.01	0.06	.807

of the four discriminating themes can be calculated from the preference data, and in terms of this calculation it is possible to identify each student as 'male' or 'female'. If there are true sex differences in expressed preferences this identification should accord with the students' natural sex. The relation of sex predicted on the basis of expressed preferences, i.e. using the appropriate combination of the four interest themes, and the actual sex of the students is indicated in the results shown in Table 2. Using this combination of interest themes 81.26 per cent of the students are correctly classified as male or female. This suggests that in this group of students the expressed preferences do discriminate substantially between the sexes. In terms of the themes that are characteristic or typical of the sexes, male interests are more Realistic and Enterprising while female interests are more Social and Artistic.

It must be emphasized that these results are from this particular group of students from these particular schools. There are no logical or statistical grounds on which they can be held to represent general trends. However, within their context it is apparent that there are substantial sex differences that accord with traditional stereotypes of sex role.

TABLE 2

Group Classification

| Actual Group | N | Predicted Group | |
		Male	Female
Male	501	393	108
		(78.4%)	(21.6%)
Female	406	62	344
		(15.3%)	(84.7%)

2. Independent schools

The RIASEC scores on the Career Assessment Inventory (CAI) derived from the expressed preferences of the 3999 students from independent schools were analysed by similar methods to the analysis of data from government schools. The results are summarized in Figure 3. Again they are represented on a 0–10 standardized distribution, and the themes are presented in the order of the amount of variance each accounts for.

(a) Social Interests. This interest theme accounted for 39.08 per cent of the total variance over all themes. Clearly the male and female groups are separated, with the Social interests of the females being considerably greater than those of the males. This result is comparable with that obtained from the government school data.

(b) Realistic Interests. This interest theme accounted for 29.19 per cent of the total variance. Again the male and female groups are clearly separated, though the range of means among the male groups (1.5 to 9.3) is much greater than among the females (–3.9 to –4.8). This indicates that these females express a uniformly lower interest in Realistic themes than did the males, and that there was a much wider range of expressed interest among the males.

(c) Artistic Interests. The variation in Artistic interests accounted for 12.30 per cent of the total variance. The ranges of expressed interest were rather wider among the female (0.5 to 5.9) than among the male (−1.9 to −5.1) groups. Once more the sexes were separated with the females showing greater interest **overall in Artistic themes.**

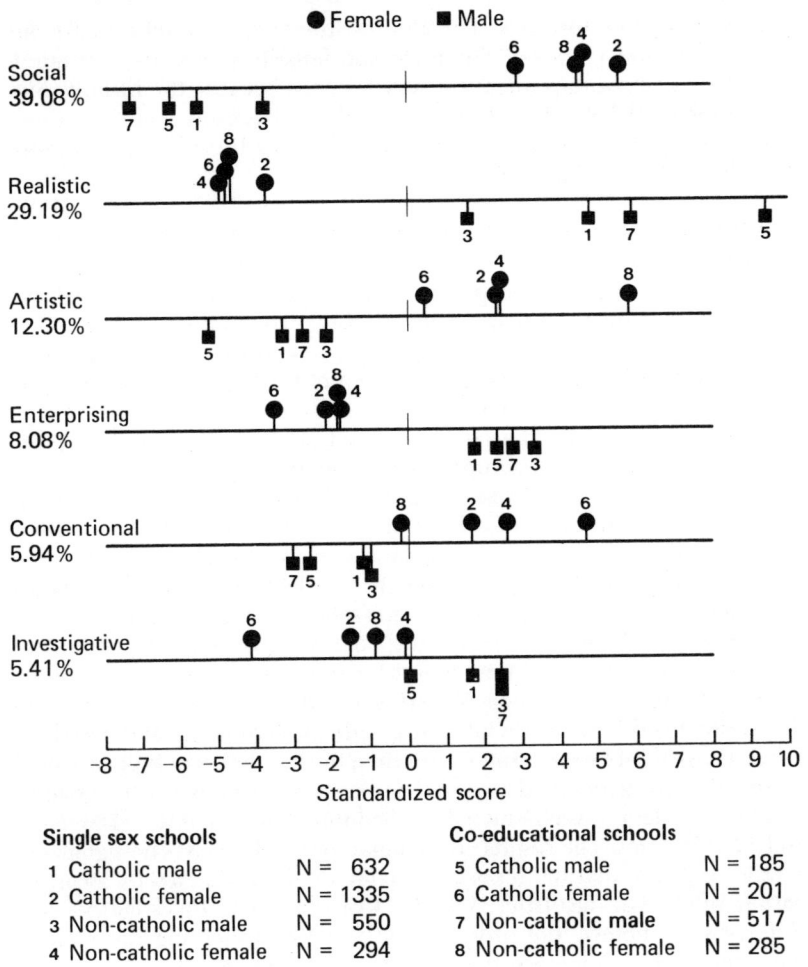

Figure 3.   Plots of Independent school **results**

(d) Enterprising Interests. This theme accounted for 8.08 per cent of the total variance. The separation between male and female groups was clearly present. Within sexes the group means indicate a possibly strong similarity: the range for females was –2.0 to –3.7, while that for males was 1.7 to 3.3.

(e) Conventional Interests. Sex differences were again apparent in the Conventional interest theme. The variation in the theme accounted for 5.94 per cent of the total variance. In general, the males expressed lower interest in this theme.

(f) Investigative Interests. This interest theme accounted for 5.01 per cent of the total variance. The male and female groups are separated, but the lack of overlap might be very tenuous because the mean values for groups 4 (–0.2) and 5 (0.0) are practically the same. Nonetheless there is a tendency for the male and female averages to spread in opposite directions from the mid-point.

This brief descriptive summary of the data does suggest some interpretations that are not dissimilar to those derived from the government school data. The first and obvious point is that sex differences in interest are clearly more manifest than differences arising from school type, whether Catholic versus non-Catholic or single-sex versus co-educational. The Social and Realistic themes together account for over 68 per cent of the total variance in interests, compared with approximately 75 per cent in the government schools. This suggests that both these themes are important in understanding the nature of sex differences in interests.

Several results showed some apparent regularity. Group 3 consisted of male students from non-Catholic single-sex schools. On average their results were the highest for males in Social, Artistic, Enterprising and Conventional themes, and the lowest in the Realistic theme. The results of females from co-educational Catholic schools were in general the lowest among the female groups for the Social, Artistic, Enterprising and Investigative themes; and the highest for the Conventional theme.

The results strongly suggest that sex differences are important in describing the differences in interest among these students, and that these differences might be more important than the influences of type of school attended. A more detailed analysis, similar to the analysis of the government school data, was conducted on the interest scores of the 1768 males and 2250 females. The results are summarized in Table 3. The significant F ratios indicate that the sexes are maximally discriminated by a combination of Social, Realistic, Artistic, Conventional, Investigative and Enterprising themes, the order of the ratios representing the relative importance of each interest theme in discriminating the sexes. An appropriate calculation enables us to identify each student as 'male' or 'female'.

TABLE 3

Discriminant Analysis: Independent Schools

Theme	Standardized Coefficient	Correlation	F(1,4016)	Significance
Realistic	−.63	−.48	780.60	<.001
Investigative	−.27	−.17	102.10	<.001
Artistic	.46	.31	323.80	<.001
Social	.90	.52	912.00	<.001
Enterprising	−.68	.04	5.53	<.02
Conventional	.27	.20	137.70	<.001

If there are true sex differences in the preferences expressed by these students, this identification should accord with their actual sex. The results of this analysis are shown in Table 4. From this combination of the six interest themes 82.50 per cent of the students are correctly classified as male or female. This figure is comparable with the results of the classification of government school data (Table 2) where 81.26 per cent of the students were correctly classified. Again it must be emphasized that the results pertain only to those students that were actually tested, and there are no statistical grounds in these results for inferring general trends. However, it is clear that within the context of the schools and the inventories there are substantial differences between the sexes.

TABLE 4

Group Classification: Independent Schools

Actual Group	N	Predicted Group Male	Female
Male	1768	1447 (81.8%)	321 (18.2%)
Female	2250	382 (17.0%)	1868 (83.0%)

Discussion

The differences between the two data sets provide very little as a basis whereby the results from them might be compared. However, they do share a common theoretical framework, that of Holland's conceptualization of persons and occupational environments,[43] and it is within this framework that some speculations about the results might be warranted.

In both data sets two things are quite clear. First, most of the variability in interests is accounted for by differences within Realistic and Social interests. It will be recalled that these interests lie at opposite points on the hexagon that provides a model of the relations among RIASEC themes. In terms of the theory, this indicates that there is no relation between Realistic and Social interests, and therefore we cannot predict the degree of interest in one from an expressed interest in the other.

From a consideration of the Realistic dimensions in Figures 2 and 3 it is clear that the variability among the males is much greater than among the females. According to the theory, the Realistic occupational environment and its associated type of person express typically and traditionally those kinds of attitudes, values and behaviours that are regarded as masculine. These include the capacities and attributes to deal with the physical demands of environments, and the psychological characteristics that those demands encourage and reinforce. These characteristics embrace shyness and conformity, genuineness and stability, and a practical and self-effacing approach to the world and the problems it presents. Values tend to be very concrete or tangible and involve the acquisition of material possessions. There tends to be an aversion to educational activities unless they involve the acquisition of manual or technical competencies.

Given these theoretical propositions it is not surprising that the males and females in these schools and school groups differ in their Realistic interests. What is suggested by the results is that the schools themselves, conceived either as individual schools or as belonging to some a priori type of school, have little apparent impact in moderating these differences. In some cases they may even intensify them.[44] One should regard the present data very tentatively, and there is certainly a need for them to be replicated. In no formal sense can statistical trends be inferred. But in the government schools there are intriguing possibilities that should not be ignored. The results for the students from school 5, the co-educational technical school, show that on average the males and females are placed at opposite poles of the Realistic dimension, while those males and females showing greatest congruence of Realistic interests are from a co-educational high school (school 3). It is obvious from the other high school data that no inferences from this difference between two schools are justified. But the results do raise the question of whether particular kinds or types of school, as against a particular school, do intensify or moderate the traditional differences between males and females in Realistic interests. And do they do this by curriculum, organization, subject-matter, or do these educational variables merely reinforce psychological traits that are somehow pre-selected by a particular kind of schooling?

In the independent school data the highest average Realistic interests are shown by the male students from the Catholic co-educational schools. The lowest Realistic interests among the male groups belong to students from non-Catholic single-sex schools. This difference might in part be related to the background differences between these two groups. Of these, socio-economic differences and all that they imply in terms of educational advantage, might play a very critical role as pre-selecting variables. It might be of some importance that the latter group obtained or shared on average the highest score among the males for every other interest theme. It could be argued that since in these data we are dealing with aggregations of interest scores across so-called types of schools rather than within particular schools, the types might tend to be more stable than the individual schools that contribute to them. In other words the aggregations would give a better approximation to the true state of affairs because the errors pertaining to the peculiar influences of particular schools might tend to cancel one another out.

There are other grounds also on which a types-of-school argument might be compromised. When dealing with single-sex schools the types are coherent enough. Here, when comparing male and female students, it is quite implicit in the comparison that the sexes are in different school environments. Such is not the case with co-educational schools, however. Here males and females are, in some sense, in the same school environment, and in the development of their interests they would presumably be affected in similar ways by that environment.[45] Allowing for the overall sex differences, we might expect males and females to be equally placed in relation to their like-sex peers within interest themes. There are some intriguing congruences, but the picture is far from being coherent and we cannot assess the reliability of what appears in the present data. Thus females from the Catholic co-educational schools share with their male class-mates the lowest interests in Artistic and Investigative themes. Yet those same girls have the highest Conventional and the lowest Enterprising interests, and are not clearly distinguished from their sex-peers in Realistic interests. A coherent account of the influence of the Catholic co-educational school on interest development might need to take these incongruencies into account.

With the non-Catholic co-educational schools the picture as it appears in these data is no more coherent. Here the girls have the highest Artistic interests and, within their sex, apparently the highest Investigative and Enterprising interests. In addition they appear to have the lowest Conventional interests among the females. This appears to be the mirror image of the pattern among the Catholic girls, which is interesting but hardly illuminating. Indeed, in a search for the effects of single-sex versus co-educational schools on interests these differences between Catholic and non-Catholic students would tend to cancel out. But the other differences between these two groups, and particularly the hypothesized socio-economic ones, seem bound to be important in accounting for any differences between them.

The results for single-sex schools provide no real support for a distinction between these Catholic and non-Catholic students in relation to patterns of interest. The females in particular have very coherent results, and any apparent differences within the sexes are manifestly minor when compared with the between-sex differences. The search for consistent, systematic and theoretically explicable differences between single-sex and co-educational schools on the one hand, or Catholic and non-Catholic schools on the other, seems unlikely to lead to unqualified outcomes.

The major qualification that seems unequivocal is the over-riding nature of sex differences in expressed preferences. This is the second major attribute of both sets of data. In the data from government schools the sexes are clearly and significantly separated on four of the six interest themes: Realistic, Social, Enterprising and Artistic. In the independent school data the sexes separate clearly on all the interest themes.

In the government school data the males express greater interest in the Realistic and Enterprising themes, while the females express more interest in the Social and Artistic themes. For the independent schools the females are ahead in the Social, Artistic and Conventional themes, while in the Realistic, Enterprising and Investigative themes males express more interest.

It is arguable that the two data sets, separated in time, system and circumstance providing different educational environments and curricular content and milieux, and subject to all the vagaries of sampling referred to before, produce remarkably consistent pictures. In addition the interests were measured in quite different contexts by different instruments, though both of these shared a common theoretical framework. The possibilities of influences in these results due to error, i.e. the effects of sources of variation unforeseen, uncontrolled and uncontrollable, are legion. That they cohere with Holland's theory in any respect reflects well on the power of the theory and the validity of the measuring instruments.

The results raise many more questions than they answer. The first is whether the results remain merely artefacts of the inventories, groups, methods of data representation and analysis, and error. Replication is clearly desirable methodologically, and the results suggest that it is reasonable to expect an analogously interpretable outcome. The results certainly provide a firm basis for predicting sex differences in occupational interest. It is also clear that these differences permeate the Realistic and Social themes. In so far as these themes represent so-called sex stereotypes into which people are locked by gender, it appears that this stereotyping is firmly entrenched in the education system. At least in relation to these two interest themes the influences of school type, whether government, independent, Catholic, single-sex or co-educational, might be to intensify rather than moderate differences. Education for an androgynous outcome in relation to occupational interests might have a long way to go.

Traditional sex-role socialization is also suggested by the Artistic-Enterprising sex distinction. The Social-Artistic combination that provides a synthesis of nurturant and creative attributes is highly significant in the preferences expressed by females and connotes the whole gamut of qualities signifying femininity. By contrast the Realistic-Enterprising synthesis of action and persuasion possesses all the macho robustness of the John Wayne stereotype.

The sex differences in the Conventional and Investigative themes that appear in the independent school data reinforce the stereotypes even further. Conventional occupations are routine and structured, with clearly defined tasks and a minimum of ambiguity. Investigative occupations tend to thrive on ambiguity, require intellectual effort, rational analysis and scientific skill. Such people resist the imposition of structure and order. It is appropriate to speculate that the development and maintenance of Investigative interests might require substantial levels of appropriate skills and knowledge. In so far as females might be steered away from scientific subject-matter, their opportunities to develop these interests will be correspondingly curtailed. But the interesting question is: who is in the driver's seat?

The questions of who controls what, and how, and particularly the role of the school in the formation of the young, vary according to the ends, aims, priorities and principles that motivate policy formation and application. That the interests of students are critical in determining their responses to educational policy seems indubitable. Policies that ignore their expressed interests and insist on prejudging what those interests are likely to be, or insist that they should be of a particular character, might be ineffective in promoting appropriate educational outcomes. The choice seems twofold. Policy can respond to the interests students express by the creation of educational environments where they can be expressed further and reinforced, where they can be nurtured and developed. Or, it may be believed that schools are only properly concerned with particular kinds of interests, and that education should be concerned to develop these to the full in each student.

The present data suggest that sex differences in interests might be intransigent. This does not mean that they are inevitable, it merely implies that they might take a long time to go away. A policy designed to foster this has to work within what is possible. If recent theorizing about occupational aspirations is close to the mark,[46] it seems that sex differences and their associated gender stereotypes will continue to be characteristic of emerging occupational interests.

NOTES

[1] See J. O. Crites, 'Interests', in R. L. Ebel (ed.), *Encyclopedia of Educational Research*, 4th edition (Macmillan, London, 1969).

[2] A. M. Kroll, L. B. Dinklage, J. Lee, E. D. Morley and E. H. Wilson, *Career Development: growth and crisis* (Wiley, New York, 1970) review and integrate some important sources.

[3] Some aspects of these have been investigated by H. D. Grotevant, 'Family Similarities in Interests and Orientation', *Merrill-Palmer Quarterly*, 1976, pp. 61-72. The results suggest that patterns of interest within families are complex, and are influenced by the interests of parents and birth order.

[4] J. L. Holland, 'Vocational Preferences', in M. D. Dunnette (ed.), *Handbook of Industrial and Organizational Psychology* (Rand McNally, Chicago, 1976), chapter 12, reviews the pertinent evidence.

[5] F. Parsons, *Choosing a Vocation* (Houghton Mifflin, New York, 1909).

[6] D. P. Campbell, *Handbook for the Strong Vocational Interest Blank* (Stanford University Press, 1971) includes a history of the development of the SVIB.

[7] E. K. Strong, Jr, 'Differentiation of Certified Public Accountants from Other Occupational Groups', *Journal of Educational Psychology*, 1927, pp. 227-38.

[8] D. P. Campbell and J. C. Hansen, *Manual for the Strong-Campbell Interest Inventory*, 3rd edition (Stanford University Press, 1981).

[9] C. B. Johansson, *Manual for the Career Assessment Inventory*, 2nd edition (National Computer Systems, Minneapolis, 1982).

[10] It is not clear who first coined the phrase 'dust-bowl empiricism', but it seems to have been accepted as an appropriate appellation by some psychologists at the University of Minnesota in the 1950s. It implied the anti-theoretical stance that to seek for explanations was futile, and that prediction should proceed on the basis of what was empirically established. In his presidential address to the Midwestern Psychological Association (Chicago, 29 April 1955) P. E. Meehl refers to the 'dust-bowl empiricism with which we Minnesotans are traditionally associated'. However, in his introduction to *Clinical versus Statistical Prediction* (Minneapolis, 1954) he specifically disavows such a 'clear, monolithic "Minnesota line"'.

[11] U.S. Department of Labor, *Dictionary of Occupational Titles*, 4th edition (U.S. Government Printing Office, Washington, D.C., 1977).

[12] A. Roe, *The Psychology of Occupations* (Wiley, New York, 1956), p. 148, and N. S. Cole and G. Hanson, *An Analysis of the Structure of Vocational Interests*. American College Testing Program, Iowa City, January, 1971 (Research Report no. 40).

[13] J. L. Holland, 'A Theory of Vocational Choice', *Journal of Counseling Psychology*, 1959, pp. 35-44.

[14] J. L. Holland, *Making Vocational Choices: a theory of careers* (Prentice-Hall, Englewood Cliffs, New Jersey, 1973).

[15] Ibid.

[16] Coding and its reliability are quite complex. The ultimate test of the accuracy of a code is empirical. Most coding seems to be intuitive, based on a rational analysis of occupational characteristics.

[17] G. D. Gottfredson, J. L. Holland and D. K. Ogawa, *Dictionary of Holland Occupational Codes* (Consulting Psychologists Press, Palo Alto, 1982).

[18] On the basis of the hexagonal model it would be anticipated that most three-letter occupational codes would involve themes adjacent on the hexagon.

[19] F. Naylor and T. Mount, 'Issues in the Generality of Holland's Hexagonal Model'. Paper prepared for the seminar/workshop—Making Vocational Choices: Research on the Application of Holland's Typology in Australia (Australian Council for Educational Research, February 1982).

[20] In a recently completed study of 'hit rates' for Australian occupations, 65% of workers were correctly identified by their primary theme on the Vocational Preference Inventory and 72% by their primary theme on the Strong-Campbell Interest Inventory (Naylor, in preparation).

[21] J. L. Holland, *Manual for the Vocational Preference Inventory* (Consulting Psychologists Press, Palo Alto, 1975).

[22] J. L. Holland, *The Self-Directed Search, Professional Manual*, 1979 edition (Consulting Psychologists Press, Palo Alto, 1979).

[23] Holland, op. cit., 1973.

[24] The secondary concepts of differentiation, congruence, and consistency are particularly important to an understanding of occupational adjustment and work satisfaction.

[25] M. E. Bernard and F. D. Naylor, 'Vocational guidance consultation in school settings', in T. R. Kratochwill (ed.), *Advances in School Psychology*, vol. 2, chapter 7 (Erlbaum Associates, Hillsdale, 1982).

[26] The assistance of various sources of data and research funding is gratefully acknowledged. Dr K. F. Taylor provided the government school data from the Melbourne Careers Project which was supported by a grant from the Australian Research Grants Committee (no. A75/15361). Career-Wise Pty Ltd donated data tapes. The gathering of further data was facilitated by funding from the Percy Baxter Charitable Trust, Career-Wise Pty Ltd, and the Department of Education, University of Melbourne.

[27] Bernard and Naylor, op. cit.

[28] Department of Employment and Youth Affairs and the Australian Bureau of Statistics, *ASCO Information Paper* (Australian Government Printer, Canberra, 1982).

[29] See note 20.

[30] Bernard and Naylor, op. cit.

[31] Empirical approaches to educational and psychological research are based on methodologies of data collection and analysis which, in principle, are meant to safeguard the researcher against error. Error is at least twofold, expressed as Type I or Type II, and consists of mistakenly inferring that there is an effect or relationship present when in fact there is not; or mistakenly inferring that there is no effect or relationship present when in fact there is. The statistical null hypothesis states that the samples under observation are all random samples from the same population. This means that there are no real differences between the samples, and any observed or apparent differences are merely due to chance. Generally errors arise because the assumptions underlying the test of the null hypothesis have been violated. The assumptions regarding the influences of sampling procedures are particularly crucial here, and their violation in behavioural and social research might be more common than we tend to believe. These are not the only assumptions that affect the interpretation of results. Assumptions relating to the effects of measurement error are also important. Error is assumed to be random and thereby does not affect the results. However, one should be aware of the possibility of systematic biases due to non-random influences in a data set.

[32] See note 26.

[33] See note 26.

[34] Johansson, op. cit.

[35] Campbell and Hansen, op. cit.

[36] The rational aspects of the CAI are based on Holland's theory. The inventory yields standardized T scores, statistically derived units of measurement which indicate the degree of departure from the average score, for each one of the RIASEC themes, and for 22 Basic Interest Scales. Each one of the latter is regarded as an aspect of one of the RIASEC themes. In this report we will be concerned only with the scores derived from the RIASEC themes themselves. Each student has six of these scores, one for each theme. All other scores were ignored.

[37] Holland, op. cit., 1975.

[38] This does not imply any criticism of the methods of the Melbourne Careers Project. Doing any kind of psychological or educational research in the field is a difficult enterprise that forces the researchers into inevitable compromises.

[39] A review of research and discussion of sex stereotyping is contained in E. E. Maccoby and C. N. Jacklin, *The Psychology of Sex Differences* (Stanford University Press, 1974).

[40] M. B. Ormerod with D. Duckworth, *Pupils' Attitudes to Science* (National Foundation for Educational Research, Slough, 1975) reviews research on sex differences in attitudes to science. In general, the results indicate that boys prefer physics and chemistry while girls prefer biology.

[41] J. D. Moss, *Towards Equality: progress by girls in mathematics in Australian secondary schools* (ACER, Hawthorn, 1982).

[42] This analysis uses a similar methodology to that which was used for the descriptive results that are shown in Figure 2. In this case, however, the method is applied for its appropriate purpose, i.e. to find an optimum combination of the RIASEC variables that discriminates between two groups, males and females. The method is extendable to many variables and groups but, logically, where g equals the number of groups, then g-1 or the number of variables, whichever is the less, places an upper limit on the number of discriminants. In the present case, therefore, there is only one optimum combination of the RIASEC variables that discriminates between the male and female students. The rationale and mathematics of the method is contained in William C. Cooley and Paul R. Lohnes, *Multivariate Data Analysis* (Wiley, New York, 1971).

[43] Holland, op. cit., 1975.

[44] Ormerod with Duckworth, op. cit., p. 68, report that co-educational schools tend to polarize the preferences of secondary boys and girls for science, while boys and girls in single-sex schools show no significant differences. A finding reported by Shelley Phillips (*Young Australians*, Harper & Row, Sydney, 1979 p. 100) suggests that single-sex schools moderate sex-role stereotyping for girls while co-educational schools tend to intensify it. The reverse appears to be the case for boys.

[45] But this presumption is confounded by the findings reported by Ormerod with Duckworth, op. cit.

[46] L. S. Gottfredson, 'Circumscription and Compromise: A Developmental Theory of Occupational Aspirations', *Journal of Counseling Psychology Monograph*, 1981, pp. 545-79.

INDEX